THE RIGHT CONDITIONS

THE WORLD BANK, STRUCTURAL ADJUSTMENT, AND FOREST POLICY REFORM

FRANCES J. SEYMOUR
NAVROZ K. DUBASH

WITH:

JAKE BRUNNER
FRANÇOIS EKOKO
COLIN FILER
HARIADI KARTODIHARDJO
JOHN MUGABE

WORLD RESOURCES INSTITUTE
WASHINGTON, DC

CAROLLYNE HUTTER
EDITOR

HYACINTH BILLINGS
PRODUCTION MANAGER

FRANCES J. SEYMOUR
COVER PHOTO

Each World Resources Institute report represents a timely, scholarly treatment of a subject of public concern. WRI takes responsibility for choosing the study topics and guaranteeing its authors and researchers freedom of inquiry. It also solicits and responds to the guidance of advisory panels and expert reviewers. Unless otherwise stated, however, all the interpretation and findings set forth in WRI publications are those of the authors.

CONTENTS

BOXES

TABLES

FIGURE

ACKNOWLEDGMENTS

The creation of this report was a team effort. We wish to thank our colleagues who researched and wrote the background case studies for this project and co-wrote the country case studies: Jake Brunner, François Ekoko, Colin Filer, Hariadi Kartodihardjo, and John Mugabe. In addition, we are grateful to Kilyali Kalit, George Krhoda, and Benson Mak'Ochieng for providing considerable analytical assistance with the background papers.

Lily Donge managed the writing, production, and review process, while also providing research assistance. Her work has made the report possible and we deeply appreciate all her efforts. We also wish to thank Nathan Badenoch, Lily Donge, Tony La Viña, Richard Payne, and Nigel Sizer for their contributions to the text boxes on Cambodia, the Philippines, Solomon Islands, and Suriname.

This report is built on the collective reflection and feedback of many people in borrower country governments, nongovernmental organizations, industry, and the World Bank. We wish to thank our sources who generously gave their time and insights in not-for-attribution interviews and correspondence. Special thanks to colleagues and partners who participated in a World Resources Institute workshop in April 1999 to review our preliminary results.

This report has greatly benefited from experts who reviewed the entire manuscript and we are grateful for their helpful comments: David Kaimowitz, Joan Nelson, Dan Ritchie, Michael Ross, and Angela Wood. We also appreciate detailed reviews of portions of the report by Mubariq Ahmad, Mark Baird, Jean-Marc Bouvard, David Brown, Jean-Christophe Carret, Lafacadio Cortesi, Laurent Debroux, Peter Dewees, Jim Douglas, Joanna Elliott, Vicente Ferrer, Marianne Haug, Korinna Horta, Lisa Jordan, Alain Karsenty, Jean-Jacques Landrot, Nick Menzies, Boniface Essama Nssah, Eavan O'Halloran, Simon Rietenbergen, Wahidah Shah, Hinrich Stoll, Fred Swartzendruber, Meg Taylor, Rod Taylor, Tom Walton, and Nurina Widagdo.

In addition, we wish to thank our WRI colleagues who reviewed and helped with this report: Duncan Austin, Chip Barber, Paul Faeth, Debbie Farmer, Tony Janetos, Tony La Viña, Jesse Ribot, Nigel Sizer, and Peter Veit. We greatly appreciate the reviewers' comments and suggestions, which have helped strengthen the report. The authors assume full responsibility for any remaining errors of fact and interpretation.

Hyacinth Billings, Debbie Farmer, and Carollyne Hutter provided valuable support in editing, production, and publication of the report. We thank them and the rest of WRI's Communications staff for their assistance in distribution and outreach.

We are grateful for financial support from the Charles Stewart Mott Foundation, the Netherlands Ministry of Foreign Affairs, the Spencer T. and Ann W. Olin Foundation, and the Wallace Global Fund.

FRANCES J. SEYMOUR
NAVROZ K. DUBASH

FOREWORD

O ver the last 15 years, the World Bank has come under a steady stream of criticism for the negative impacts of its policy advice and lending operations on environmental sustainability, social equity, and good governance in borrower countries. An important question facing reformers inside and outside the World Bank is whether the institution's significant analytical capacity and financial leverage can be harnessed to promote those goals in collaboration with domestic constituencies for reform.

Two of the most contentious issues raised by critics of the World Bank's performance have been the institution's involvement in the forest sector and its promotion of structural adjustment. Both of these issues are high on the policy agenda in the year 2000, as the World Bank concludes a two-year Forest Policy Implementation Review and Strategy process, and considers the implications of unprecedented levels of adjustment lending in the wake of the financial crises of the late 1990s.

In *The Right Conditions: The World Bank, Structural Adjustment, and Forest Policy Reform*, Frances Seymour, Navroz Dubash, and their colleagues in Papua New Guinea, Cameroon, Indonesia, and Kenya address the intersection of these two controversial arenas by asking the question: to what extent, and under what conditions, can the World Bank be an effective proponent of forest policy reform through adjustment lending?

A key finding of the report is that under certain circumstances, the World Bank has been effective in supporting domestic constituencies for reform against entrenched vested interests in unsustainable logging. The World Bank's engagement of stakeholder groups and ability to sustain its commitment to the reform agenda are identified as key elements of effectiveness. However, where institutional capacity is weak, the World Bank has been much less successful in utilizing adjustment lending to leverage implementation of agreed policy changes. The report identifies changes in World Bank policy and practice that would improve the institution's effectiveness, credibility, and legitimacy as a proponent of forest policy reform.

The report challenges the conventional World Bank wisdom in several respects. First, with respect to forest policy, the report recommends that the Bank move beyond efficiency-oriented reforms within an industrial forest management paradigm to embrace more fundamental reforms oriented toward equity and environmental sustainability. Second, with respect to the effectiveness of conditionality in adjustment lending and borrower commitment to reform, the report finds that the process by which the World Bank engages the borrower in the reform agenda is significant. A strict application of the principle of selectivity—in which the World Bank only lends to governments already fully committed to reform—would result in missed opportunities for the World Bank to "tip the scales" toward embattled constituencies for reform.

Finally, the report sheds light on the World Bank's new governance agenda, articulated in President Wolfensohn's 1999 Annual Meetings address. The report concludes that in order to be an effective proponent of reform in the forest sector, the World Bank must address governance issues. Conversely, in countries where forests are important, for the World Bank to be a credible proponent of good governance, forest issues must be addressed front and center.

WRI has addressed the changing international political economy of the forest sector in several reports including: *Logging Burma's Frontier Forests: Resources and the Regime* by Jake Brunner and colleagues; *Tree Trade: Liberalization of International Commerce in Forest Products* by Nigel Sizer and colleagues; and *Trial by Fire: Forest Fires and Forestry Policy in Indonesia's Era of Crisis and Reform* by Charles V. Barber and colleagues.

Support for this report, companion reports and events in case study countries, and for WRI's International Financial Flows and the Environment Project has been provided by the C.S. Mott Foundation, the Wallace Global Fund, the Spencer T. and Ann W. Olin Foundation, and the Netherlands Ministry of Foreign Affairs. I am pleased to express our appreciation for their generosity and foresight.

JONATHAN LASH
PRESIDENT
WORLD RESOURCES INSTITUTE

EXECUTIVE SUMMARY

PURPOSE AND APPROACH

Over the last 15 years, two of the most contentious issues faced by the World Bank have been its involvement in the forest sector and its structural adjustment lending. Concern about the World Bank's role in contributing to forest degradation in borrower countries led to a ban on World Bank finance for logging in primary tropical forests in 1991, but the impact on forests of lending in other sectors and structural adjustment remains controversial. Critiques of structural adjustment lending have focused on the unintended negative consequences of macroeconomic reform and fiscal austerity for the poor and for the environment, as well as on the World Bank's infringement on national sovereignty and democratic process.

The late 1990s witnessed a spike in structural adjustment lending in absolute terms and as a proportion of overall World Bank lending, as well as a revival of debates about the effectiveness of conditionality, spurred by the World Bank report, *Assessing Aid*. And in 1998, the World Bank initiated a two-year Forest Policy Implementation Review and Strategy process, designed to assess the World Bank's experience in the forest sector, as well as to develop a forward-looking strategy.

This report addresses the intersection of these two controversial arenas by asking the question: to what extent, and under what conditions, can the World Bank be an effective proponent of forest policy reform through adjustment lending? The report focuses on experience in a few exceptional cases where the World Bank has explicitly included forest policy reform conditions in adjustment lending operations: Papua New Guinea, Cameroon, and Indonesia. In addition, the report includes an analysis of what happened in Kenya, where the World Bank proposed, but did not move forward on, an adjustment operation focused on environmental policy reform.

Previous World Bank forest policy reviews have focused on the positive and negative impacts on forests of project-specific loans, while past reviews of adjustment lending have examined the unintended, usually negative, social and environmental consequences of macroeconomic policy change. By contrast, this analysis concentrates on the few examples of the World Bank's intentional use of structural adjustment as an instrument to bring about changes in forest policy.

Our approach is to examine the process by which the World Bank has attempted to promote policy change, which illuminates the roles of international and domestic actors in formulating and implementing the reform agenda. Our objective is to identify the right conditions, within the World Bank as well as in the borrower country, under which the World Bank can be an effective proponent of forest policy change through adjustment lending.

FINDINGS

The cases in this report demonstrate that under the right conditions, the World Bank has been able to catalyze key forest policy changes in the context of adjustment lending, tipping the scales toward reformist elements and away from vested interests. Under the wrong conditions, the World Bank's efforts have been met with frustration for both it and the borrower, and have led to a stalemate in the reform agenda.

In Papua New Guinea, progressive forces in the government bureaucracy and their allies in the World Bank were successful in using adjustment lending to consolidate policies that reined in rampant logging, and for several years prevented attempts by vested interests to roll back those reforms. In Indonesia, the World Bank and the International Monetary Fund took advantage of the 1997 financial crisis to shine a spotlight on governance issues in the forest sector, and force the dismantling of forest product marketing monopolies.

These limited successes are counterbalanced by significant failures and omissions. In Indonesia and Cameroon, the World Bank has so far been unable to transform government commitments into meaningful change in concession allocation and management systems. The cases provide little evidence of the World Bank effectively promoting reforms focused primarily on equity or environmental objectives. In Kenya, an attempt to promote a more broadly conceived environmental adjustment program never even reached the point of an identification mission, much less a lending operation.

Taken together, the case studies provide insight into the conditions under which the integration of forest policy reform objectives into adjustment lending can precipitate or consolidate desired policy change. On the part of the borrower, those conditions include constituencies for reform within the borrower government or civil society and opportunities for meaningful policy changes that do not require extensive institutional reform to implement. On the part of the World Bank, those conditions include strong and consistent commitment to the reform agenda and engagement with key stakeholders to define and communicate the objectives and strategy for reform.

The case studies challenge the emerging conventional wisdom that conditionality cannot be effective without full government commitment to the reform agenda, or borrower ownership. This view assumes that borrowers either do or do not have sufficient ownership, that it is reasonable to expect the World Bank to accurately assess the degree of that ownership in advance, and that there is little the World Bank can do to influence ownership. The experiences in Papua New Guinea, Cameroon, Indonesia, and Kenya illustrate the complexity and dynamics of constituencies for and against reform, inside and outside government, and how variables within the World Bank's control can influence the domestic politics of forest-related issues. While sustained policy reform and implementation ultimately depend on domestic political forces, forest-related conditions imposed by the World Bank have been effective in raising the profile of forest issues on the national agenda, prodding governments to commit themselves to new policies, and providing support to domestic constituencies' efforts for reform.

However, the cases suggest that conditions attached to adjustment lending are less effective in addressing the long-term institutional challenges characteristic of the forest sector that often constrain the implementation of agreed reforms. This is a significant finding, since in every case-study country, the World Bank singled out the lack of institutional capacity as a principal impediment to long-term sustainable forest management. Because of its short time frame, adjustment lending is poorly suited to supporting implementation and institutional reform. In addition, while the World Bank's principal interlocutors in adjustment lending, ministries of finance and planning, are often able and willing to effect changes in policies such as taxation that affect forests, ministries of forestry tend to be much less amenable to reforming themselves. There is not yet a record of experience to judge whether follow-on sectoral and project lending can be effective vehicles for implementing policy changes agreed to during adjustment operations.

The case studies also highlight the importance of the World Bank's ownership of the reform agenda, as evidenced by its willingness to be firm about forest-related conditionality. The World Bank was not an effective proponent of policy change when its commitment to reform was inconsistent up the institution's chain of command or over time. When the World Bank wavered in its commitment, it undermined the efforts of constituencies for reform in the borrower country.

In addition, the case studies indicate that the quality of the World Bank's engagement with stakeholders was also a significant factor. When it failed to engage key constituencies, the World Bank rendered reform efforts vulnerable to misunderstandings and design flaws in structural adjustment conditions, and allowed opponents of reform to dominate public debate.

While confirming that forest policy reform ultimately depends on domestic political variables, the case studies indicate that there are opportunities for the World Bank to cultivate coalitions for change. It can achieve this by broadening the scope of the reform program objectives beyond economic efficiency to include environmental, equity, and governance concerns. The World Bank can increase its effectiveness by reaching out to a larger group of stakeholders in the policy formulation and implementation process, and by insisting on conditions that open up forest policy decisionmaking to public scrutiny and participation.

RECOMMENDATIONS

The case study experience summarized in this report has implications for the World Bank at two levels, operational and strategic.

OPERATIONAL IMPLICATIONS

Safeguard policies: The World Bank's lack of credibility as a proponent of environmentally positive policy change is highlighted when internal contradictions in a reform package undermine environmental objectives. Environmental assessment procedures should be applied to structural adjustment loans to identify unintended negative environmental consequences.

Sustained sectoral engagement: The prospects of successfully promoting forest sector reform are increased when the necessary analysis and contacts are in place prior to launching an adjustment operation. The World Bank should conduct and disseminate analysis that addresses the social equity and environmental implications of proposed changes in the forest management regime, rather than limiting its analysis to efficiency objectives, in order to improve the effectiveness and legitimacy of adjustment operations.

Stakeholder engagement: World Bank should invest more resources in communicating with key stakeholder groups about the nature and purpose of adjustment lending, and in understanding their priorities and concerns. Equally important is that the World Bank move beyond an outreach mode to establish a dialogue with key stakeholders, and to incorporate their insights into the design and implementation of the proposed reform program.

Conditionality engineering: Adjustment conditionality has been more successful in leveraging a small number of high-profile policy changes than in effecting a large number of incremental steps necessary for their implementation. The World Bank should explore the use of conditions that specify the outcome to be achieved and characteristics of the decisionmaking process in order to increase transparency and public participation in policy design and implementation.

Staffing and incentives: If the World Bank is to broaden the adjustment agenda to include nontraditional issues and constituencies, it needs a different set of skills and attitudes: to conduct stakeholder analyses, more social scientists will be required; to move beyond efficiency objectives, macroeconomists will need to share responsibility for the reform agenda with others; to avoid alienating potential members of coalitions for change, perceived arrogance will need to be replaced by collegiality.

STRATEGIC IMPLICATIONS

Selectivity: An influential World Bank research report, *Assessing Aid*, asserts that donors should selectively focus their resources on countries with governments that have already demonstrated a commitment to reform. This proposition ignores the possibility that there are latent constituencies for reform even in countries where there is little overt support for the reform process, and that conditionality can empower these constituencies. Conditionality can alter the political dynamics of forest issues, if only by raising their profile on the national agenda, and can cause setbacks to those with vested interests in unsustainable logging.

The governance agenda: For the World Bank to be effective in promoting reform in the forest sector, it must centrally address governance issues. The World Bank was able to catalyze reforms where existing corrupt practices were challenged, as in Indonesia and Papua New Guinea, while the reforms were relatively ineffective where these practices were not firmly condemned, as in

Cameroon. Conversely, in some countries where forest issues are of material and symbolic significance nationally, it is incomplete for the World Bank to talk of good governance without reference to forest sector reform. This suggests that the environment and natural resources arena is a particularly suitable place to pursue a governance agenda.

Under the right conditions, in the borrower country and on the part of the World Bank, the World Bank can be an effective proponent of forest policy reform through adjustment lending. These findings suggest that adjustment lending, the World Bank's most significant instrument, presents an important opportunity for mainstreaming social, environmental, and governance objectives into the World Bank's work. The findings also offer a sobering challenge to the institution to get the conditions right.

1

INTRODUCTION

In 1998, a logjam that had blocked forest policy reform in Indonesia for decades was finally loosened when the World Bank, acting with the International Monetary Fund (IMF), included forest policy reforms among the conditions attached to a financial crisis assistance package. While the need for change had long been promoted in Indonesia and abroad by the World Bank and others, the deep political entrenchment of logging interests within Indonesia's political economy always stymied action. Backed by the political and economic weight of a structural adjustment program, the World Bank seized this moment of political opportunity to catalyze change.

The Indonesia case is the most recent of a small number of examples where the World Bank, often acting with the IMF, has sought to use structural adjustment lending to bring about forest policy reform. *(See Box 1.1 for a definition of structural adjustment lending.)* In principle, one could construe inclusion of forest-related objectives in structural adjustment programs as evidence of progress in implementing the World Bank's long-standing commitment to mainstream environmental concerns into the full range of its activities.[1] Proponents of this approach argue that adjustment lending provides a powerful tool with which to dismantle entrenched forest interests that block shifts to more environmentally and socially sound management regimes. Those who are more skeptical point to the limited credibility of the World Bank as an agent of progressive change based on its checkered history of engagement in the forest sector, and the controversial legacy of past structural adjustment.[2]

BOX 1.1 | STRUCTURAL ADJUSTMENT DEFINED

Structural adjustment loans (SALs)—also referred to as adjustment lending—support economy-wide policy change and institutional reform, rather than a specific project. Sectoral adjustment loans (SECALs) support reforms that are limited to a specific sector. The objectives of SALs are to

- provide balance-of-payments support,
- promote economic growth and poverty alleviation by stabilizing the macroeconomic environment,
- increase efficiency in the use of resources, and
- improve the scope for private sector development.

Sources: Jayarajah, 1995; World Bank, 1992

In this report, we examine the empirical record of the World Bank's attempts to apply structural adjustment lending to forest policy reform in Papua New Guinea, Cameroon, Indonesia and Kenya, and ask the following question:

To what extent, and under what conditions, can the World Bank be an effective proponent of forest policy reform through structural adjustment lending?

Our approach is to examine a limited set of cases where the World Bank has intentionally attempted to incorporate forest policy goals into adjustment lending, in order to understand the political economy behind the reform process. While most other reviews of adjustment lending have focused on a comparative assessment of outcomes, our primary interest is in the *process* by which adjustment lending is initiated, formulated, negotiated, and

implemented. This attention to the process of reform allows us to assess how different actors, international and domestic, affect the formulation of reforms and contribute to the progress of a reform agenda.

This approach raises at least two methodological issues.[3] First, in this study we restrict ourselves to the analysis of forest policy reform, which is necessary, though not always sufficient, to achieve environmentally sound forest outcomes. Moreover, in our emphasis on the process of reform, we do not enter into the debates over the specific content of those reforms. Second, we limit our focus to forest policy, while acknowledging that the fate of forests is often influenced as much or more by decisions taken outside the forest sector and by macroeconomic policy decisions. *(See Table 1.1 for a comparison of macroeconomic lending and forest project lending in the case study countries.)* Our approach

---

TABLE 1.1 | **WORLD BANK LENDING IN THE CASE STUDY COUNTRIES, 1980–1998**
(IN TOTAL COMMITMENTS US$ MILLION)

Country	Lending for Forest Projects *		Macroeconomic Lending		Total Lending ***	
	1980–1991	1992–1998	1980–1991	1992–1998	1980–1991	1992–1998
Papua New Guinea	0	0	50	50	436	135
Cameroon	39	0	150	432	1,052	767
Indonesia	54	57	600	1,000**	14,165	8,988
Kenya	57	61	186	171	1,889	1,146

*   Lending for Forest Projects includes direct lending for forest projects and indirect lending for forest development (projects with forests components).
** During fiscal year 1998, the World Bank approved a US$1 billion adjustment loan to Indonesia which was not included in the data sources referenced for this table.
*** Total lending includes non-forest project lending which is not summarized here.
Source: World Bank, 1998b

BOX 1.2 | SURINAME: INTERNATIONAL SUPPORT BUYS TIME
FOR FOREST POLICY REFORM

Background

In 1975, Suriname won independence from the Dutch. By 1982, relations between the former colony and the Netherlands had deteriorated following a military coup and serious human rights abuses. Dutch aid was partially suspended and Suriname entered a period of economic and political instability that has continued until today. Repeated failure to meet IMF and World Bank loan conditions led to withdrawal, over time, of these institutions and of the Inter-American Development Bank (IDB). Foreign assistance was largely limited to grant aid driven by the complex Netherlands-Suriname relationship.

In the mid-1990s, aid politics took a new twist in Suriname, one of the most heavily forested countries in the world and home to traditional Amerindian tribal societies. In 1994–95, following a visit by the President of Suriname to Asia, the government embarked on negotiations with several of Southeast Asia's most rapidly expanding logging enterprises. Local and international environmental, social developmental, and human rights groups were alarmed about the proposed massive logging investments, which at one time totaled over US$500 million. It was even revealed that some senior elected officials had received substantial bribes to promote the investments and were linked through family members to subsidiaries of the Malaysian and Indonesian firms.

International Intervention

Responding to pleas from overseas environmental groups, IDB's President, Enrique Iglesias, took a personal interest in the issue. He spoke with Suriname's head of state, Ronald Ventiaan, and offered to provide substantial financial support through loans and grants for technical cooperation, if the government would consider suspending logging expansion plans. News of the offer quickly reached the democratically elected National Assembly of Suriname where an already loud minority opposition to the logging deals was growing. The National Assembly, which had to formally approve the deals with a simple majority vote, became gridlocked between one group urging rapid approval and the other demanding that the IDB proposal be properly aired and reviewed as a viable alternative. During this period, the World Bank also sent letters expressing concern about the deal, though these carried very little weight, as it had no program in Suriname at the time. As the country began preparations for national elections, which an emerging opposition coalition would eventually win, any further debate of the logging deals was dismissed and no contracts were signed.

Results and Analysis

Since 1995, the IDB has continued to boost its environmental program in Suriname and has since helped to create a national environmental protection agency. In March 1998, the IDB approved a US$1.38 million grant, with additional cofinancing by the European Union, to support Suriname in its efforts to develop a national legal and institutional framework for environmental policy and management. This was followed in November 1998 by a US$30 million policy-based sector loan to Suriname for agriculture and trade with a component that addressed the need for forest policy implementation and reform. Under this component, Suriname had to ensure stakeholder participation in a long-term forest policy, and develop regulations to implement the Forest Management Act of 1992. These activities included efficiency pricing, actual collection of royalties and fees, and enforceable regulations for concessions.

IDB's intervention raised the political profile of the threats to forests. It offered the possibility of meeting cash needs through donor support rather than logging expansion, which strengthened domestic opposition to the logging deals. The IDB was able to play this role because, unlike other donors, it had maintained a presence in Suriname. This timely and sustained intervention helped head off a round of rampant logging in Suriname.

Sources: Sources from the Inter-American Development Bank, Environment and Natural Resources Division 3.

Inter-American Development Bank. 1998. *Agriculture and Trade Policy Reform Loan: Environmental and Social Impact Report.* Washington D.C.: Inter-American Development Bank.

Nigel Sizer and Richard Rice. 1995. *Backs to the Wall in Suriname: Forest Policy in a Country in Crisis.* Washington D.C.: World Resources Institute.

and methods are described further in the Appendix.

We have focused on a single institution, the World Bank, but many of the findings apply equally to other aid institutions, such as the intervention by the Inter-American Development Bank in Suriname described in Box 1.2. In some cases, notably Indonesia and Cameroon, the IMF has also been an important actor.[4] In these situations, since the IMF has drawn heavily on the World Bank for the content of forest reform conditions, as well as engagement with relevant stakeholders, we have maintained our focus on the World Bank.

The Right Conditions was shaped by two important contextual factors. First, in 1998, the World Bank initiated a comprehensive review of its engagement in the forest sector, the "Forest Policy Implementation Review and Strategy" (FPIRS), to assess its 1991 forest policy. This exercise will likely influence future World Bank lending in the forest sector. This study is designed as an indepen-

The poverty alleviation agenda has led the World Bank to embrace good governance, environmental protection, and human rights as legitimate concerns of both project lending and structural adjustment lending.

dent effort to examine the intentional use of adjustment lending to bring about forest policy reform, and is timed to make the results available as an input to the FPIRS.

Second, the World Bank's structural adjustment lending has changed—qualitatively and quantitatively—in recent years. A stated shift toward a poverty alleviation agenda has led the World Bank to embrace good governance, environmental protection, and human rights as legitimate concerns of both project lending and structural adjustment lending. In the wake of the Asian financial crisis of 1997, adjustment loans as a proportion of World Bank lending have more than doubled from their historical levels *(See Figure 1.1)*, an increase that suggests the need for additional attention to how this instrument is used.

WORLD BANK FOREST POLICY

Forest policy has long been a politically charged issue for the World Bank. While direct lending to the forest sector accounts for less than two percent of the World Bank's portfolio, it contributes, in the plaintive words of a senior World Bank manager, "98 percent of the headache" (World Bank,

1998b, p. 5). This disproportionately high profile of the forest sector arises primarily from the attention the international environmental movement has brought not only to forest projects, but also to the World Bank's broader engagement in the sector. Examples include large infrastructure projects, such as the Polonoreste road-building project in Brazil, macroeconomic policy lending that leads to unanticipated shifts in the incentives for patterns of forest use, and World Bank involvement in the controversial Tropical Forestry Action Plan (TFAP)—a joint exercise initiated by the World Resources Institute, the United Nations Development Programme, and the World Bank.[5]

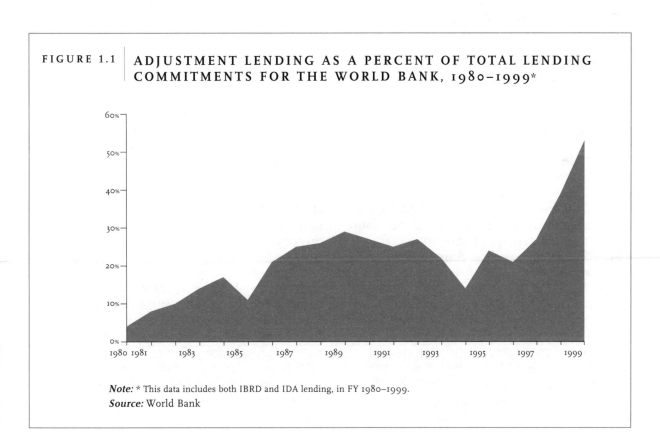

FIGURE 1.1 | ADJUSTMENT LENDING AS A PERCENT OF TOTAL LENDING COMMITMENTS FOR THE WORLD BANK, 1980–1999*

Note: * This data includes both IBRD and IDA lending, in FY 1980–1999.
Source: World Bank

Evolution of World Bank Forest Policy

Initiated in 1985 to halt the loss of tropical forests, the TFAP increased the volume and visibility of the World Bank's involvement in the forest sector. The World Bank played an important role in assisting with and funding national TFAP planning processes in several countries. Five years later, however, many analysts pronounced that TFAP had delivered less than its promise. A review by the World Resources Institute noted that while its originators had conceived of TFAP as a means to address the root causes of deforestation, it became instead a vehicle to harmonize donor assistance (Winterbottom, 1990). As a result, the TFAP was used to justify increased investment in the forest sector without fundamentally challenging existing forest management regimes. This perspective was too narrow to effect long-term change.

In 1991, the World Bank undertook a review of its lending experience in the forest sector, and developed a new policy paper to guide its involvement. The review, according to the authors, was stimulated by a realization that development thinking had moved beyond a preoccupation with mobilizing capital for industrial development, and had come to embrace the ecological value of forest resources, as well as their economic value to local communities (World Bank, 1991a; World Bank, 1991b). The review process sparked a debate over the appropriate role of the World Bank in supporting logging, and led to a policy that the World Bank would under no circumstances fund commercial logging in primary moist tropical forests (World Bank, 1991a). In addition to the ban on World Bank finance for logging, there were several other controversial issues at stake, including institutional and sociological aspects of control over and access to forests.

The 1991 review process concluded that the World Bank should emphasize program rather than project lending in the forest sector. The goal of sectoral program lending, it was argued, should be to structure incentives appropriately, develop an organizational structure, and establish the basis for participation by various stakeholders (World Bank, 1991b). The World Bank should only undertake projects that were embedded within a clear sectoral framework. Until this time, it had not undertaken program lending in the forest sector, with the exception of an influential sectoral adjustment loan (SECAL) to the Philippines in 1991. *(See Box 1.3.)*

Implementation of the 1991 policy was reviewed in 1994, but as the review document itself notes, the time span between formalization of the policy and the review was too short to identify the impacts of the new policy (World Bank, 1994b). For our purposes, it is relevant to note that this interim review did not address the impact of adjustment lending and macroeconomic policies in any systematic way, and relied instead on an existing World Bank study (later published as Cruz and Repetto, 1992) for conclusions on this topic.

The Forest Policy Implementation Review and Strategy (FPIRS), initiated in 1998, is a response to a commitment made by the World Bank in 1994 to engage in a more substantive review of the impact of its work on the forest sector. The early days of the FPIRS were controversial. First, internal documents were publicized that suggested that some World Bank staff sought to use the new review to revisit and remove the prohibition

BOX 1.3 | PHILIPPINES: BORROWER OWNERSHIP THROUGH FOREST SECTOR LENDING

Background

In the early 1980s, massive commercial logging and conversion of forests into agricultural lands caused severe deforestation in the Philippines. Over a 20 year-period, forest cover shrunk from half of total land area to less than a quarter, an ecological crisis that affected millions of Filipinos, including many of the seven to eight million indigenous peoples. Despite the scale of the problem, donors were reluctant to provide assistance for Philippine forest activities because of rampant corruption and the existence of politically powerful logging cartels. In 1986, the political conditions changed dramatically with the fall of President Marcos. In 1987, Fulgencio Factoran, a human rights lawyer, was appointed to head the Department of Environment and Natural Resources (DENR), and embarked on a campaign to reform the forest sector.

Adjustment Experience

At the same time, the new government of Corazon Aquino faced pressing macroeconomic problems, in particular a debt burden which by 1988 was consuming 32 percent of the nation's foreign exchange earnings. Her first order of business was to address balance-of-payments problems.

During the 1970s the forest sector had been an important source of foreign exchange earnings, accounting for 18 percent of exports in 1973. By 1987, although this proportion had dropped to five percent, the sector became an essential indirect part of the solution to the macroeconomic crisis by attracting donor dollars. By 1992, the DENR was one of the country's leading recipients of international aid. The World Bank, the Japanese government, and the Asian Development Bank (ADB) approved five forest-related loans totaling US$731 million, and the U.S. Agency for International

Development (USAID) provided an additional grant of US$125 million.

Forty percent of these funds, half of which came from a World Bank sectoral adjustment loan, were allocated to balance-of-payments support conditioned on a series of forest policy reforms. The government was required to increase logging fees, ban logging in primary forests, and enforce logging regulations. The logging companies were against these conditions and put extreme pressure on several influential members of the Philippine congress to oppose the reforms.

This opposition was overcome through clever strategic use of donor funds by the reformers. First, although most of the forest conditions were drafted collaboratively by the DENR and the World Bank, DENR staff presented the conditions as externally imposed, thereby displacing the political unpopularity of the conditions onto the shoulders of the donors. Second, DENR officials made allies of economic planners and the Central Bank of the Philippines who desperately needed balance-of-payments support. Third, the ADB loan allowed DENR staff to allocate funds by congressional district to compensate them for the loss of their patronage privileges, winning them over to the pro-reform side. Finally, the DENR mobilized the support of the local NGO community, and won public support through high-publicity raids on illegal loggers.

Outcomes

By tying forest reform to conditions mandated by multilateral and bilateral donors, the pro-reform stakeholders were successful in executing and institutionalizing their reform agenda despite political forces opposing the changes. The use of environmental conditions had three major effects: the political power of the logging companies was

BOX 1.3 | (CONTINUED)

broken on the national and regional levels; the logging industry's economic strength was undermined by denying loggers access to the country's most valuable timber in old-growth forests; and the capacity and institutions needed to enforce the reforms and conditions were created.

On the negative side of the ledger, critics noted that the need to repay large sums in foreign exchange to donors would be likely to place additional pressure on exports of environmentally sensitive resources. In addition, the massive scale of forestry funds made available in a short time-span outstripped state capacity to use these funds effectively. The result has been conflicts among various stakeholders, including local and international NGOs, private interests, and forestry communities.

Yet, some positive results are real and measurable. From 1987 to mid-1994, the number of timber licensees was drastically reduced from 154 licensees, with a combined annual allowable cut of 8.1 million cubic meters, to 31 licensees, with a cut of 878,000 cubic meters. The remaining licensees are better monitored, taxed at a higher rate, and are required to post bonds. Furthermore, over the last decade Philippine forest policy has shifted

from an emphasis on industrial forestry to the prioritization of community-based forest management as the best strategy toward sustainable forestry and social justice.

In the Philippines case, the essential conditions to make such a reform agenda work were a strong reform constituency within the country and politically sophisticated leadership, open public consultative processes and access to information to engage the NGO constituency, and pressure, both internationally and from individuals within the ADB and the World Bank, to engage in environmental reform.

Sources: Michael Ross. 1996. "Conditionality and Logging Reform in the Tropics." In *Institutions for Environmental Aid,* edited by R. Keohane and M. Levy. Cambridge, Massachusetts: MIT Press.

Frances Korten. 1994. "Questioning the Call for Environmental Loans: A Critical Examination of Forestry Lending in the Philippines," *World Development,* Vol. 22, No. 7: 971–981.

Interviews with Antonio G.M. La Viña, former Undersecretary of the Department of Environment and Natural Resources, on March 11, 1999 and May 11, 1999.

---

on direct support for logging in primary moist tropical forests. In this context, some World Bank staff expressed the opinion that the policy has precluded strategic financing to promote sustainable forest management practices.[6] Others were more concerned that many World Bank managers interpreted the policy in a manner that has allowed them to disengage from a controversial sector. Second, preparations for the forest review were overshadowed by a controversial set of

meetings initiated in 1998 by the president of the World Bank with the leaders of large logging companies. This rocky start illustrates the charged atmosphere within which discussions over the World Bank's role in forest issues are conducted.

World Bank Forest Policy: The Debates

As mentioned earlier, debates over the World

Bank's approach to forest issues have been contentious in part because of a failure to address the impact of lending in nonforest sectors (Kaimowitz and Angelsen, n.d.), and

---

The World Bank's critics have called for greater attention to the institutional, political, and sociological questions around who controls forest access and use.

---

macroeconomic policies on forests (Cruz and Repetto, 1992).[7] However, the policies that are explicitly directed at forests have not been free of contention either. World Bank foresters have tended to focus their attention on the promotion of an effective system for the management of industrial forestry. By contrast, the World Bank's critics have called for greater attention to the institutional, political, and sociological questions around who controls forest access and use, how environmental issues are addressed, and how forest resources are tied to the national political economy.

In 1989, the World Bank commissioned a study of forest pricing and concession systems with an emphasis on West and Central Africa. The results outline the issues, current practices, and recommendations for use by staff preparing loans to countries in this region, and capture a conventional wisdom of the time in the World Bank on reform of industrial logging operations. *(See Box 1.4.)* This view informed the policy reforms described in the chapters that follow and remains an important component of World Bank thinking on the forest sector.

This conventional wisdom has been the subject of an ongoing debate within and outside the World Bank, a debate which has raised questions as to whether the proposed policies are practical or will achieve the desired outcomes.[8] In addition, there are serious concerns as to whether a general approach such as this set of reforms can sufficiently address the diversity of forest issues and experiences in different countries.[9]

Beyond the specifics of the debate over the policies, however, there are two points that are relevant to this discussion. First, the conventional wisdom addresses equity issues only indirectly, by assuming that enhanced rent capture from the forest sector by the state will allow for greater reinvestment for poverty alleviation and equity-oriented programs. By contrast, World Bank critics from civil society stress more direct approaches to the objective of poverty alleviation and the explicit incorporation of participatory processes into decisions over forest use (Bank Information Center et al., 1999). This theme includes concerns over who has access to and control over forest resources, industrial loggers or community dwellers, and issues over the rights of forest-dwelling and indigenous communities.

Second, the conventional wisdom only addresses environmental issues indirectly. Reformist logging policies are aimed at intensifying logging in a limited area, thereby freeing other forest areas from logging pressures. In addition, the conventional wisdom assumes that increasing the value of standing timber provides incentives for less wasteful logging practices and better protection against encroachment. In rebuttal, conservationists argue that conservation interests are better served more directly,

BOX 1.4 | ## WORLD BANK CONVENTIONAL WISDOM ON FOREST POLICY

The Diagnosis

"(F)orest revenue and concessions systems in West and Central Africa and probably in many other developing countries too, are characterized by unmanageable complexity, timber fees that are considerably below what the concessionaires are willing to pay, very low tax collection rate, arbitrary allocation of concessions, failure to make use of market mechanisms, forest destruction due to lack of forest management, enormous waste of wood, and financial irregularities."

Recommendations

USE AUCTIONS TO ALLOCATE CONCESSIONS

Administrative allocations of concessions based on mutual agreement between the government and the company lead to concessions of short duration and with no forest management requirements. This approach has tended to greatly undervalue the resource, leading to inefficiency and generation of low tax revenues. This system is also susceptible to political pressure. By contrast, auctions allow the market to determine the highest value of the resource. Moreover, in theory, auctions are transparent (because any qualified company can bid and the criteria for allocation are predetermined), objective (because the company, not the government, decides what price to pay for the concession), and efficient (because it favors those companies that can make the most money, and pay the most tax, from the concession). Concessions should be allocated for at least 30 years.

REPLACE VOLUME-BASED TAXES WITH AREA TAXES

Area taxes are an instrument to increase revenue collection (because they are easy to collect) and a useful regulatory tool (because they act as a disincentive to companies that want to acquire huge concessions for speculative purposes). They are particularly powerful when coupled with an auction system because they force companies to reveal how much they consider the forest to be worth. This is important in those countries where the companies usually have much better data on the commercial value of the forest than does the government. Under these conditions, an area tax-based auction system serves as a disclosure mechanism.

REMOVE EXPORT BANS AND REDUCE EXPORT TAXES

Many countries have introduced log export bans and high log export taxes in an effort to promote industrialization. These measures depress the price of logs on the domestic market, which has several negative consequences: it encourages wasteful logging and wood processing, reduces incomes of logging companies and logging-dependent communities, implies revenue forgone from log exports, and reduces the implicit value of the standing forest with consequent higher risks of agricultural conversion.

REQUIRE FOREST MANAGEMENT PLANS

Whereas the use of auctions and higher area taxes are part of a sound forest policy, there is little empirical evidence of their impact on harvesting practices, which some fear will intensify. Allocation and taxation reforms should, therefore, be coupled with a requirement for forest management plans to mitigate the potential negative impacts caused by higher volume harvesting. This requirement also responds to growing domestic and international support for the notion of sustainable forest management. The private sector and NGOs should also be involved in monitoring and reporting on forest management practices and forest conditions.

Source: Grut, Gray, and Egli, 1991

through the establishment of protected areas (Bowles et al., 1998).[10]

While the World Bank has increased its forest-related project lending aimed at equity and environmental concerns following the 1991 forest sector policy (World Bank, 1994b), the institution has lagged behind in explicitly integrating these concerns into policy prescriptions. The center of the World Bank's agenda remains a reformist one: given the reality of industrial logging, the policy prescriptions are designed to ameliorate both equity and environmental concerns by improving the efficiency of industrial logging.

THE CHANGING FACE OF STRUCTURAL ADJUSTMENT LENDING

Debates over Adjustment Lending

SALs and SECALs are the World Bank's primary means to induce policy reform in borrower countries. Three features of structural adjustment loans distinguish them from other types of aid instruments.[11] First, since SALs relate to the economy as a whole and are usually large relative to the size of an economy, they are negotiated directly with ministries of finance and top economic officials, an audience that does not typically make the links between their economic briefs and forest issues. Second, inserting forest conditions into a SAL serves to structurally link forest policy reforms to high-profile macroeconomic adjustment issues. Forest issues could either be heightened by the linkage or overshadowed, depending on the particular case. Third, SALs must be designed and disbursed quickly, calling into question

whether they can support long-term reform measures.

Between 1984 and 1992, about one quarter of World Bank funds were committed to structural adjustment loans annually (Kapur, Lewis, and Webb, 1997). However, SALs absorbed a "disproportionate amount of the time and nervous energy" (Kapur, Lewis, and Webb, 1997, p. 517) of the World Bank's management and Executive Board for two reasons.

First, adjustment lending increased the accountability of governments to donors and potentially weakened the accountability of governments to their domestic constituents. Many of the proposed policies introduced through adjustment lending were politically unpopular, with few short-term benefits and political rewards; borrower governments resented being forced to implement policies that often undermined their political base of support. While adjustment is a means of holding borrower governments accountable to donors, the donors in turn are largely accountable only to wealthy industrialized countries. As Kapur et al. put it in their history of the World Bank: " 'accountability' is not a particularly symmetrical variable" (Kapur, Lewis, and Webb, 1997, p. 704).[12]

Moreover, greater accountability to donors does not necessarily foster greater accountability to domestic constituents and can even undermine it. The potentially negative effects of adjustment lending on accountability are particularly problematic when adjustment loans are perceived as propping up illegitimate regimes.[13] As governance concerns have been given greater prominence in the World Bank's stated agenda, this concern could be explicitly addressed by structuring adjustment loans to promote greater transparency in reform processes in borrower countries. Whether the benefits from doing so will be greater than the potential costs of sustaining illegitimate governments can only be determined on a case by case basis.

Second, the content of adjustment lending programs was controversial. Through the 1980s and beyond, there was a steady stream of external criticism of the process, priorities, and outcomes of adjustment lending both from other international institutions,[14] academics,[15] and from civil society organizations.[16] A primary reason for discontent over adjustment lending is that the instrument has typically been used to promote a limited menu of macroeconomic reforms with little attention to social and environmental implications. These criticisms raise an important question: can adjustment lending overcome its perception as a harbinger of short-term societal harm?

For the purposes of this study, a particularly salient criticism is that neither negative nor positive environmental impacts are systematically addressed in structural adjustment loans. *(See Box 1.5.)* Yet, previous analyses have concluded that responsible adjustment lending must not only assess and mitigate potential negative consequences of macroeconomic reforms, but should also include measures designed to maximize social and environmental benefits (Cruz and Repetto, 1992; Munasinghe and Cruz, 1995; Reed, 1996). The World Bank's Operational Directive on adjustment lending does indeed instruct staff to "consider the implications for the environment" and "take into account" findings about linkages between the reform program and the environment (World Bank, 1992, p. 3). However, a recent internal World

Neither negative nor positive environmental impacts are systematically addressed in structural adjustment loans.

Bank study reported that less than 20 percent of loans approved in FY98 and FY99 had any substantial mention of potential environmental impacts arising from the loans (World Bank, 1999). By contrast, sectoral adjustment loans are currently subject to the stronger requirement of an environmental assessment under the World Bank's Environmental Assessment Policy (World Bank, 1999).

These two concerns, regarding accountability and content, are central to current debates within civil society groups on adjustment lending.

On the one hand there are those who recognize the need for ownership and sovereignty but regard some governments as unresponsive to the wider needs of their populations and therefore support some form of "poverty focused" or "social" conditionality, which if done right could strengthen civil society; on the other, there are those who regard all conditionality imposed from outside as undermining the democratic system and abusing the sovereignty of the borrower country (Wood and Lockwood, 1999, p. 3).

In this study, we examine the empirical record to ask if the content of adjustment lending can be changed to address social and environmental problems, and undertaken in

THE ENVIRONMENTAL IMPACTS OF STRUCTURAL ADJUSTMENT

The environmental impacts of structural adjustment operate through a variety of pathways. First, in extractive economies, incentives to trade on the world market intensify extraction of natural resources without a corresponding set of safeguards to mitigate environmental costs (Reed, 1996). Second, macroeconomic policies change incentives across sectors, which lead to depleting unpriced or underpriced natural resources and environmental services in favor of accumulating relatively unproductive industrial capital (Cruz and Repetto, 1992).

Third, in the agricultural sector, while commercial farmers are able to respond to new price signals to intensify and increase the efficiency of production with some environmental gains, subsistence farmers and agricultural workers respond by extensifying production, placing additional stress on natural resources, or are forced into the ranks of the urban informal sector (Reed, 1996). In the Philippines, for example, Cruz and Repetto report that macroeconomic policies depressed agricultural incomes, which caused farmers to migrate to ecologically sensitive areas and put pressure on the natural resources of those regions (Cruz and Repetto, 1992). Finally, the weakening of state institutions and fiscal reductions often accompany adjustment lending, which circumscribes the ability of the state to manage natural resources and enforce environmental laws (Reed, 1996).

Several studies conclude that some macroeconomic policies can also be environmentally beneficial, and can be made more so if they are intentionally designed with environmental objectives in mind (Cruz and Repetto, 1992; Munasinghe and Cruz, 1995; Reed, 1996). Examples of environmentally positive measures include removal of price distortions that result in perverse incentives for natural resource use, awareness of and compensation for market failures where environmental services are under-priced, measures to strengthen environmental monitoring and enforcement units at national and sub-national levels, and legal provisions to appropriately delegate authority for natural resource management, such as community forestry measures (Cruz and Repetto, 1992; Munasinghe and Cruz, 1995; Reed, 1996). Pricing, monitoring and enforcement, and the delegation of management authority are all reform measures of central importance to the forest sector.

a manner that encourages governance reforms.

Beyond Macroeconomics: Adjustment Lending Extended

Although the definition of adjustment lending emphasizes only growth rates and balance-of-payments as legitimate goals, the experience of adjustment lending, dominated by unsuccessful efforts in Sub-Saharan Africa in the 1980s, forced the World Bank to reconsider. An important review of the African experience concluded that African governments must "go beyond the issues of public finance, monetary policy, prices and markets to address fundamental questions relating to human capacities, institutions, governance, the environment, population growth and distribution and technology . . . ordinary people should participate more in designing and implementing development programs" (World Bank 1989, p. 1).[17] Moreover, as Nelson and Eglinton (1992) point out, this shift in thinking was widespread across the aid community and was triggered in no small part by geo-political events such as the collapse of the Soviet bloc.

Despite the officially apolitical mandate of the World Bank, the triumph of liberal democracy opened the door to a variety of objectives—good governance, environmental protection, human rights—seen as necessary preconditions to economic well-being and also as positive outcomes in their own right.[18] The extent to which the World Bank could expand its mandate to achieve these broader objectives became the object of study not only within the World Bank, but also by outside academics and NGOs (Bosshard et al., 1996; Nelson and Eglinton, 1993). Because achieving these new objectives of adjustment lending is facilitated by and dependent on good governance (Nelson and Eglinton, 1993), defining the role of the state was, then, an important part of articulating this new vision. The World Bank's 1997 *World Development Report* articulates this vision as the need to match the state's role to its capability, and reinvigorate public institutions so as to boost their capability (World Bank, 1997). As discussed earlier, reforms required in the forest sector rely on state capability and fall squarely within the category of reforms that depend on good governance.

The Adjustment Paradox

From the inception of adjustment lending, the viability of tying policy reform to loans has been questioned. If borrower governments are not committed to reform, then will an adjustment loan convince them to re-evaluate policies? And if they are already committed to change, then why do they need an adjustment loan to implement reform (Mosley, Harrigan, and Toye, 1995)?[19] For much of the history of adjustment lending, the two sides—the World Bank and borrower governments—have refused to recognize this paradox that potentially undermines the viability of adjustment lending.

The World Bank has publicly characterized its approach to the formulation of adjustment loans as apolitical, consensual, and noninterventionist. As Kahler (1989, p. 140) sums up the official line: "Programs are designed by governments to meet their own needs; if they also meet the IMF and World Bank criteria, then they will be supported financially." But in such cases, what is the money for, and what purpose does the conditionality serve? By contrast, from a borrower country's perspective, formulating an adjustment loan is a bargaining process—how much money is being exchanged for what measure of policy reform. Implicit in the bargaining perspective is that borrower governments have little or no ownership over the reform process, and have an incentive to side-step politically difficult reforms wherever possible.[20]

In reality, the adjustment paradox rests on an assumption of unitary political actors on both sides of the bargaining table (Kahler, 1989). Yet, as the case studies in this report illustrate, within both the World Bank and the borrower government are different actors with sometimes conflicting motivations and incentives. Acknowledging multiple actors and interests shifts the debate beyond the dichotomy of borrower versus World Bank control, to an exploration of the political tensions involved in adjustment lending processes. The middle ground of negotiation, political struggle, and dialogue between the extreme models of World Bank and borrower ownership is the terrain that most adjustment

---

The middle ground of negotiation, political struggle, and dialogue between the extreme models of World Bank and borrower ownership is the terrain that most adjustment programs must in reality negotiate.

---

programs must in reality negotiate. This is particularly true in the forest sector, which is often riven by overlapping and contentious tenure regimes, competing uses of industrial and community forestry, and weak enforcement of existing laws and regulations.

Conditionality Engineering

The World Bank's ability to induce and cajole governments, and to strengthen different constituencies within borrower countries rests, in part, on its application of conditionality to projects, policies, or as a screen to determine aid eligibility (Nelson and Eglinton, 1993). Conditionality for policy reform can have three main objectives.[21] First, the World Bank can use conditionality to induce reform where a borrower does not want to undertake reform. Second, conditioned aid can serve to keep borrowers committed to reforms already undertaken by threatening to withdraw aid. Third, agreement with conditions can be a signal to other donors and investors that a credible policy program is in place.

To achieve any of these goals, both sides must believe that the underlying contract between the World Bank and the borrower government will be enforced. However, it is extremely difficult to maintain the credibility of this contract (Wood and Lockwood, 1999). First, policy conditions are often hard to monitor, open to interpretation, and the extent of compliance with them may require subjective assessment. Second, donors such as the World Bank often have incentives to keep lending money, which lead them to avoid declaring a borrower out of compliance. Moreover, since stopping funding could produce a macroeconomic crisis and result in the borrower defaulting on repayment, the lender has an incentive to avoid imposing a penalty and instead to provide additional loans to stem crises irrespective of policy performance (Collier et al., 1997). Third, it is difficult to prevent reform processes from stalling once conditionality has lapsed and funds have been disbursed, if there is no domestic commitment to the policy reform. These difficulties are amplified in governance-rich arenas, such as forestry, that are relatively less amenable to irreversible reforms implemented by a stroke of the pen.

Given this situation, both the World Bank and independent studies report low degrees of conditionality effectiveness. In a study of the effectiveness of tranche conditions, the release of tranches was delayed in three-quarters of World Bank adjustment loans between 1980 and 1988 because of noncompliance (cited in Collier et al., 1997, p. 1401).[22] In this context, one line of thinking emphasizes the need for dialogue to bring the objectives of the borrower and the donor more in line with each other, and specifically for the borrower to develop ownership over the reform program.[23]

Borrower Ownership

While borrower ownership is widely and approvingly invoked in studies of adjustment lending, there have been few attempts to define the concept. One exception, a World Bank discussion paper by Johnson and Wasty (1993), identifies four components by which borrower ownership may be measured: locus of initiative (borrower or World Bank); level of intellectual conviction among key borrower policymakers; expression of political will at the top; and effort toward consensus building among various stakeholders.

This definition suggests that the role of World Bank task managers should be to build intellectual conviction within government, encourage expression of this conviction through political expression, and engage nongovernmental constituencies in formulation of reform efforts. A goal of this report is to assess the extent to which World Bank staff attempted to and were able to pursue this approach, and to comment on the results of such an approach where it was attempted.[24]

New Thinking in Development Assistance

A recent influential study by the World Bank, *Assessing Aid*, finds that using conditionality to twist the arms of governments does not work, and that the borrower's ownership of a reform program is critical to its success. The primary conclusion, in an echo of earlier debates over allocative conditionality, is that donors should be more selective, and aid dollars should be sent to countries with sound economic management.[25] In positive environments, reformist governments can use policy-conditioned lending to protect reforms from special interests and to signal their seriousness of intent to the outside world (World Bank, 1998a).

Based on a regression analysis, the study concludes that whether adjustment lending succeeds depends on existing political and economic variables, and minimally on variables under the World Bank's control such as size of the loan, number of conditions, resources used to prepare the loan, and resources used for analytical work in the four years prior to the loan (World Bank, 1998a). Thus, the study adamantly counters the suggestion that "if the World Bank works harder or puts more resources into an adjustment loan, a failed reformer can somehow be turned into a successful one" (World Bank, 1998a, p. 59).

The variables used in *Assessing Aid* to represent World Bank effort fail to measure its sophistication in negotiating the political terrain in borrower countries. However, to build borrower ownership the World Bank must engage political actors by finding and supporting reformers within governments, supporting knowledge creation, and engaging civil society. Although they find no place in the regression analysis, these are precisely the measures recommended in the report for countries with poor policy environments, a recommendation that runs counter to the primary conclusion that the World Bank cannot turn a failed reformer into a successful one. Hence, the report contradicts itself. Instead of the dichotomous view of borrowers as either likely successes ripe for Bank intervention or likely failures, it is more fruitful to consider a spectrum of ownership over policy reform across borrower countries, and to explore the alternatives available to the World Bank for intervention across this spectrum.

*   *   *   *

The next three chapters summarize the findings of case studies of the World Bank's experience with forest policy reform and adjustment lending in Papua New Guinea, Cameroon, and Indonesia. Chapter Five describes the case of Kenya, where an entire adjustment operation related to environmental policy reform was proposed, but never realized. The concluding chapter synthesizes the findings, lays out the conditions under which the World Bank can be an effective proponent of forest policy reform through adjustment lending, and suggests the implications of those findings for the World Bank's policies, practices, and strategies.

REFERENCES

Bank Information Center, Consumer's Choice Council, Environmental Defense Fund, Forest Peoples' Programme-UK, Urgewald-Germany, World Rainforest Movement. 1999. "NGO Comments on the OED Design Paper." Mimeo.

Boscolo, Marco, and Jeffrey R. Vincent. 1998. "Promoting Better Logging Practices in Tropical Forests." Washington D.C.: The World Bank.

Bosshard, Peter, Carlos Heredia, David Hunter, and Frances Seymour. 1996. *Lending Credibility: New Mandates and Partnerships for the World Bank.* Washington D.C.: World Wildlife Fund.

Bowles, Ian A., R.E. Rice, R.A. Mittermeier, and G.A.B. da Fonseca. 1998. "Logging and Tropical Forest Conservation." *Science* 280 (19 June): 1899–1900.

Collier, Paul, Patrick Guillaumont, Sylviane Guillaumont, and Jan Willem Gunning. 1997. "Redesigning Conditionality." *World Development* 25 (9):1399–1407.

Cornia, Andrea, Richard Jolly, and Frances Stewart. 1987. *Adjustment with a Human Face.* Oxford: Oxford University Press.

Cruz, Wilfrido, and Robert Repetto. 1992. *The Environmental Effects of Stabilization and Structural Adjustment Programs: The Philippines Case.* Washington D.C.: World Resources Institute.

Development GAP. 1995. *Structural Adjustment and the Spreading Crisis in Latin America.* Washington D.C.: The Development GAP.

Grut, Michael, John A. Gray, and Nicolas Egli. 1991. *Forest Pricing and Concession Policies.* Washington D.C.: The World Bank.

Grynberg, Roman. (no date.) "Not Even the Hewers of Wood: Export Taxes, Downstream-Processing and the Bretton Woods Consensus." Mimeo.

Horta, Korinna. 1999. "Governance Issues: The Achilles Heel of International Financial Institutions." Paper read at World Resources Institute's Workshop on Environmental Governance in Central Africa, at Washington DC.

Johnson, John H., and Sulaiman Wasty. 1993. "Borrower Ownership of Adjustment Programs and the Political Economy of Reform." Washington D.C.: Operations Evaluation Division, The World Bank.

Kahler, Miles. 1989. "International Financial Institutions and the Politics of Adjustment." In *Fragile Coalitions: The Politics of Economic Adjustment*, edited by J. M. Nelson. New Brunswick, NJ: Transaction Books.

Kaimowitz, David, and Arild Angelsen. (no date.) "The World Bank and Non-Forest Sector Policies that Affect Forests." Bogor, Indonesia: CIFOR.

Kapur, Devesh, John P. Lewis, and Richard Webb. 1997. The World Bank: Its First Half Century. 2 vols. Vol. I. Washington D.C.: Brookings Institution Press.

Karsenty, Alain. 1998. "Environmental Taxation and Economic Instruments for Forest Management in the Congo Basin." London: International Institute for Environment and Development.

Killick, Tony. 1997. "Failings of Conditionality." *Journal of International Development* 9 (4):483–495.

Mosley, Paul. 1987. "Conditionality as Bargaining Process: Structural-Adjustment Lending, 1980–86." Princeton, NJ: Princeton University, International Finance Section.

Mosley, Paul, Jane Harrigan, and John Toye. 1995. *Aid and Power: The World Bank and Policy-Based Lending.* New York: Routledge.

Munasinghe, Mohan, and Wilfrido Cruz. 1995. *Economywide Policies and the Environment: Lessons from Experience.* Washington, D.C.: The World Bank.

Nelson, Joan M., and Stephanie J. Eglinton. 1992. *Encouraging Democracy: What Role for Conditioned Aid.* Washington D.C.: Overseas Development Council.

—1993. *Global Goals, Contentious Means: Issues of Multiple Aid Conditionality.* Washington, D.C.: Overseas Development Council.

Reed, David, ed. 1996. *Structural Adjustment, the Environment, and Sustainable Development*: Earthscan Publications.

Rich, Bruce. 1994. *Mortgaging the Earth: The World Bank, Environmental Impoverishment and the Crisis of Development.* Boston: Beacon Press.

Seymour, Frances. 1996. "The World Bank and Environmental Sustainability." In *Lending Credibility: New Mandates and Partnerships for the World Bank*, edited by P. Bosshard, C. Heredia, D. Hunter and F. Seymour. Washington D.C.: World Wildlife Fund.

Stern, Ernest. 1991. "Evolution and Lessons of Adjustment Lending." In *Restructuring Economies in Distress: Policy Reform and the World Bank*, edited by V. Thomas, A. Chibber, M. Dailami and J. d. Melo. Oxford: Oxford University Press.

Wade, Robert. 1997. "Greening the Bank: The Struggle over the Environment, 1970–1995." In *The World Bank: Its First Half Century*, edited by D. Kapur, J. P. Lewis, and R. Webb. Washington D.C.: Brookings Institution Press.

Walker, R.T., and T.E. Smith. 1993. "Tropical Deforestation and Forest Management under the System of Concession Logging: A Decision Theoretic Analysis." *Journal of Regional Science* 33:387–419.

White, Howard, and Oliver Morrissey. 1997. "Conditionality when Donor and Recipient Preferences Vary." *Journal of International Development* 9:497–505.

Winterbottom, Robert. 1990. *Taking Stock: The Tropical Forestry Action Plan after Five Years.* Washington D.C.: World Resources Institute.

Wood, Angela, and Matthew Lockwood. 1999. "The 'Perestroika of Aid'? New Perspectives on Conditionality." Bretton Woods Project and Christian Aid.

World Bank, The. 1989. *Sub-Saharan Africa: From Crisis to Sustainable Growth.* Washington D.C.: The World Bank.

—1991a. "The Forest Sector." Washington D.C.: The World Bank.

—1991b. "Forestry: The World Bank's Experience." Washington D.C.: Operations Evaluation Division, The World Bank.

—1992. "Operational Directive: Adjustment Lending Policy." Washington D.C.: The World Bank.

—1994a. *Adjustment in Africa: Reforms, Results and the Road Ahead.* Oxford: Oxford University Press.

—1994b. "Review of Implementation of the Forest Sector Policy." Washington D.C.: The World Bank.

—1995. "Mainstreaming the Environment: The World Bank Group and the Environment since the Rio Earth Summit." Washington D.C.: The World Bank.

—1997. *World Development Report.* Oxford: Oxford University Press.

—1998a. *Assessing Aid: What Works, What Doesn't, and Why.* Washington, D.C.: The World Bank.

—1998b. "Forests and the World Bank: An OED Review of the 1991 Forest Policy and its Implementation." Washington D.C.: The World Bank.

—1999. "Social and Environmental Aspects: A Desk Review of SECALs and SALs Approved during FY98 and FY99." Washington D.C.: Environmentally and Socially Sustainable Development, The World Bank.

NOTES

1. A World Bank report entitled, "Mainstreaming the Environment," notes that in addition to specific environmental programs, the challenge for the institution is to ensure that "environmental concerns are incorporated into the *entire* portfolio of the World Bank's activities" (emphasis in original) (World Bank, 1995). See Seymour (1996) and Wade (1997) for a discussion of such efforts to integrate environmental concerns into the World Bank's policies and projects.

2. For a sweeping critique of the World Bank's environmental policies, see Rich (1994).

3. We are grateful to David Kaimowitz (CIFOR) for raising these issues.

4. The IMF has also been involved in Cambodia (*see Box 4.4*).

5. A second precursor was the Food and Agriculture Organization's (FAO) Tropical Forest Action Plan, and FAO later became the coordinator of the TFAP (Winterbottom, 1990).

6. Based on comments made at World Bank meetings attended by one of the authors.

7. These themes also emerge from NGO commentaries on World Bank policy and letters to World Bank staff, most recently summarized in a letter from a group of NGOs commenting on the OED Design Paper for the 1998–99 FPIRS (1999).

8. For example, Walker and Smith (1993) show that a long duration of concession is neither a necessary nor sufficient condition for good forest management. What matters to logging companies is not the official concession duration, but rather their expectations about how long they will be allowed to log in an area. In another example, Boscolo and Vincent (1998) challenge the conventional wisdom on longer concessions, by arguing that because of discounting, longer concessions in reality provide little incentive to adopt reduced-impact logging or to comply with minimum limits on the diameter of trees cut. Karsenty (1998) argues that many of the proposed reforms, such as forest taxation, require a level of technical capacity and public accountability that is lacking.

9. Grynberg (n.d.) argues this position from the perspective of the Solomon Islands. For details of this case, see Box 2.1.

10. See the exchange between Bowles et al. (1998) and others in the September 4 issue of *Science*.

11. The authors are grateful to Joan Nelson for this succinct characterization of the features of SALs.

12. This point is developed further in Horta (1999).

13. Horta (1999), in a paper that makes reference to both Cameroon and Indonesia as problematic cases, asks, "Could it be that by supporting national governments which often have little legitimacy in the eyes of their own populations and which are not accountable to their own citizens, the World Bank and other donor agencies are actually undermining the possibilities for democratic change, i.e., governance reform?"

14. Particularly influential was the report by UNICEF, *Adjustment with a Human Face*, which focused on the social costs of adjustment as measured by adverse changes in social indicators (Cornia, Jolly, and Stewart, 1987).

15. The most comprehensive of the academic studies is Mosley et al. (1995).

16. See, for example, Development GAP (1995).

17. Interestingly, this trend toward a more expansive definition of the goals of adjustment lending was reversed in a subsequent report on Africa which reinforced the importance of investment in human capital, institution building, and governance, but reinstated macroeconomic conditions as the primary objective by adding: "The objective of structural adjustment programs thus is to establish a market-friendly set of incentives that can encourage the accumulation of capital and more efficient allocation of resources" (World Bank, 1994a, p. 2).

18. As the history of the World Bank notes, "environmental protection has joined poverty alleviation and social-sector improvement as a major amendment to the macroeconomic goals of policy-based lending" (Kapur, Lewis, and Webb, 1997, p. 534).

19. This paradox troubled the World Bank's Board in the early days of adjustment lending. One often heard response is that an adjustment loan enables proper sequencing of reform, and serves as an insurance policy in the event that reforms fail to work. Mosley et al. (1995) note that neither of these considerations was given much weight when the idea of adjustment lending was formally discussed by the World Bank's Board. For Ernest Stern, who, along with Robert McNamara, was the originator and main proponent of adjustment lending in the early years (Kapur, Lewis, and Webb, 1997), the rationale for adjustment lending was, and remains, clear: structural adjustment lending is quick disbursing and "ought to be anchored in balance-of-payments problems." As such, Stern argued there should be a clear distinction between adjustment lending and the need for policy reform (Stern, 1991). This restrictive definition would certainly clarify the rationale for adjustment lending. Unfortunately, it would also place the World Bank in the position of poaching on IMF territory; the second reason for the Board's early skepticism of adjustment lending (Mosley, 1987).

20. One, albeit incomplete, indicator of the relative ineffectiveness of adjustment lending, is that the World Bank's independent Operations and Evaluation Department reports that 36 percent of reform programs evaluated between 1980 and 1995 were deemed not to have met their reform objectives (World Bank, 1998a). Moreover, the history of the World Bank notes dryly that internal assessments of the impact of adjustment lending on growth have "not been euphoric" (Kapur, Lewis, and Webb, 1997, p. 543). On this last indicator, it is fair to note, however, that there is no clear counterfactual—what would have happened in the absence of adjustment lending—against which to measure success or failure.

21. This list is drawn selectively from Collier et al. (1997) and White and Morrissey (1997).

22. One donor reaction has been to tighten the contractual framework by tying release of funds to a pre-specified sequence of policy reforms—short-leash lending—and even to tie release of specific amounts of program aid to specific reforms (Collier et al., 1997). Another reaction has been to sidestep the explicit condition negotiation process altogether and provide aid as a reward for successful policy reform. Collier et al. (1997) take this logic one step further to suggest that adjustment lending be conditioned on the achievement of outcomes rather than on the implementation of policies. However, devising mutually agreeable, nonbiased, and measurable indicators of success is far harder for outcome conditions than policy conditions, a challenge that is even greater for poverty, environment, or governance conditionality than for macroeconomic conditionality.

23. Thus, Kahler (1989) argues for persuasion, dialogue, and joint problem solving. Killick (1997) calls for selectivity, ownership, support and dialogue. White and Morrissey (1997) conclude that the only constructive roles for conditionality are monitoring and support.

24. It is important to note that Johnson and Wasty do not find the nature of government interac-

tion with the World Bank to be a significant determinant of borrower ownership. However, interaction was measured by the frequency and amount of World Bank engagement on the basis of review of secondary documents, not by quality of engagement. Moreover, their study did not examine the role of engagement with non-state stakeholders. This study will seek to rectify these omissions through detailed case studies. Other factors that were found to be of limited, or no, significance to borrower ownership include the nature of the political regime, the

intensity of external shocks, and the initial condition of the economy (Johnson and Wasty, 1993).

25. In an interesting alternative formulation of selectivity, Montes (cited in Wood and Lockwood, 1999) suggests the application of selectivity among governments based on good governance and a commitment to poverty reduction rather than on macroeconomic management.

2

PAPUA NEW GUINEA

Navroz K. Dubash
Colin Filer

I n 1995 and 1996, disputes over land and forests became the determining factor in Papua New Guinea's (PNG) macroeconomic health. Always simmering just below the surface, fights over forest policy became the epicenter of a macroeconomic crisis in PNG, as the World Bank held up disbursement of desperately needed foreign assistance pending resolution of disputed forest legislation. Some elements of civil society and the PNG bureaucracy supported the move, while PNG politicians uniformly decried the World Bank's attack on their sovereignty. At the heart of the dispute was the World Bank's new-found determination to enforce environmental policy reform through adjustment lending, combined, in the case of PNG, with an explicit strategy to reach out to civil society organizations. What generated this determination, how did the different sectors in PNG view it, and how successful was this tactic in reforming national forest policy?[1]

BACKGROUND

Papua New Guinea, a densely forested country, has a unique system of land tenure. Natural and highly diverse forests cover about two thirds of PNG. Exports of raw logs from these forests provide considerable economic value. At their peak in 1994, PNG's raw log exports totaled three million cubic meters and accounted for 18 percent of export earnings (Filer and Kalit, 1999). The collection of export taxes on these logs contributed about 10 percent of non-grant revenues to the PNG government coffers. Forests in PNG contribute significantly to the nation's economy.

To access these resources, however, logging companies must negotiate a complex, variable, and often undocumented land tenure system, which governs more than 99 percent of forest lands (Filer and Kalit, 1999). The political and cultural significance of customary tenure arrangements cannot be overstated. Customary tenure does not only govern access to forest and land resources, but is also tied to forms of social organization and cultural property (Filer, 1998). Consequently, formal state institutions intended to govern forest resources have to be shaped around, and are constrained by, these customary tenure arrangements. A similar situation exists in the neighboring Solomon Islands, where the World Bank and International Monetary Fund also attempted to reform the forest sector through adjustment lending. This experience is described in Box 2.1.

SOLOMON ISLANDS: BORROWER OWNERSHIP NECESSARY TO 'TIP THE SCALES'

Background

The forest sector in Solomon Islands over the past decade shares many similarities to that in PNG. As in PNG, most of the country's land and forests are held under customary ownership, unsustainable harvesting by foreign timber companies has been rampant, state capacity to monitor logging operations has been inadequate, and there have been charges of corruption against government officials. Unlike PNG, logging completely dominates the Solomon Islands' economy. In 1996–97, timber sales accounted for 50 percent of goods export earnings and 20–30 percent of the total budget, making the Solomon Islands the most log export-dependent country in the world. However, customary landowners have reaped few benefits from industrial, export-oriented forestry. A combination of preferential export tax exemptions and transfer pricing has limited the rents that accrue to the government, exacerbating the debt crisis, while at the same time encouraging unsustainable logging practices. World Bank attempts to reform this situation have advanced, or receded, based on the position of the government in power. As in PNG, the political situation in the Solomon Islands has been highly fluid, with few governments completing their elected terms.

Adjustment Experience

In 1993, the government of Prime Minister Solomon Mamaloni lost the parliamentary elections and the National Coalition Partnership (NCP) government of Francis Billy Hilly came to power. Responding to the past administration's destructive forest policy, the NCP government made forest reform a top priority, introducing a number of policies to reduce pressure on the country's forests. Many of the recommended reforms were made by a joint World Bank and IMF mission that went to the Solomon Islands at the request of the NCP government. At that time, the IMF and the World Bank attempted to develop a structural adjustment package for Solomon Islands, which included sustainable forest management. However, the loan process was not completed, in part because the World Bank believed that there was inadequate government commitment to the forest policy reform process. The proposed reforms proved to be politically unpopular because of short-term economic costs, and ultimately contributed to a vote of no confidence in the NCP government in 1994.

With the demise of the NCP, Mamaloni returned to power as head of the Solomon Islands National Unity, Reconciliation, and Progressive Party (SINURP). During Mamaloni's tenure, log exports rose to three times sustainable yields, and licenses were issued to raise logging rates even higher. Moreover, increased logging did not translate into greater government revenues. Although budget projections increased, the combination of transfer pricing and export tax remissions to loggers, particularly those associated with senior government officials, led to a decrease in revenues realized. In addition, the new government also moved to dismantle the proposed NCP reforms by decreasing log export taxes, decreasing surveillance of foreign logging firms, and pushing back a proposed log export ban. The resulting tension between the government and donor agencies was exacerbated by the ballooning fiscal deficit, which eventually led the government to suspend debt payments. Matters came to a head in 1995 when SINURP ejected international donor organizations from the country, in the process destroying the Australian Agency for International Development (AusAID) funded unit in charge of monitoring log exports.

BOX 2.1 | (CONTINUED)

A new coalition government, the Solomon Islands Alliance for Change (SIAC), came into power in 1997, and immediately faced a downturn in log prices from the East Asian crisis. In the forest sector, the SIAC government has reversed the export tax exemptions of the Mamaloni government, instituted a moratorium on new licenses, and re-established the Timber Control Unit with the assistance of AusAID. The government has thus demonstrated substantial commitment to reform and has also re-established relations with international agencies.

In mid-1999 the World Bank approved a Structural Adjustment Credit with substantial forest reform content that echoes the reforms promoted in PNG: institution of a logging Code of Practice; enactment of new forestry legislation; reactivation of the Forest Management Unit; and implementation of forest taxation reforms. The long-term goal of the credit is to bridge the transition to a diversified economy that reduces dependence on log exports.

Results and Analysis

The current government is attempting to pay off massive debt arrears, even while trying to reduce logging—its primary foreign exchange earner—and transfer to a more sustainable pattern of natural resource use. As log exports are the only short-term source of revenue, this leaves a very limited set of options for the government, and makes it heavily dependent on donor capital to decrease dependence on log exports. Yet, the current situation represents a considerable improvement over the policies of the Mamaloni government.

In the absence of government support for and ownership over the reform process, the World Bank and other donor agencies were unable to effectively promote forest policy reform in the Solomon Islands. During the Mamaloni government, donors were unable to exercise any leverage over forest policy despite growing indicators of macroeconomic crisis. It was not until a new, and more committed, national government came to power that reform of forest policies became viable.

Sources: Ian Fraser. 1997. "The struggle for control of Solomon Islands forests." *The Contemporary Pacific* 9 (1):39–72.

Roman Grynberg. (no date.) "The IMF and the Solomon Islands: Structural Adjustment Under Binding Environmental Constraints." *Pacific Studies.*

Phillip Montgomery. 1995. "Forestry in Solomon Islands." *Pacific Economic Bulletin* 10 (2):74–76.

Hilda Kari, Minister of Forests for Solomon Islands, statement to Parliament, October 1998.

World Bank sources.

The primary actors, then, in the forest arena in PNG are local peoples, or so-called "resource-owners." Local communities are spatially, politically, and socially fragmented. Any other actors who wish to access forest resources must, at some point, deal with the demands and desires of resource-owners. Resource-owners are represented by politicians whose loyalties are primarily to narrow local constituencies and highly personalized political factions, rather than to political parties or to any specific policies,

BOX 2.2

CHRONOLOGY OF ADJUSTMENT AND FOREST POLICY REFORM IN PAPUA NEW GUINEA

NAMALIU GOVERNMENT (JULY 1988 – JULY 1992)

- 1987   Barnett Commission of Inquiry initiated.
- 1988   PNG requests TFAP review.
- July 1989   Final Report of Barnett Inquiry released.
- January 1990   National Alliance of NGOs (NANGO) established.
- February 1990   Final TFAP report.
- April 1990   TFAP donor roundtable.
- November 1990   Draft Forest Policy prepared; TFAP renamed National Forestry Action Plan (NFAP).
- July 1991   Parliament enacts Forestry Bill. NFAP renamed National Forestry and Conservation Action Plan (NFCAP).
- April 1992   World Bank expresses concern over delay in gazettal of Forestry Act.
- June 1992   Forestry Act gazetted.

WINGTI GOVERNMENT (AUGUST 1992 – AUGUST 1994)

- August 1993   Bill to amend the Forestry Act in favor of loggers introduced in parliament.
- March 1994   Amendments to Forestry Act defeated. Finance minister introduces mini-budget to address growing fiscal crisis.

CHAN GOVERNMENT (SEPTEMBER 1994 – JULY 1997)

- February 1995   PNG reaches agreement with World Bank and IMF on an Economic Recovery Program (ERP).
- July 1995   World Bank mission arrives to finalize ERP conditions. NGOs and students protest ERP's land reform conditions.
- August 1995   World Bank approves ERP and releases first tranche.

BOX 2.2 | (CONTINUED)

February 1996	Forest Minister proposes amendments to Forestry Act to weaken Forest Board; World Bank mission departs prematurely after failure to implement first tranche conditions.
April 1996	World Bank serves 90-day notice of default on ERP; Prime Minister announces opposition to new forest revenue system, which is included in ERP conditions.
July 1996	Parliament approves Forest Minister's amendments to Forestry Act.
August 1996	World Bank applies pressure for government to rescind amendments.
October 1996	Parliament withdraws amendments to the Forestry Act; World Bank extends loan agreement.
January 1997	Second and final tranche of ERP released.

SKATE GOVERNMENT (AUGUST 1997 – JULY 1999)

September 1997	World Bank mission to design Forestry and Conservation Project.
May 1998	Dr. Pirouz Hamidian-Rad, former World Bank economist, appointed as Chief Economic Adviser to the Prime Minister.
July 1999	Skate government falls.

which results in highly unstable coalition governments.

Another set of actors are bureaucrats who serve the politicians, but in reality play several additional roles. Among bureaucrats it is possible to identify some reformist elements who serve as policy brokers within the bureaucracy. These policy brokers often have the insider knowledge of political and bureaucratic processes necessary to advance a reformist agenda, and put this to good use in their role as mediators between politicians and other stakeholders. It is also useful to distinguish between national bureaucrats and expatriate bureaucrats, each of whom bring with them different connections and incentives; reformers may come from either strata.

Next come logging interests, which Malaysian companies dominate in PNG and the Forest Industries Association represents in domestic politics.[2] Of growing importance, are NGOs which may be divided into national and international categories, and are involved in policy advocacy and specific conservation projects with groups of resource-owners.[3]

Finally, there are the international donor organizations. Among these, the Australian aid agency (AusAID) and the World Bank play the most significant roles.[4] In its efforts to shape forest policy reform, the World Bank has had to engage all the actors described above. The process, and outcomes of that engagement *(listed chronologically in Box 2.2)*, forms the substance of this chapter.

The Early Days of National Forest Policy Reform: Borrower Ownership?

Commercial forestry in Papua New Guinea received its first major boost from the demand for timber generated by post-World War II reconstruction efforts. In subsequent years, this production steadily increased, encouraged by, among others, the World Bank who called for "an aggressive policy of commercial development" of PNG forests (quoted in Filer, 1998, p. 88).

Independence from Australian rule in 1975 provided PNG the opportunity to rethink the model of industrial forestry, in ways suggested by the Fourth Goal of the constitution: "For Papua New Guinea's natural resources and environment to be conserved and used for the collective benefit of us all, and to be replenished for the benefit of future generations." During this period, parliament passed the Forestry (Private Dealings) Act, which allowed resource owners to cut deals directly with logging companies—a significant change from the colonial model.

The discussions over the broader vision of forest use in PNG during the post-indepen-

dence years foreshadowed much of the current debate over forest policy and use in PNG: industrial logging versus small-scale village forestry; round log export versus domestic processing; and customary tenure as an obstacle versus customary tenure as a guard against rampant logging (Filer, 1998). While a small community of PNG intelligentsia participated in these discussions, many of the influential voices were those of colonial administrators and Australian environmentalists. These debates did not result in the development of institutional mechanisms and died down in the decade after independence. In the interim, log export volumes increased three-fold, facilitated by politicians with ever-closer ties to the logging companies.

It was the increasing evidence of these ties that led to a Commission of Inquiry in 1987 into improprieties in the logging sector.[5] The Barnett Commission, led by an Australian member of the PNG judiciary, was zealous in its two-year investigation, and revealed many illustrations of what Barnett later pungently described as the "heavy odour of corruption, fraud and scandal arising from the timber industry" (quoted in Filer, 1998, p. 93). The report recommended names for prosecution for criminal and leadership offences and suggested measures to clamp down on corruption. Specifically, Barnett called for a national forest policy, revised forestry legislation, and a unified national forestry service. He also urged the involvement of landowners in permit allocation processes, a review of existing permits, measures to reduce transfer pricing, an emphasis on domestic processing of timber, and an increase in benefits for landowners. Seriously implicated in the report was the then Forests Minister which suggests that the rot uncovered in PNG's forest sector spread right to the top.[6]

There are two important conclusions to be drawn from the lengthy, detailed, and hard-hitting Barnett inquiry. First, there was substantial domestic impetus for forest reform in PNG before the World Bank became engaged in the sector. This momentum spread beyond actors in national politics to the general public, who were drawn into the process through the publication of Barnett's often sensational findings. Second, that Barnett, an Australian who had played an important role in formulating the constitutional agenda in PNG, was once again playing a central role almost 15 years after independence, speaks to the continued importance of expatriates in PNG policy circles.

Early Days of World Bank Involvement: The Tropical Forestry Action Plan

Barnett's preliminary findings created a considerable impetus for reform. In reaction, the government announced steps to create a new Forest Policy and Forestry Act, and also sought international assistance under the Tropical Forestry Action Plan (TFAP). The TFAP was the entry point for the World Bank into the forest sector in PNG. Before the Barnett Commission report had been released, the World Bank undertook its own study under TFAP auspices, and released its

draft report a few months later, also in 1989. From then on, the World Bank assumed a central coordinating role in policy dialogue and forest project preparation.

Both reports pointed in the same direction but with a notable difference. Barnett had suggested subsidizing timber processors while penalizing log exporters, a set of policies aimed at transforming the export-oriented nature of the timber industry into one more rooted in adding value domestically.[7] This view has retained much currency with NGOs in PNG. By contrast, the people at the World Bank saw no logic in granting a subsidy to domestic processing (Filer and Kalit, 1999). The result, they felt, would be an inefficient domestic processing industry that would require perpetual subsidies to compete on the international market. This difference of opinion between many NGOs and the World Bank drove a wedge between the two. Some NGOs argued that the World Bank's reluctance to countenance incentives for domestic processing illustrates the limits of its reformism.[8] From this perspective, the Bank's involvement is aimed at an efficient log export industry, rather than at the NGO vision of small-scale domestic timber processing.

Nonetheless, given the desperate situation in 1989, the interests of the World Bank, reformist bureaucrats, and the few domestic environmentalists of the time were sufficiently aligned to work together on reining in rampant logging. The Barnett inquiry and the TFAP process came together in two interconnected sets of activities: preparation and enactment of a new Forestry Act, and the establishment of a set of forest projects under the umbrella of the National Forestry Action Plan (NFAP).

A task force consisting of staff of the Department of Forests, other bureaucrats, and select outside experts drafted the National Forest Policy. The content of the policy was dictated most directly by Barnett's recommendations, but these did not contradict those articulated in the World Bank-led TFAP.[9] The World Bank's contribution was two-fold. First, it provided detailed comments on drafts of the Forestry Act that emerged from the Policy, most of which were aimed at ensuring the independence of the proposed Forest Authority from political interference. This emphasis anticipated many of the subsequent battles between the World Bank and national politicians, including the one that led to the imbroglio over the structural adjustment loan in 1996. Second, when the Forest Minister dragged his feet on gazettal of the Act in response to logging industry pressure,[10] the World Bank's Country Director for PNG wrote a letter to the Forest Minister pointing out that the donor community would unfavorably view this delay.[11]

The Act considerably complicated the process of industrial logging.[12] The highly complex institutional processes put in place by this legislation tied up the logging industry in red tape.[13] Indeed, this could be interpreted as a deliberate exercise led by the national bureaucrats, who, with their detailed knowledge of local politics and institutions, selectively mobilized the World Bank for political support.[14]

However, the World Bank, with the support of AusAID, was the lead coordinator in the second set of activities spurred by the Barnett Commission and the TFAP—the National Forestry Action Plan (NFAP). The World Bank initiated this process by convening a roundtable in April 1990. This meeting

The World Bank's lead role ensured that it was continuously engaged in the forest reform process, but also made it the lightning rod for criticism related to the process.

sought to orchestrate negotiations between government agencies—primarily the Department of Environment and Conservation and the Department of Forests—and donor organizations interested in funding specific projects.

The World Bank's lead role ensured that it was continuously engaged in the forest reform process, but also made it the lightning rod for criticism related to the process. First, environmentalists and reformist bureaucrats were concerned about the absence of a conservation focus in the original NFAP. In response, national bureaucrats introduced two major conservation projects that the World Bank had left out of its initial list proposed to the 1990 roundtable of donors (Filer and Kalit, 1999). At about this time, however, the World Bank was undergoing internal changes aimed at raising the institution's profile on environmental issues. In 1990, it established the Global Environment Facility in collaboration with other agencies. In addition, the World Bank's own internal Forest Policy had been rewritten in 1991 to give more weight to conservation. These factors combined to rename the NFAP the National Forestry and Conservation Action Plan (NFCAP) in mid-1991.

Second, the role of NGOs in the NFCAP was proving contentious, and the World

Bank, as the lead coordinator of the process, was implicated in failing to solve this problem. Specifically, the NGOs were envisioned as playing a critical role in promoting landowner participation in the NFCAP, yet despite funds earmarked for this purpose, this component did not get going until mid-1993 (Filer and Kalit, 1999). Moreover, an independent review of the NFCAP interpreted the World Bank's promotion of the newly formed National Alliance of Non-Governmental Organizations (NANGO) as a key stakeholder in the national NFCAP process as distracting NGOs from the task of engaging landowning communities (Taylor et al., 1994). While the review likely did have a point, it is also true that this outcome has as much to do with the small number of NGOs in PNG stretched too thin, and with internal divisions about goals and methods within the national NGO community, as with any mismanagement on the part of the World Bank.

By 1994, it became clear that the battle over a legislative and regulatory structure to govern forest access and use had not been won. From 1992–94, the forest industry was engaged in all-out warfare with the new Forests Minister, Tim Neville, a businessman whose wealth was independent of forest interests. Neville made it clear that his goal was to phase out raw log exports in favor of domestic processing within five years. The loggers responded by stage-managing a bill in Parliament that would have repealed key provisions of the Forestry Act.[15] A coalition of national NGOs and other national policy brokers who rallied behind the Forest Minister stymied the move, but this episode pointed to the fragility of the reforms. While the reformers emerged victorious from several skirmishes, the war had by no means been won.

What lessons can we draw from these early days of forest policy reform in PNG? First, there is a vibrant community of domestic reformers drawn from national bureaucrats, NGOs, and national politicians who crystallized around the Barnett Commission. While all these segments do not always agree, they have been active in defining the substance of the reforms and negotiating the political terrain to implement these reforms. Second, the World Bank has played a leading role in coordinating the projects that were meant to provide substance to the NFCAP. Third, the World Bank, until 1994, also played a supporting role in the process of national policy reform by commenting on the substance of the reforms, and by breaking political logjams by cajoling and occasionally by invoking its power as the coordinator of the international donor community. The World Bank supported national bureaucrats and NGOs because they shared the same immediate goal. In 1994, when the logging companies nearly managed to roll back the reforms, the need was for additional political muscle in

There is a vibrant community of domestic reformers drawn from national bureaucrats, NGOs, and national politicians in PNG.

defense of the reforms. The World Bank, as an actor deeply engaged in the reform process, and with deep reserves of financial and institutional power, was well placed to play that role. The opportunity to place the final seal on the forest reform process came in 1995, and the World Bank was ready to take advantage of it.

ADJUSTMENT LENDING

By the end of 1994, PNG faced a macroeconomic crisis. External balance-of-payments had deteriorated, external debt was high, domestic public debt had tripled from 1989, and foreign exchange reserves were depleted, undermined by an abatement in the oil boom (World Bank, 1995). The government devalued and then allowed the kina (the local currency) to float, cut expenditures, and introduced measures to shrink the deficit. Nonetheless, outside help was required to ease the cash flow crisis that had paralyzed state functioning, and PNG approached the World Bank and IMF for help with an Economic Recovery Program (ERP).

The ERP and Forest Conditionality

Following the ominous macroeconomic portents that became clear during 1994, the World Bank and PNG entered into negotiations over a loan in early 1995. The ERP loan document that emerged in August 1995 promised PNG US$50 million in two equal tranches, but also bound the country to about 50 conditions, arranged in five main groups. One of these groups, Promoting Sustainable Development, laid out five conditions *(see Box 2.3)* which were to "promote long-term sustainable private sector-led growth in income and employment" (World Bank, 1995). These conditions had three aims, all of which were consistent with a vision of reforming industrial forestry: to stop interference with the Forestry Act or the National Forest Board; to limit the physical damage inflicted by selective logging practices allowed under timber permits; and to maximize the share of the resource rent accruing to the government and local landowners.

Why were sustainable development conditions incorporated into the ERP?[16] As suggested above, the continued commitment by the politicians in power to forest policy reform was certainly suspect, as evidenced by the attempt in 1994 to rollback the reforms. Moreover, the Forest Minister, appointed in 1994, was elected to parliament from a constituency that accounted for nearly half of the country's log exports. As such he could be expected to be sympathetic to logging interests, and made statements confirming these

---

BOX 2.3 | **SUSTAINABLE DEVELOPMENT CONDITIONS IN THE ERP POLICY MATRIX**

1. Refrain from introducing amendments to the Forestry Act of 1991, which will in any way reduce or qualify the present allocation of powers and responsibilities to the Board, or the Authority, for the approval, issue or suspension, or modification, of timber licenses, permits or authorities.

2. Ensure that areas of natural forests that are used for log production are managed on a sustainable basis.

3. Introduce a logging revenue system.

4. Provide the Forest Authority with an operating budget equal in real terms to that allocated in 1995, in timely disbursements. Provide separate and adequate funding for the surveillance of log exports.

5. Ensure that the Forest Authority formally adopts a forestry and operational code of conduct for implementation in the field.

Source: Government of PNG. 1995. "World Bank Economic Recovery Loans."

---

tendencies soon after his appointment, and before the ERP was finalized (Filer and Kalit, 1999). The ERP provided the opportunity to draw a line in the sand in the face of a potential rollback, and did so by raising the costs to the government of retrograde forest policies.

National bureaucrats in PNG point out that they took the lead in formulating the sustainable development conditions in the ERP, suggesting ownership by at least one national constituency over the direction of reform.[17] During this period, many (although certainly not all) of the reformist bureaucrats were senior expatriate contract officers.[18] These expatriates often have the same professional training and background as donor agency staff and consultants, and approach problems in a similar manner. Moreover, expatriates in PNG receive a higher salary than nationals do, and although many have been in PNG for several years, they nonetheless occupy a gray area between insider and outsider. By contrast, bureaucrats from a national background juggle their identity as technocrats with that as landowners in PNG, and can also enter formal politics. This is not to suggest that expatriates are necessarily more likely to be reformers, but that they face different incentives than do national bureaucrats. Hence, borrower ownership is complex, and is based on support for an adjustment program driven in large part by expatriate bureaucrats.

Two elements of this defensive strategy are worth noting. First, at this stage, the ERP was the only instrument the World Bank had with which to defend the reforms. Although the World Bank had offered the government a separate project loan to strengthen the capacity of the Forest Authority, the govern-

ment was not interested in loans for this purpose, even at concessional rates, because other donors were pouring grant money into the country (Filer and Kalit, 1999). But the World Bank had no competitors for an adjustment loan, and so could dictate the terms of the ERP. Second, none of the conditions themselves introduced new ideas, but were merely intended to defend, with new and more potent weaponry, key features of the institutional terrain that had been a battleground for many years.

Land Reform: A Public Relations Debacle for the World Bank

The reformers in the bureaucracy, and perhaps also many of the national NGOs, supported the sustainable development conditions. Yet the ERP was hugely unpopular in PNG. Part of the explanation rests in a broadly negative perception of the adjustment process in general, with the African experience—which was perceived to have resulted in large social costs—a particularly vivid example. This section, which deals with a controversial land reform condition, describes another reason for the unpopularity of the loan.

One condition in an early draft of the ERP called for completion of legislation to enable customary land registration. According to sources in the World Bank, the condition was an attempt to mop up a Land Mobilization Program that had been dragging on in one form or another since 1985, but was not a major component of the loan.[19] The roots of the issue lay in domestic debates dating back to 1973 over how land registration could serve as a way of mobilizing land as a source of collateral for credit, while maintaining intact customary land tenure (Filer and Kalit,

1999). Land registration was, and remains, a controversial subject for a large cross-section of PNG society. On receiving the draft of the ERP, the national bureaucracy immediately flagged it as politically controversial, whereupon it was dropped from the list of conditions, but not before a draft containing this condition was leaked.

The land reform condition served as potent ammunition for populist opponents of the ERP. Students upset at being asked to bear some of the costs of their higher education, unions upset at abolition of the minimum wage, and public servants upset at the prospect of job retrenchment seized on land registration as a way to mobilize the rural masses and relate the ERP to their concerns. A sample of one letter to the press illustrates the depth of anger directed at the World Bank: "the assumption that a country's age-old traditional system can be wiped out at the whim of a financial institution shows the contempt of outsiders for this growing nation" (quoted in Filer and Kalit, 1999).[20] Wild stories circulated around the country, including one that had the Government of PNG offering the peoples' land to the World Bank as security for the ERP loan.[21] The populists were successful, and the World Bank undertook an outreach campaign to ease the fears of a hostile population.

Three lessons emerge from this episode. First, the land reform conditions, which World Bank staff characterize as a minor component of the early draft ERP, were introduced without an adequate understanding of the major political sensitivities involved.

Second, the potential benefits of the sustainable development conditions to rural populations were not sufficient to outweigh the

Even though resource owners potentially stood to gain a larger share of revenues by implementing sustainable development conditions, this was not the public perception of the conditions, suggesting a failure in communication.

mistrust generated by the land reform condition. Although the conditions were not unilaterally imposed by the World Bank, but jointly shaped by the World Bank and national bureaucrats, the ownership of those conditions was limited to policy brokers within the bureaucracy and not shared by the public. Thus, even though resource owners potentially stood to gain a larger share of revenues by implementing the sustainable development conditions in the ERP, this was not the public perception of the conditions, suggesting a failure in communication.

Third, even if the World Bank had been able to communicate the extent to which the sustainable development conditions promoted rural interests, structural adjustment lending inevitably imposes costs on certain segments of the population, who usually express their opposition through political dissent. As Filer (1998, p. 138) notes: " (T)he pain of structural adjustment will be felt by several groups of national stakeholders (politicians, public servants, other wage-earners) whose interest in forest policy bears no comparison to their interest in 'bread-and-butter' issues." Yet, for rural populations, forest policy is a bread-and-butter issue, and the World Bank not only missed the opportunity to illustrate how rural populations stood to gain from the sustainable development conditions, but handed the populists the means by which to mobilize that population against the ERP.

A Stand-off over the Second Tranche of the ERP

The fact that the country was in an uproar over the land reform condition made it easier, in 1996, for Prime Minister Julius Chan and his cabinet to publicly defy the World Bank in 1996 over the sustainable development conditions. At stake were two issues: a new forest revenue system, which had the logging industry up in arms; and another set of proposed amendments to weaken the Forestry Act.

The conditions on a forest revenue system included in the ERP bound the government to institute a marginal tax rate on log exports, along with payment of royalties to landowners, both based on the export price of the logs. The government's resolve to contest this system was stiffened by the visit of the Malaysian Primary Industries Minister to PNG, and Prime Minister Chan's visit to Malaysia, from where he returned determined to defy the World Bank. It took a notice of default by the World Bank and further implementation missions before the government gave in to these conditions (Filer and Kalit, 1999).

The amendments to the Forestry Act were carried even further. The new Forest Minister fired the Managing Director of the Forest Authority who had refused to speed up the allocation of timber permits. He then issued amendments to the Act that would have stacked the Forest Board in the Minister's favor and granted him powers over allocation of concessions that the Act was explicitly structured to avoid. For a while the Prime Minister and the cabinet stood tough, invoking the sovereign right of independent PNG to control its own policy. By following this position, the government stood to lose not only the second tranche of US$25 million, but also several other donor loans that were tied to the ERP, and to suffer a loss in reputation. By late 1996, the government could hold out no longer. It introduced amended legislation to reverse the earlier changes, and the second tranche was finally released in early 1997 (Filer and Kalit, 1999).

The ERP and its history is notable for two reasons. First, it is one of the earliest instances where the World Bank included environmental conditions in a structural adjustment loan. Second, the World Bank, which does not always strictly enforce its conditions, was willing to hold up the entire adjustment loan, thereby threatening much-needed budgetary support and creating ill-feeling within PNG while defending sustainable development conditions. As the World Bank's Implementation Completion Report states regarding the sustainable development objectives of the loan: "Certainly this was the main reason for the almost year long delay in release of the second tranche" (World Bank, 1997, p. 6).[22] What were the politics behind these events within the World Bank? How was the decision to break with precedent and

---

Neither the decision to include sustainable development conditions in the Economic Recovery Program nor the decision to stand firm on these conditions were uncontroversial at the World Bank.

---

impose environmental conditions made, and, once made, how was the decision made to back them up forcefully?

Debates within the World Bank[23]

Neither the decision to include sustainable development conditions in the ERP nor the decision to stand firm on these conditions were uncontroversial at the World Bank. Adjustment lending has traditionally been the preserve of the macroeconomists at the World Bank, and loans have typically been tied to such macroeconomic policy levers as monetary policy, fiscal reform, and reduction of export barriers. This macroeconomic focus has led to an emphasis on fairly straightforward loans that can be prepared rapidly. In this context, inclusion of forest conditions requires more time than other adjustment loans since, in the words of a World Bank macroeconomist, "Sociological aspects are more important when it comes to forest conditions."[24] This is a problem in the World Bank, where there have been, and still are, considerable incentives to rapidly disburse loans.

In the PNG case, these obstacles were overcome by a combination of factors. First, forest sector staff had a history of engaging in debates over forest policy reform in PNG, and were in a position to recognize the opportunity the ERP provided to cement reforms.[25] Second, the PNG country director was willing to embrace this bold step and played a mediating role between sector staff with forest experience and macroeconomists with experience in structural adjustment loans.[26] Third, reformist bureaucrats in PNG were aware of the additional leverage that forest conditionality would bring to their

cause, and worked with the World Bank staff to shape the appropriate conditions.[27]

Fourth, while the World Bank's macroeconomists were skeptical at first, they became increasingly converted to the need for these conditions.[28] The reasons for their initial skepticism are worth noting. Forest conditions introduced factors that were beyond their expertise. Moreover, this particular set of structural reforms directly affected one large constituency in PNG—forest communities—while with macroeconomic policy adjustment, the economists had hitherto been able to claim a technocratic and objective distance.[29] Finally, during this period, the World Bank as an institution was seeking to incorporate the lessons of the adjustment experience in Africa, which pointed to greater attention to social and environmental factors during the adjustment process.

The inclusion of the sustainable development conditions was controversial, but the forceful enforcement of them was even more so. As World Bank staff describe internal incentives, there is a culture of not enforcing conditions placed on borrower governments.[30] Externally, this can lead to a deterioration in relations with the borrower and a series of protracted negotiations. Internally, it slows down the loan disbursement pipeline and can also slow down project lending in the country, which exposes the staff crafting the loan to the ire of their colleagues.

When it became clear that PNG would not meet the conditions of the ERP, opinion within the World Bank was polarized. The country staff who put together the loan were firm on withholding funds until the conditions were met. Opposed were some elements within senior management who argued that a delay in disbursement of funds would seriously harm the relationship with the borrower government, and that the issue of forest policy reform should not hold up the adjustment loan. Then, the Australian government pleaded PNG's case directly to the World Bank's president, which heightened internal pressure at the World Bank to accede.[31]

From the perspective of the Government of PNG, the World Bank's position on the loan conditions was as unexpected as it was unwelcome. Sources within the World Bank concede that the government may indeed have received contradictory signals from within the World Bank.[32] At an early stage in the ERP negotiation process, senior World Bank management had met with senior PNG politicians to deliver the unequivocal message that this loan would be rigorously monitored. On the other hand, at least one influential member of senior management with responsibility for the region had repeatedly indicated that the social and environmental conditions attached to the loan were of no great concern. The government's contribution to the final report of the ERP shows that they were receiving mixed messages. Under the category "lessons learnt" they note: "greater caution should be exercised regarding commitments undertaken in the policy matrix and the letter of development policy. It eventuated that statements of very general intent in the letter were subsequently treated as legally binding by the World Bank's lawyers" (World Bank, 1997, p. 33).

Given the internal pressures for the World Bank to submit and the signals sent by senior management that the sustainability conditions would not be taken too seriously, why did the PNG country staff hold the line?

Part of the answer lies in the World Bank staff at the helm of the ERP. In place was the rare combination of a team who had followed the twists and turns of forest policy over the years, who were aware of the blatant bad faith of the government, and a country director willing to back them up on their decision. In addition, however, the PNG case was a high visibility case within the World Bank because of the sustainable development conditions—conditions the World Bank had widely publicized within PNG. There was certainly some anxiety that for the World Bank to take the bold step of incorporating sustainability objectives explicitly in its loan conditions, only to back down under pressure would draw the unwelcome attention of environmental NGOs and other critics of the World Bank.[33] Moreover, if the World Bank could claim to have acted boldly in defense of sustainable development, then it would have legitimately won the right to seek praise from these same critics.

Indeed, the World Bank disbursed the second tranche after the sustainability conditions had been met, even though another three of the nine loan covenants were not fulfilled. Two of these were relatively minor, while the third had to do with macroeconomic details of budgetary allocations and an investment program that would be "acceptable to the World Bank" (World Bank, 1997, p. 19–20). What this suggests is that it is harder for the World Bank to ignore a breach of conditionality on such issues as forestry, than a similar breach in the more esoteric world of macroeconomics, particularly when it is backed by public statements of commitment to interested parties such as NGOs.

Failure to stand firm on the sustainable development conditions would likely have empowered corrupt politicians and their pay-masters in PNG, disheartened bureaucratic reformers and NGOs, and rolled back a half-decade of gradual reform in PNG's forest policy. However, the World Bank's persistence in seeing these conditions through came at a cost. World Bank staff spent more than three times the planned amount of time on supervision of the ERP and five times the planned amount, if the time required for preparation, appraisal, negotiation, and supervision of the loan are included (World Bank, 1997, p. 25). Although the loan was successful at enforcing policy reform, from a strict accounting perspective it was a loan with very low financial returns to staff time. The World Bank will only be encouraged to go down this path again if the internal metric of success for adjustment loans gives greater weight to the former rather than the latter.

IMPLEMENTATION EXPERIENCE

The ERP put a halt to the slide back to pre-Barnett inquiry days in PNG's logging sector. But internal and external observers of the forest sector in PNG doubted if the new institutional structures were self-sustaining. The World Bank appears to have shared these doubts and initiated a number of follow-up activities. Before these could be completed, the World Bank's lead economist for

---

Although the loan was successful at enforcing policy reform, from a strict accounting perspective it was a loan with very low financial returns to staff time.

PNG and the architect of the ERP, Pirouz Hamidian-Rad, left the World Bank to become the Chief Economic Adviser to the Prime Minister of PNG. Since Hamidian-Rad's move was in contravention of the World Bank's own internal regulations, this change halted further application of adjustment lending in PNG.

Before the ink was quite dry on the ERP, the World Bank and the government negotiated a follow-up adjustment loan, the Social and Economic Development Program (SEDP) loan, which also included forest conditionality, and a project loan targeted at forestry, as part of a Forestry and Conservation Project (FCP). Both were aimed at deepening and strengthening the governance framework for industrial logging; the FCP added a conservation dimension.

Early versions of the SEDP policy matrix, drafted by Hamidian-Rad before he left the World Bank, contained a numbing 171 conditions, of which 26 were tied to forestry and conservation outcomes (World Bank, 1998a). Many of these conditions were structured to reinforce the gains made during the ERP. The number of conditions suggests that in the opinion of the World Bank, or more specifically Hamidian-Rad, very little could be left to the discretion of the government. On the other hand, encasing a government in a web of conditions to restrict its discretionary power implies a fairly minimal level of borrower ownership. The World Bank acknowledged that a major risk to the program could be the degree of government commitment to the SEDP.[34] Yet, the Government of PNG was not a homogeneous entity, and the Forest Authority and the Department of Environment and Conservation, both of which derived support from the World

Bank's conditions, substantially endorsed the conditions.

The Forestry and Conservation Project (FCP) was explicitly structured to support forest sector reforms achieved under the ERP and planned under the SEDP (World Bank, 1998b). It is important to note two important points about the FCP. First, it contained measures designed to limit further irregularities in commercial logging operations, but also introduced significant new conservation mechanisms. The centerpiece of the latter was the proposed establishment of a Conservation Trust Fund, which would provide communities with the means to realize the economic value of their forest resources without resort to logging. International environmental NGOs and their PNG affiliates were to help establish this component. Second, the FCP was structured as an Adaptable Program Lending instrument, under which funds are disbursed subject to performance. This mechanism imports dimensions of adjustment lending into project lending. Moreover, five conditions on forestry were included in both the FCP and the SEDP, which served to make the two loans conditional on each other.

This careful process of building on the ERP stopped when Hamidian-Rad left the World Bank to take on his new role as Chief Economic Adviser in PNG, just months after he had been central to negotiation of the SEDP. Because his new position violated the World Bank's internal rules about potential conflicts of interest, the World Bank refused to proceed with the SEDP, despite the government's urgent need for budgetary support, until the controversy over Hamidian-Rad's role in governing PNG was settled.[35]

Since the early days of the ERP, Hamidian-Rad had been a forceful presence in PNG. He had faced down a horde of angry students during the land reform unrest of 1995, and had developed a reputation for hard-headedness both among his World Bank colleagues and those on the other side of the table in PNG.[36] In a country where personality politics dominates, Hamidian-Rad became the personality that defined the World Bank's politics. When he switched sides in 1998, the same quality he had brought to his dealings with the government over the ERP was focused on the World Bank. This shift had two important implications for the development of forest policy in PNG.

First, in an effort to secure approval of the SEDP, the government refused to allow the FCP to go forward without the SEDP.[37] Sources within the World Bank suggest that Hamidian-Rad was behind this move, which demonstrates insider knowledge of the pressure the World Bank would face from international NGOs if the most important conservation program in PNG were to be stopped in its tracks.[38] As a result, negotiation of both the conservation-focused FCP loan and the SEDP loan were suspended for over a year.

Second, Hamidian-Rad led a policy of radical restructuring along with an increase in development expenditures controlled by members of parliament that caused a short-term financial crisis.[39] To boost export revenues, Hamidian-Rad was complicit in a series of measures taken to increase log exports: tax relief to the industry; cancellation of independent log surveillance procedures that limited transfer pricing by log exporters; fast-track approval of logging concessions; and restructuring of the Forest Service to side-line reformist elements

(Filer and Kalit, 1999). These measures represented a complete turn-around from the policies supported by Hamidian-Rad while at the World Bank.

In July 1999, the impasse between the Government of PNG and the World Bank was overcome only by the resignation of Prime Minister Skate, and the removal of Hamidian-Rad from his position as Chief Economic Advisor.[40] This change at the national political level helped resume the dialogue and negotiation between the World Bank and PNG.

The injection of the personalized politics around Hamidian-Rad considerably complicates an assessment of the success of the ERP and the subsequent implementation efforts. Moreover, the FCP, which was designed to cement and implement the legislative and institutional gains achieved through the ERP, is yet to be implemented, which renders any assessment premature. However, even putting aside Hamidian-Rad's role, it is clear that the gains achieved in the ERP required constant defense through continued conditionality and cross-conditionality across the SEDP and FCP.

THE ROLES OF OTHER STAKEHOLDERS

By the mid-1990s, the World Bank had announced that attention to stakeholder interests and insights would form an important component of how the World Bank now did business in borrower countries. In its own assessment of the ERP, the World Bank credits its initiative in "deepening the dialogue with the various stakeholders and policy makers to overcome the adverse influence of vested interest groups in seeing

several important conditions through" (World Bank, 1997, p. iv).

Nongovernmental Organizations: Domestic and International

In PNG, the World Bank made an explicit commitment to civil society engagement. In the midst of the crisis over disbursement of the second tranche of the ERP, a letter was circulated from an NGO in PNG stating strong support for the World Bank in holding the line on the second tranche. A simple reading of this engagement is that the World Bank's efforts paid off in the form of civil society support for the World Bank's role in facing down a wayward and corrupt government in defense of institutional reform in the forest sector. This is the story line the World Bank sketches in its Implementation Completion Report. While this version has elements of truth, the story is actually far more complex, as the World Bank found itself embroiled in the politics of Melanesian society.

In PNG, one can draw a distinction between groups who explicitly focus on environmental outcomes, and other groups organized around religion, social concerns, and service delivery. Of the latter, churches are by far the strongest element of civil society, but have not hitherto been heavily engaged in environmental debates. Among environmentalists, there is a broad distinction between advocacy groups who tend to have a somewhat radical bent (expressed in the forest sector as an opposition to export-oriented forestry), and groups engaged primarily in community-oriented conservation projects and only secondarily in policy reform.[41] A similar distinction may be made between the international environmental groups that have a presence in PNG. While Greenpeace works closely with the more radical groups on policy reform issues, The Nature Conservancy, Conservation International, and the World Wide Fund for Nature all maintain local offices that are engaged in conservation work at the project level.

In 1995, World Bank President Wolfensohn had a heated meeting with NGOs in Australia, during which the topic of the World Bank's engagement in PNG was heavily featured. Wolfensohn reportedly pledged to make PNG a test case for how the World Bank did business with NGOs, but also made it clear that in the case of PNG, he and his staff would deal with domestic NGOs in PNG, rather than with Australian NGOs.[42] This was a turning point for the World Bank's civil society engagement in PNG. Until this point the World Bank had simply kept lines of communication open with NGOs and supported the representation of the National Alliance of Non-Governmental Organizations (NANGO) on the National Forest Board. After Wolfensohn's statement, the frequency and intensity of NGO-related activities went up dramatically, and the World Bank appointed a staff person to build and manage relations with NGOs. In the midst of the controversy surrounding the land reform condition, the World Bank had promised to hold regular meetings with an umbrella group of civil society organizations, the National Council for Socio-Economic Justice (NCSEJ), which was formed to contest the whole program of structural adjustment. One of these was a three-day meeting, which focused specifically on the forest conditions of the ERP.

In mid-1996 when the government aggressively pursued actions in violation of the forest conditions, there was a strong reaction from some elements of civil society in PNG in support of these conditions. The General Secretary of the PNG National Forest Resource Owners Association (FROA) sent out a letter to international environmental NGOs in his capacity as "a representative of civil society in PNG." In strong language, he backed the position of the World Bank and other donors in withholding the second tranche until the sustainable development commitments had been met and placed the blame for the impasse squarely at the government's door (Ariku, 1996). This was an extraordinary letter in that it explicitly dismissed concerns over national sovereignty and baldly stated that the World Bank, through the ERP, was doing far more to support the interests of the citizens of PNG than were the elected representatives in the PNG government. This was followed up with a celebratory letter in the local press when the government eventually caved in to the conditions, which stated: "World Bank's adamant stand on forestry reforms is in the best interest of the nation" (quoted in Filer, 1998, p. 161). For the World Bank, it appeared to be a vindication of its attempts at engaging with civil society. Within PNG, however, the author of these letters was a controversial figure, whose legitimacy as spokesperson for a broad constituency was suspect.[43] Soon thereafter, his credibility with other sections of civil society was further damaged when the World Bank appointed him as its NGO Liaison Officer.

There were other, albeit more equivocal, voices of support for the sustainable development conditions. A letter from Greenpeace to other international NGOs, drawing on documentation from the Individual and Community Rights Advocacy Forum (ICRAF) in PNG, noted that while there was widespread opposition to the SAP, and particularly to the land reform conditions, the conditions covering the forest sector were consistent with the positions taken by some sections of civil society in PNG and were thus deserving of support (Cortesi, 1995). This support was not shared by all international NGOs; a 1996 report by an Australian NGO, AID/WATCH, argues that the failure to consider the consequences of industrial logging demonstrates the hollowness of the World Bank's claim to play the "good environmental cop" in PNG (AID/WATCH 1996).

That this support for the sustainable development conditions was relatively muted and conditional was due to the level of popular opposition to non-forest components of the ERP, the closed and non-transparent process of negotiation of the loan, and the content of the World Bank's forestry agenda in PNG. Many environmentalists within PNG believed that the World Bank's intervention was limited to promoting more efficient and sustainable industrial, export-oriented forestry. By contrast, written materials and interviews suggest considerable agreement among NGOs in PNG that the country should question the paradigm of industrial logging and turn toward an expansion of investment in small-scale logging and domestic processing of timber (ICRAF, 1997).

The point here was not whether a shift away from exports and toward domestic processing made economic sense (which the World Bank denied), or whether it might be desirable for reasons of good governance alone (as the NGOs claimed), but that the NGOs believed the ideological dogmatism of the World Bank had prevented this discussion from taking place. While none of the NGOs interviewed for this report denied that

Many environmentalists believed that the World Bank's intervention was limited to promoting more efficient and sustainable industrial, export-oriented forestry.

the sustainable development conditions were useful in placing checks on a government that was poised to hand over PNG's forests to Malaysian loggers, many also expressed disappointment at the perceived lack of openness exhibited by the World Bank to models other than industrial forestry.

There are recent signs that this stalemate has been broken. Since 1997, several NGOs in PNG who had been calling for an outright ban on log exports were signaling their willingness to settle for a moratorium on new concessions. Meanwhile, international NGOs with offices in PNG were calling for the World Bank to include a moratorium on new concessions as one of the conditions attached to the FCP or to a new adjustment loan (Cortesi, 1999)—a recommendation which was also one of the outcomes of a workshop held in PNG in May 1999 jointly sponsored by the World Bank and the World Wide Fund for Nature (WWF, 1999). The moratorium was ultimately included in the draft policy matrix proposed for the next structural adjustment program, and was endorsed by the new PNG government in November 1999 (Independent, 1999; National, 1999).

In addition to undertaking consultations with civil society groups, the World Bank was also responsible for inserting a condition in the ERP that committed the government to establish an alternative civil society based mechanism for delivery of social, agricultural, and infrastructure services to rural populations.[44] While the World Bank did not directly fund this mechanism, it did fund meetings aimed at mobilizing and organizing civil society to take on this role. The World Bank particularly engaged the NCSEJ, which prominently included the leaders of the anti-land reform protest and its successor, the PNG Watch Council. The Watch Council received funds from the government and some logistical support from the World Bank.

International pressures partially drove the World Bank to be more open, pressures that were made very real by President Wolfensohn's promise to make PNG a test case for how the new World Bank does business.

However, the group's claims to represent the public interest were considerably shaken when it became known that funds disbursed by the government to the Watch Council for social programs were used to oil the wheels of an election campaign mounted by the Watch Council's leaders. The campaign was ultimately successful and resulted in some of these erstwhile members of civil society occupying parliamentary seats. For these aspiring politicians, there were few votes to be won from a sympathetic portrayal of the World Bank; rather more to be gained from representing the World Bank and the government as "a single Janus-faced oppressor" (Filer and Kalit, 1999, p. 39). In hindsight, the World Bank's actions could be interpreted as an attempt to undertake damage control following the land reform incident, and suggests a lack of understanding of PNG politics. The World Bank most proactively engaged those elements of civil society that had been most vocal around the land reform issue, while comparatively less attention was paid to church groups with a much broader popular base, or to environmental groups, with their more specific focus on sustainable development.

What do we make of these various attempts at engagement with civil society? First, international pressures partially drove the World Bank to be more open, pressures that were made very real by President Wolfensohn's promise to make PNG a test case for how the new World Bank does business. Second, the misrepresentation, deliberate or otherwise, of the land reform condition by populist elements in PNG certainly punctuated the need for the World Bank to do a better job of engaging civil society and disseminating information about the implications of adjustment-led reforms. This outreach was subsequently undertaken, with mixed results. Third, while the World Bank did receive some civil society support for the forest conditions of the ERP, the unpopularity of the broader set of adjustment conditions and the perceived ideological rigidity of the World Bank on the future of forestry in PNG led an important constituency for reform to be lukewarm in its support for the World Bank.

Despite assertions in the World Bank's Implementation Completion Report concerning the importance of civil society engagement, this engagement was only partially successful. The World Bank received vocal support from one individual who did represent a segment of civil society for a period, but whose claim to representation grew weaker over time. The environmental NGOs, the World Bank's most likely supporters, did not loudly voice their approval because they believed that the World Bank was not truly open to the ideas of civil society actors and had already decided on promoting an orderly log export system. And in attempting to engage the populists who raised the land reform alarm, the World Bank found itself manipulated by a small leadership segment with political designs; in keeping with PNG's political culture, the goal of service delivery was turned into a political donation. In sum, engaging civil society, while a necessary first step, is no guarantor of success. Whom the World Bank engages, and how they are engaged, are crucial to the final outcome.

Private Sector

The forest industry, as represented by the Forest Industries Association, tended to perceive the World Bank as firmly aligned with environmental interests. It complained of a lack of consultation over the design of the Forestry and Conservation Project (Filer and Kalit, 1999). Moreover, the industry followed a political strategy of portraying itself as allied with the interests of landowners who sought to derive economic benefits from their land, and contrasted this with a conservationist perspective that would call on landowners to forego logging income.

World Bank missions made a point of consulting both NGOs and industry representatives, but the degree of outreach to NGOs exceeded that to industry. From the perspective of the World Bank, this is justified because the industry's views are easier to

glean than are those of the more disparate NGO community.[45] It is important to recall that the Barnett report, which stressed the need to control the industry, set the stage for this engagement. Moreover, the timber tycoons' behind-the-scenes manipulation of successive forest ministers to undermine World Bank conditions did not predispose the World Bank to accommodate the loggers. Finally, the government actively discouraged the World Bank from meeting the forest industry, perhaps because they were concerned that direct communication between the two would upset the patronage relationship between industry and some politicians.[46] In this climate, the World Bank kept the lines of communication to industry open—as when it conceded the need for adjusting the forest revenue system in 1998 to accommodate a downturn in the world log market—but for much of the period described above, the World Bank and the reformers shared a goal of bringing the logging industry under control.

Other International Aid Donors

Australia continues to play an important political and economic role in PNG. As such, the Australian government's support for any World Bank program in PNG is a precondition for success. In the early 1990s, relations between the two were strained over two issues. From the World Bank's perspective, Australia retained far too strong a colonial relationship with PNG.[47] Specifically, PNG provided special tax incentives for Australian companies, and AusAID's program was heavily tied to the use of Australian firms and consultants. As a result, the World Bank saw the Australians as unwilling to undertake bold measures in PNG, such as reforming the tax code, preferring instead to provide project assistance.

From the Australian perspective, the stability of PNG society, separated from Australia by only a narrow channel, was and remains a key imperative. In addition, with respect to the ongoing aid program, there was some friction over the World Bank's management of AusAID funds committed to the NFCAP process. As a result, in the mid-1990s, Australia decided to directly fund some projects that were originally intended to be channeled through the World Bank. The complications were a source of some friction in the early 1990s.[48] Since 1994, however, the sides are more in agreement. Although we have not been able to find any further details of engagement, it is clear that the ERP would not have proceeded without at least tacit Australian support for broader structural reform.

THE BOTTOM LINE

A surface reading of the World Bank's engagement with forest policy reform in PNG might hold that the World Bank faced down a wayward and corrupt government to successfully protect important institutional reforms in the forest sector backed by strong civil society support. While elements of this story hold true, a more detailed reading suggests a more complex story.

First, the World Bank, reformers in the bureaucracy, and environmental NGOs did share an interest in passing legislation and instituting regulation to place checks on the logging industry and distribute rents from logging in a more equitable manner. The history of the adjustment experience suggests that the application of conditionality to envi-

The Australian government's support for any World Bank program in PNG is a precondition for success.

ronmental outcomes in the context of a structural adjustment loan was essential to achieving this outcome. This result illustrates the ability of the adjustment lending instrument to achieve defined objectives through a stroke of the pen. Moreover, it shows the ability of adjustment lending to raise forest issues to the top of the national agenda, bringing them to the attention of powerful ministries. The result, in this case, was that negative outcomes in the forest sector were reversed because the costs of inaction would have had ripple effects at the macroeconomic level if the ERP had been cancelled.

Second, the proposition that this achievement was built on solid borrower ownership of the adjustment loan is partially supported by the material presented here, but with caveats. The PNG case illustrates the difficulties in evaluating ownership in binary terms. The Barnett inquiry and subsequent efforts by reformist bureaucrats provide substantial evidence of ownership of a reform agenda by actors from within PNG. Yet, national politicians were driven by a completely different agenda. They were almost always opposed to a process of institutionalization that depersonalized control over forest assets and removed them as sources of patronage within the political system. Moreover, many of the reformist bureaucrats who formulated the forest conditions were senior expatriate contract officers whose training and background match that of donor agency staff. The important role of these expatriates confuses the issue of borrower ownership.

Third, the World Bank's engagement with civil society proved contradictory. A central feature of the ERP was the World Bank's efforts to engage civil society and build a measure of support for the ERP within this sector. Here, the World Bank did win some support from elements of civil society, although this was confused both by the controversial reputation of one of the key supporters, as well as by the simultaneous reservations expressed by other supporters of the forest conditions in the ERP. Moreover, the World Bank directly engaged populists who simply used the World Bank to leverage financial support from the government with which to contest elections.

Perhaps most significant, dialogue with the World Bank's most obvious constituents—environmental NGOs—foundered on substantive issues. The World Bank's agenda initially focused on distributing the resource rents from export-oriented logging in an efficient and equitable manner, and over time expanded to apply institutional brakes to the rampant logging of PNG's forests. Worthwhile as these goals are, the World Bank did not, until recently, appear willing to challenge the neo-liberal prescription of export-led growth as applied to the forest sector, an unwillingness that set limits to engagement with NGOs whose vision of the future rested on community forestry and domestic log processing.

Fourth, the World Bank's success in holding the line on the forest conditions depended on several factors internal to the World Bank. The first necessary condition

was contacts within PNG and the detailed information on the forest sector necessary to formulate the appropriate loan conditions. This in turn was facilitated by the World Bank's continued and sustained participation in forest debates through the NFCAP process

---

The World Bank's efforts to engage civil society and build a measure of support was a central feature of the Economic Recovery Program.

---

and donor coordination efforts throughout the early 1990s. This involvement allowed the World Bank to anticipate not only technical problems but also, to some extent, political obstacles to forest policy reform. The second condition was firm support at the managerial level within the World Bank, which only resulted after an internal struggle. This episode suggests that future efforts should examine internal incentives to staff. Additionally, firm support from senior World Bank management is essential if conditionality of this nature is to be credible with governments.

Finally, subsequent events have shown how fragile forest policy reforms are in PNG—fragility that is evident in another round of tough conditionality in the latest structural adjustment program. The PNG case suggests then, that structural adjustment lending can play an important supportive role in giving political power to reformers through the indirect channel of World Bank conditions, but that ultimately that sustainable policy reform requires commitment to become entrenched within the national political system. If the reform process needs to be supported by a series of structural adjustment loans with similar content, then it can hardly be characterized as successful. The next few years will tell if forest policy reform in PNG is self-sustaining or not. To be supportive, the World Bank has to be genuinely open to civil society prescriptions and visions. Only then can it play an important role in supporting relationships and new political forces that are strong enough to represent conservation interests effectively.

REFERENCES

AID/WATCH. 1996. "Pawa na Pipel! People and Power in Papua New Guinea." Woollahra, Australia: AID/WATCH.

Ariku, Noah Javen Ariku. 1996. "Release of Tranche Two of World Bank ERP/SAP Loan to Papua New Guinea." Mimeo.

Cortesi, Lafcadio. 1995. "Letter to several NGOs." Greenpeace.

—1999. "Untitled email to World Bank staff." 29 July.

Filer, Colin, and Kilyali Kalit. 1999. "Environmental Adjustment: Opportunity for Policy Reform in the Forestry Sector? Papua New Guinea Case Study." Port Moresby, PNG. Mimeo.

Filer, Colin with Nikhil Sekhran. 1998. *Loggers, Donors and Resource Owners. Policy That Works for Forests and People.* Edited by J. Mayers. London: International Institute for Environment and Development.

ICRAF. 1997. "Justice and Freedom." Port Moresby, PNG: Individual and Community Rights Advocacy Forum.

Independent. 1999. "Greenpeace Praises Forests Moratorium." *Independent*, December 21.

National. 1999. "WWF Lauds Moves for Stricter Forestry Laws." *National*, December 17.

Taylor, Meg, Philip Siaguru, John Millet, and Lance Hill. 1994. "Review of the National Forest and Conservation Action Programme." Port Moresby, PNG: United Nations Development Programme.

World Bank, The. 1995. "Report and Recommendation of the President of the IBRD to the Executive Directors on a Proposed Loan of US$50 million to the Independent State of Papua New Guinea for an Economic Recovery Program." Washington D.C.: The World Bank.

—1997. "Implementation Completion Report: Independent State of Papua New Guinea Economic Recovery Program Loan." Washington D.C.: The World Bank.

—1998a. "Papua New Guinea: Social and Economic Development Program Loan." Washington D.C.: The World Bank.

—1998b. "Project Appraisal Document on a Proposed Loan to Papua New Guinea for a Forestry and Conservation Project." Washington D.C.: The World Bank.

World Wildlife Fund. 1999. "Strategies for Sustainable Forestry: Summary of Discussions and Recommendations from the WWF-World Bank Sustainable Forestry Workshop, Madang, Papua New Guinea, 26–28 May 1999." Unpublished report.

NOTES

1. This chapter draws on "Environmental Adjustment: Opportunities for Progressive Reform in the Forest Sector? Papua New Guinea Case Study," by Colin Filer and Kilyali Kalit (1999), which is available at http://www.wri.org/wri/governance/iffeforest.html as well as on interviews conducted by the authors in Papua New Guinea and Washington, D.C., on a not-for-attribution basis.

2. One Malaysian company, Rimbunan Hijau, controls half the log export volume and has diversified into wood processing and even into ownership of a national newspaper.

3. Churches are the most active and widespread form of civil society organization in PNG, but have not, thus far, played an active role in forest processes (Filer, 1998).

4. Over the past decade, grant aid has accounted for about 10 percent of GNP in PNG. Three quarters of this have come from the Australian government, which over time has been shifting its aid contribution from general budgetary support to specific projects implemented usually by Australian contractors (Filer and Kalit, 1999).

5. The then Prime Minister who initiated the review was relatively insulated from charges of impropriety since his own political base lay in a coffee-growing region, which may explain his willingness to initiate the inquiry.

6. However, it was only in 1991, two years later, that this particular politician was found guilty of eighty charges of misconduct by a Leadership tribunal and forced to give up his parliamentary seat (Filer, 1998).

7. There was also a second point of difference: the World Bank was skeptical of Barnett's assumption that resource owners are innocent victims of loggers, and therefore potential allies of reformers (Filer and Kalit, 1999).

8. Not-for-attribution interview with several NGOs in PNG, December 1998.

9. The task force also included representatives of the Forest Industries Association which, at the time, was not dominated by Malaysian logging interests. These representatives argued for a set of rules that would allow for long-term secure concessions and a regulatory structure that would not require them to compete for concessions with bribes. (Personal communication from a member of the National Forest Policy task force, December 1999.)

10. This was accomplished, in part, by logging companies mobilizing landowner company directors from six provinces. These landowners formed the Forest Resource Owners Association (FROA) and effectively represented the interests of logging companies (Filer and Kalit, 1999.)

11. In addition, there was a second letter from the Prime Minister to the Forest Minister communicating the same message (Filer and Kalit, 1999).

12. The key provisions of the act that followed from the policy were establishment of the following: a National Forest Board with representation from government departments, provincial government, the Forest Industry Association, and NGOs; provincial forest management committees; a National Forest Service; a process of

resource acquisition which required the Forest Authority to enter into Forest Management Agreements with customary owners; a process of a multi-stage resource allocation, which included a development options study; conditions of development that included a logging plan, and payment of a performance bond. It also specified that logging should only take place in accordance with a National Forest Plan which was then unwritten (Filer and Kalit, 1999).

13. The act successfully achieved this outcome, but not before the Forest Minister had allocated 17 new timber permits the day before the act was gazetted (Filer and Kalit, 1999).

14. This is certainly the opinion of national bureaucrats, and is supported by information that the reformist elements within the bureaucracy prompted the World Bank's letter to the Forest Minister, as well as the letter written by the Prime Minister. (Not-for-attribution interview with PNG government official, December 1999.)

15. Specifically, it would repeal the resource acquisitions and resource allocation provisions that had slowed down the process of industrial logging, which would give the Forest Board a free hand in allocating permits. At the same time, they proposed to reform the Board to stack it with industry representatives and members of the industry-friendly Forest Resource Owners Association, while dropping the sole NGO representative (Filer and Kalit, 1999).

16. World Bank staff point out that the loan was innovative with respect to social sectors as well. Thus, instead of leading to budgetary cuts in these sectors as past adjustment loans had done, spending on health and education was increased. (Not-for-attribution interview with World Bank staff, July 1999.)

17. Not-for-attribution interviews with government officials in PNG, December 1998.

18. Expatriates played an important role in the government, and in NGOs and the private sector.

19. Not-for-attribution interview with World Bank staff, April 1999.

20. At one point the World Bank country economist, Pirouz Hamidian-Rad, was taken captive by a hostage crowd.

21. This rumor seems to have begun with the option, in the legislation, for landowners to lease land to a third party who could use the land as security for a bank loan. Based on this, speculation arose that "big men" could use this option to gain control over the land of others in a customary land group. Next was the possibility that politicians would lease land to Asian companies for development of palm oil estates. From there, it was but a short step to the belief that the government would offer the World Bank land as collateral for the ERP (Filer and Kalit, 1999).

22. The other reasons were the lack of progress on allocating funds for service delivery at local levels, and attempts to reverse the process of tariff rationalization (World Bank, 1997).

23. Details in this section are drawn from interviews conducted with World Bank staff and interviewees in PNG that were conducted on a not-for-attribution basis.

24. Not-for-attribution interview with former World Bank staff, December 1998.

25. Not-for-attribution interview with former World Bank staff, December 1998.

26. Not-for-attribution interview with World Bank staff, January and July 1999, and with an NGO representative in PNG, December 1998.

27. Not-for-attribution interview with PNG government officials, December 1998.

28. Not-for-attribution interview with World Bank staff, February 1999, and January 1999, and with PNG government officials, December 1998.

29. However, the macroeconomists remained more comfortable with the economic dimensions of these conditions, such as the revenue arrangement, than with the institutional issues.

30. Not-for-attribution interview with World Bank staff, January 1999.

31. Not-for-attribution interview with World Bank staff, January 1999.

32. Not-for-attribution interview with World Bank staff, January, February, and July 1999.

33. Not-for-attribution interview with former World Bank staff, December 1998.

34. An additional risk identified is the government's capacity to implement the program (World Bank, 1998a).

35. Not-for-attribution interview with World Bank staff, November 1998.

36. Not-for-attribution interview with World Bank staff, November 1998 and with an NGO representative in PNG, December 1998.

37. Not-for-attribution interview with former World Bank staff, December 1998.

38. Not-for-attribution interview with World Bank staff, December 1998.

39. Specifically, economic restructuring was introduced to cut recurrent expenditures, reduce import controls, and accelerate the privatization of government assets, all of which might be characterized as "structural adjustment without the loans" (Filer and Kalit, 1999, p. 61). In anticipation of these savings, development expenditures were increased, much of which was placed at the discretion of members of parliament. Since the total saved through cuts proved to be less than the amount already parceled out, the country faced a financial crisis. Moreover, foreign exchange reserves decreased as export revenues declined; all of which devalued PNG's currency, the kina.

40. The immediate cause for his resignation was a political crisis resulting from his attempts to raise money from Taiwan by offering diplomatic recognition.

41. An example of the former is Individual and Community Rights Advocacy Forum (ICRAF), and the latter is the Foundation for Peoples and Community Development (FPCD).

42. Not-for-attribution interview with World Bank staff, February 1999, and April 1999.

43. Both the organization and the individual have complicated histories, illustrating the complexity of NGO politics in PNG. The FROA, as a member of the NCSEJ, had aroused some controversy over its pro-logging industry stance. In protest, the Secretary of the NCSEJ, Noah Ariku, formed a competing Forest Resource Owners Association, which went by the same name but the opposite politics on forest issues. Both bodies, claiming to be the real FROA, ran newspaper advertisements—one parroting the Forest Industries Association view, the other that of the World Bank—each accusing the other of being a puppet of the originators of their respective views. Soon thereafter, these two competing FROAs struck a compromise and Ariku, the lead dissident, was named the Secretary of the merged FROA. The letters to international environmental NGOs were addressed from Ariku, both as General Secretary of the FROA and Executive Director of Mission Innovator, Inc., an organization that no one in PNG had any prior knowledge of.

44. Not-for-attribution interview with World Bank staff, February 1999.

45. Personal communication with World Bank staff, November 1999.

46. Not-for-attribution interview with World Bank staff, July 1999.

47. Not-for-attribution interview with World Bank staff, July 1999.

48. Personal communication with researcher in PNG, June 1999.

3

CAMEROON

Jake Brunner
François Ekoko

I n 1989, the World Bank initiated a major attempt to improve forest management in Cameroon by tying forest policy reforms to structural adjustment lending. The first round of negotiations between the World Bank and the Government of Cameroon culminated in the 1994 Forest Law, which introduced far reaching changes in the way that forest concessions were allocated, taxed, and managed. The law also included provisions that, for the first time in Central Africa, granted local communities the right to benefit financially from wood cut in their customary forests. Yet, despite the World Bank's substantial efforts, the government repeatedly reneged on its commitments, throwing the implementation of the reforms into disarray.

The policy reform process in Cameroon is of national and regional significance. Understanding the process, however, is complex. Stakeholders in the reform process—the various branches of government, the private sector, the World Bank, other international donors, domestic and international NGOs, and local communities—tend to hold divergent views about the reforms' success. Arriving at a balanced assessment of the World Bank's approach means calibrating among a range of conflicting opinions.[1]

BACKGROUND

From independence in 1960, Ahmadou Ahidjo ruled Cameroon under a highly centralized, one-party system. Following his resignation on health grounds in 1982, he was replaced by Paul Biya, who continued one-party rule until 1990, when he was led by popular protest and external pressure to accede to a multi-party system. The parliamentary elections in 1992 left the president's party in power, but only as part of a coalition. The presidential election in the same year, which returned Biya to power, is generally considered to have been grossly manipulated, as was the second presidential election in 1997 (Burnham and Sharpe, 1997). According to Berlin-based Transparency International's Corruption Perceptions Index, Cameroon was the world's most corrupt country in 1998 and 1999 (Transparency International, 1999).

During the 1960s and 1970s, Cameroon enjoyed a reputation as one of the more successful economies in Africa (Burnham and Sharpe, 1997). Growth over this period averaged five percent a year, driven largely by high prices for its principal exports, including cocoa, coffee, cotton, aluminum, and from the late 1970s, petroleum. But imprudent use of its oil revenues, a 65-percent decline in the terms of trade for its chief export crops, and a marked expansion in government employment led to a balance of payments crisis in the early 1980s; the inauguration of an IMF structural adjustment program in 1988; and a 50-percent currency devaluation in 1994. Gross domestic product (GDP) declined by six percent per annum on average between 1986 and 1993, producing a 50-percent fall in per capita incomes. Economic decline was accompanied by increased poverty, as poor farmers suffered the brunt of the fall in producer prices and the government cut basic health and education services (World Bank, 1996). Public debt increased from US$5.9 billion in 1989 to US$9.1 billion in 1999, of which 80 percent was external debt. The ratio of external debt to GDP rose from 33 percent in 1989 to an all-time high of 109 percent in 1994, before falling back to 80 percent in 1999. Forty-four percent of the budget goes for debt service.

The World Bank has been closely associated with Cameroon's development efforts since 1967. As Table 3.1 shows, there has been a significant shift away from project lending—which fell from US$902 million in 1980–1991 to US$154 million in 1992–1998 —toward structural and sectoral adjustment lending, which increased from US$150 million to US$612 million over the same period. Project lending has thus declined in both relative and absolute terms. The earlier generation of projects was plagued with problems, and following a portfolio review in late 1993, eight were closed and three restructured (World Bank, 1996). A US$273 million cocoa rehabilitation project had had no result whatsoever according to the World Bank's own Operations Evaluation Department.

The World Bank would like to do more work in Cameroon, but it has not disbursed project funds because of the poor management and problems linked to a lack of transparency and good governance in that country (Reuters, 1999). By the end of 1999, the World Bank had only six projects in Cameroon worth US$330 million, compared to 34 projects in Ghana worth US$1.2 billion, and 23 in Ivory Coast worth US$578 million.

TABLE 3.1 | WORLD BANK LENDING TO CAMEROON (IN TOTAL COMMITMENTS US$ MILLION), 1980–1998

	1980–1991		1992–1998	
Structural adjustment lending	Projects: 1	Loan: 150	Projects: 7	Loan: 432
Sectoral adjustment lending	Projects: 0	Loan: 0	Projects: 2	Loan: 180
Project lending	Projects: 25	Loan: 902	Projects: 6	Loan: 154
Forest projects	Projects: 1	Loan: 17	Projects: 0	Loan: 0
Nonforest projects with forest components	Projects: 1	Loan: 22	Projects: 0	Loan: 0

Source: World Bank, 1998

BOX 3.1

CHRONOLOGY OF ADJUSTMENT AND FOREST POLICY REFORM IN CAMEROON

1986	Onset of the economic crisis.
1988	TFAP completed and SAC I approved.
1992	Paul Biya wins the presidential elections.
November 1993	National Assembly debates the draft Forest Law.
January 1994	Devaluation of the CFA franc and approval of the ERC.
August 1995	Promulgation of the Implementation Decree.
February 1996	SAC II approved.
August 1997	First concession auction.
October 1997	Paul Biya wins the presidential elections.
June 1998	SAC III approved.
June 1999	Government approves new concession auction rules.

The World Bank has been involved in three Structural Adjustment Credits (SACs) in 1988, 1996, and 1998, and an Emergency Recovery Credit (ERC) following the currency devaluation in 1994. Only SAC III included detailed forest conditionalities, although SAC I and the ERC were used to ensure that the government passed the major legal texts necessary for forest sector reform. Boxes 3.1 and 3.2 summarize, respectively, the chronology of the reform process and the main forest conditionalities.

ADJUSTMENT LENDING AND FOREST POLICY REFORM

The forest sector contributes significantly to Cameroon's economy. Timber production increased rapidly after 1992 as a result of the economic crisis, the currency devaluation, and a surge in demand for logs from Asia. In 1998, the sector contributed ten percent of non-oil GDP, nine percent of all tax revenues (if transport and related activities are included), and 28 percent of all exports by value. Sixty-six sawmills were active in 1999, producing a total of 2.7 million m3 of wood and directly employing 10,400 people (MINEF, 1999).

Starting in 1989, the government, with strong World Bank support, targeted policy reform as the cornerstone of improved forest management. Cameroon's forests were declining in both size and quality. Clearing for agriculture was identified as the major

---

BOX 3.2	FOREST CONDITIONALITIES

1988   SAC I: preparation of the Forest Law.

1994   ERC: promulgation of the Implementation Decree.

1998   SAC III: definition of detailed concession auction criteria and appointment of an independent observer to report on the auction proceedings; preparation of a strategy for the allocation of logging concessions; preference given to community forests over *ventes de coupe* in the non-permanent forest zone; and implementation of an effective tax recovery program.

---

cause of deforestation, but logging, and the commercial poaching that goes with it, was considered to be the main cause of forest degradation (O'Halloran and Ferrer, 1997). The World Bank believed that if it changed the way that logging concessions were allocated, taxed, and managed, the government could prevent the worst environmental damage and increase its share of revenue to help deal with its most pressing economic and social concerns. The World Bank intended follow-up these reforms with a forest loan that would allow it to monitor policy implementation.

The regime had used the allocation of logging concessions to maintain political support, as shown by the jump in the number of registered logging companies prior to the presidential elections in 1992 and 1997. Strong vested interests were opposed to changes that would have limited the use of Cameroon's forests for political purposes. The World Bank tried to overcome these interests by tying reforms to structural adjustment lending, a powerful incentive.

The 1994 Forest Law

A detailed review of Cameroon's 1981 Forest Law had been undertaken by the 1988 Tropical Forestry Action Plan (TFAP). Between 1989 and 1993, the World Bank undertook a series of missions to Cameroon to discuss a forest and environment project that would help implement the TFAP recommendations. Gradually, however, the discussion shifted away from project activities and toward Cameroon's forest policies and the need to update the previous law. Although the Food and Agriculture Organization and the United Nations Development Programme led the TFAP preparation, it was the World Bank that pressed the government for policy reform since these agencies and the bilateral donors had neither the political will nor financial leverage to do so. While the World Bank's forest and environment project team negotiated with the government, a second team, based in Washington, started work on a new forest law. In 1993, the World Bank stated its opinion that significant reforms were needed before further project support could be justified (Ekoko, 1997).

One of the main weaknesses of the 1981 Forest Law was the lack of a legal framework for planning land use and integrating forest protection and production activities (O'Halloran and Ferrer, 1997). Under the previous system, the Prime Minister had sole discretion over the allocation of logging concessions, while the Minister of Agriculture, and later the Minister of Environment and Forests,[2] was responsible for granting smaller (2,500 ha) cutting rights (*ventes de coupe*). Larger concessions (*licenses*) were given for a period of five years (but were renewable) on the basis of requests submitted by logging companies. The *ventes de coupe* and *licenses*, which had no management requirements, were allocated based on mutual agreement between the companies and government authorities. Companies had no incentive to manage the forests efficiently because they were unlikely to derive any benefit from good management. The law did not allow the transfer of concessions, and did not guarantee long-term access so that companies could benefit from previous practice during a second felling cycle. Since export taxes were not linked to the market price of wood, and area taxes were very low, loggers were encouraged to cut only the best trees and the government received less revenue. Companies constructed roads deep into the forest to exploit the rarest and most valuable timber species, opening up these areas to agricultural settlers and bushmeat hunters.

The lack of a clearly defined forest policy hindered the drafting of the new law. The Ministry of Agriculture commissioned a set of studies of forest concessions and taxation. These studies, which were proposed by the World Bank and largely funded by Canadian development assistance, were completed in 1992.[3] In November 1993, the World Bank

and the Ministry of Environment and Forests (MINEF) agreed on the draft text of the Forest Law, which was submitted to the National Assembly.

The draft law introduced four basic reforms (O'Halloran and Ferrer, 1997). First, concessions were to be allocated by auctions on the grounds that they are less susceptible to political pressure and more economically efficient than the previous discretionary practices. Second, the law introduced changes in pricing and taxation to allow for an increase in fiscal revenue and the use of market-based incentives to improve forest management (Karsenty, 1999a). A key reform was a significantly higher area tax indexed to inflation.[4] The World Bank argued that by increasing the cost of the raw material, a higher area tax encourages greater efficiency in its use, and that a company with large margins to improve efficiency is more likely to invest in reducing waste than in acquiring larger concessions. In 1997, the World Bank also succeeded in having market prices introduced as the basis of export tax rates, which the government had rendered meaningless by manipulating the reference prices through obscure administrative decisions. These prices underestimated the value of logs by 30–40 percent and of processed wood by 90 percent, and represented a significant loss in government revenue.

Third, the draft law introduced forest management plans.[5] Whereas auctions and higher area taxes were believed to constitute sound forest policy (Grut et al., 1991), there was little empirical evidence of their impact on harvesting practices, which some feared would intensify. Forest management plans were intended to mitigate the potential negative effects of more intensive logging. They also responded to growing domestic and international support for sustainable forest management. Finally, the draft law included provisions for local communities to acquire the exclusive right to manage and exploit up to 5,000 ha of their customary forest. Local communities could earn revenue by logging their forests themselves or contracting with a logging company. They were also to receive 10 percent of the area tax, with 40 percent going to the communes, the lowest level of government administration, and 50 percent to MINEF.

Lack of Borrower Ownership

The process by which the 1994 Forest Law was drafted reflects the central role played by the World Bank and the passivity of the Government of Cameroon. Letters from the World Bank to the government between 1990 and 1992 show that the World Bank was instrumental in shaping the reform agenda (Ekoko, 1997) and maintaining the momentum of the policy dialogue. Because of poor interministerial coordination and MINEF's internal weaknesses, the government not only failed to lead the reform process, but also to participate in it effectively.

Authority over the negotiations was widely dispersed. By 1992, nine different governmental agencies had some input into, or degree of oversight over, forest policy.[6] MINEF's authority relative to the other agencies was undermined by the lack of political clout of the then Minister, who belonged to the smallest party in the governing coalition. Moreover, the establishment of MINEF in 1992 was not followed, as is normal practice, by the creation of a complementary desk in the Presidency to coordinate the activities of the Ministry with other government agencies.

Although officially responsible for coordinating the policy dialogue, the President's advisors never met with MINEF staff to discuss the proposed law, nor did they consult with the President's party to assess the political implications of the new law (Ekoko, 1997).

The process by which the 1994 Forest Law was drafted reflects the central role played by the World Bank and the passivity of the Government of Cameroon.

The lack of presidential leadership was compounded by MINEF's own weaknesses. In 1986, the President staked his prestige on his rejection of the tough austerity measures requested by the IMF, insisting that Cameroon would undertake economic reforms of its own. Budget cuts and the first of several hiring freezes were announced, but were never implemented. The crisis worsened with expenditure overruns in 1987 of 11.5 percent of GNP, and the government was forced to agree to IMF conditions that included severe reductions in administrative expenditures. Staff salaries were cut by 40 percent (and were often paid several months in arrears), virtually all perquisites (such as housing and vehicle allowance) were abolished, and the operating budgets of most ministries were slashed. In 1992, only five percent of MINEF's total budget was allocated to non-staff expenditures, and the last time the Ministry received new vehicles was in 1984. Maintenance, never adequately budgeted for, all but disappeared.

The IMF-led budget cuts were not compensated by effective donor support. A review of donor projects shows a strong orientation toward protected areas management and research (CIRAD, 1997). These tended to be of high symbolic value, but of limited practical use in strengthening the Ministry's analytical and coordination skills. Significantly, there had been little donor support for plantations, which require long-term investment and high quality management. The effect was to disperse the Ministry's resources on numerous small projects of limited potential. As one Ministry staff person put it: "On Monday we do biodiversity, on Tuesday forest taxation, on Wednesday protected areas . . ."[7]

Declining salaries, poor working conditions, and the offer of very large sums of money provided a strong incentive for corruption. The average MINEF official earned 60,000 CFA francs per month and had no means of transport or communication, but could gain millions of CFA by not reporting logging in areas for which a company had no right. According to World Bank staff, when the Ministry's computerized tax assessment system broke down in 1991, forcing the government to rely on logging company declarations, tax revenues went up, implying that the Ministry's tax reporting was even less reliable than the industry's.[8]

The collapse in MINEF's operational capacity, and the fact that many senior ministry officials benefited from the discretionary practices that the World Bank sought to end, undermined its interest in seriously engaging in the forest policy dialogue. Some ministry officials have also expressed personal hostility toward certain World Bank staff who they claimed imposed unreasonable dead-lines backed up with the threat of loan suspension (Ekoko, 1997).

Modifications to the Law: the Role of the National Assembly and France

Since the late 1960s, Cameroon's National Assembly had confined itself to rubber-stamping the President's legislation. But with the return of multi-party politics and the weak performance of the President's party in the 1992 parliamentary elections, the Assembly started to play a more independent role. Fear of jeopardizing World Bank support led the Presidency to get the forest law passed by pressuring parliamentarians to abide by party discipline, and by leaving as little time as possible for debate (Ekoko, 1997).

Despite these tactics, the Assembly modified the text of the law and effectively changed key provisions. The most important change rejected the use of auctions to allocate logging concessions in favor of a clause that read: "a forest concession shall be granted upon recommendation by a competent commission." Parliamentarians who opposed the government on this issue argued that nationals would be unable to compete with foreign logging companies in an auction, and that the forest would be sold out to foreigners.

According to the World Bank, this fear was unjustified as the draft law included a concession size category of up to 50,000 ha that was open only to Cameroonian nationals. Thus, despite the patriotic rhetoric, partisan political gains and financial self-interest appear to have motivated the opposition (Ekoko, 1997). Many parliamentarians were involved in logging, either directly, or indirectly as shareholders in logging companies or as owners of licenses leased to foreign companies. They also benefited from the discretionary allocation of *ventes de coupe,* which allowed them to participate in the lucrative business with limited capital. These forests were typically subcontracted to foreign companies (a practice known derogatorily as *fermage*). Auctions implied an increase in the cost of access to the forest, and thus a threat to parliamentarians' financial interests. They would also have eliminated an important source of patronage.

Parliamentarians also sought to capitalize on the law's unpopularity to boost their fortunes in the municipal elections scheduled for June 1994 (Ekoko, 1997). The new law was very controversial and many opposed it, because they felt it legalized the plundering of Cameroon's forests. Parliamentarians from forest regions were particularly active during the discussions and, despite representing rival political parties, were united in their opposition. Prior to the debate, many rural youth considered their representatives as traitors for allowing their forest resources to be exploited without any financial compensation. Opposition to the law allowed parliamentarians to regain support from this constituency.

In addition to challenging the auction provision, parliamentarians also proposed banning log exports as a way of promoting local processing, limiting the maximum size of concessions from 500,000 ha to 200,000 ha, and reducing the maximum duration of concessions to 15 years (renewable for another 15). These decisions contradicted the advice of both the French government, which argued that larger and longer concessions were needed for sustainable forest management (Carret, 1998), and the World Bank,

which argued that log export bans encouraged the rapid establishment of inefficient processing industries by depressing the local price of wood.

The proposed log export ban threatened French logging interests and allegedly triggered the intervention of the French government (Pearce, 1994). In November 1993, when the new forest law was being debated, the French Minister for Cooperation and Overseas Development, who happened to be in Cameroon at the time, met the President and Speaker of the National Assembly to discuss economic cooperation issues. There are indications, however, that the visit was also to lobby against a log export ban, which would have hurt the largest French companies, which accounted for over half of Cameroon's log exports. This visit could be interpreted as a reminder of the political and financial support that France has provided to the regime at crucial moments, and that France expected to receive similar support when its own interests were threatened. Significantly, the French Minister refused to meet with the main opposition leader, a move the President greatly appreciated.

This interpretation squares with the fact that the only time the Presidency intervened in the National Assembly was on the matter of the log export ban (Ekoko, 1997). Members of the President's party and other coalition members were ordered to vote against the ban. The approved version of the law states: "70 percent of logs shall be processed domestically." Immediately after the law was passed, the Presidency agreed that a ban would come into effect, but not until January 1999, five years later. Even the 70 percent rule was watered down by the provision that companies exporting more than

30 percent of their production as logs could do so if they paid a progressive surtax on the difference. This tax proved to be difficult to administer because of problems calculating logged and processed wood volumes.

According to the World Bank, its resident mission launched a publicity campaign to explain the economic benefits of the new law. In 1993, the World Bank hired the advisor to the Minister of Environment and Forests as its agriculture and natural resource officer. She brought an excellent knowledge of the forest sector and an extensive network of contacts inside and outside of government. The World Bank's resident representative also regularly appeared on television and radio to argue that the greater transparency the new law would bring was in the interests of the country. Nevertheless, the World Bank was powerless against the Assembly's opposition. Even the World Bank's special briefings proved counterproductive as parliamentarians accused it of meddling in Cameroon's internal affairs. The World Bank admits that its publicity campaign was ineffective, but when a staff member was asked what more it could have done, the reply was "Nothing short of overthrowing the government."9

Around the Parliamentary Roadblock: The Implementation Decree

The National Assembly's amendments to the draft law were inconsistent with what the World Bank considered to be a sound forest policy. At the same time, the government was negotiating an ERC following the CFA franc devaluation. The World Bank told the government that it would not accept the revised law. In response, the government sent a letter to the World Bank indicating that it would submit revisions to the law to

the parliamentary session of November 1994. But during a visit to Cameroon, World Bank staff realized that the President would not dare challenge the Assembly on the new law.

The World Bank admits that its publicity campaign was ineffective, but when a staff member was asked what more it could have done, the reply was "Nothing short of overthrowing the government."

Two reasons explained the President's reluctance. First, the President's party was part of a fragile coalition that was struggling in the face of growing political opposition. This opposition had culminated in the villes mortes campaign that closed down many cities between 1990 and 1992 and threatened the very survival of the regime. Then, in 1992, Biya's victory in the presidential elections was seriously questioned, both domestically and abroad. The Presidency did not want to further provoke the opposition by reintroducing such controversial legislation. Second, the Presidency may have been pleased with the changes, because they allowed the continuation of the discretionary practices that served the interests of some powerful individuals, government officials, and many parliamentarians.

The World Bank realized that any effort to persuade the government to challenge the Assembly and reverse the most serious changes in the law would be futile. It therefore asked MINEF to draft an Implementation Decree that would interpret the law in line with the draft that the World Bank had originally agreed to. The Ministry submitted a draft version of the decree to the World Bank in July 1994. The World Bank rejected this version and several staff spent over a year revising the decree line by line. A final version, acceptable to the World Bank, was issued in August 1995. Changes in pricing and taxation were to be addressed in subsequent finance laws.

IMPLEMENTATION EXPERIENCE

Implementation of the 1994 Forest Law has been problematic. On the face of it, the forest and finance laws have succeeded in boosting tax revenues. After accounting for the effect of the 1994 devaluation, revenues went from 10 billion CFA francs in 1990, to 14 billion in 1994, to 24 billion in 1997 (Carret, 1998). Over the same period, wood production rose from about two to three million m3. The government therefore increased its share of the value of the wood from 6,000 CFA/m3 to 10,000 CFA/m3. This increase was partly from higher area taxes and the use of market prices to determine export tax rates. But it mainly resulted from the Ministry of Economy and Finance (MINEFI) deciding to invite the Swiss company SGS in 1995 to control log exports, which accounted for 80 percent of forest taxes. This was done because of MINEF's poor tax recovery record. Implementation of other aspects of the new law has proved equally difficult, notably in the case of the concession auctions.

Concession Auctions

Allocating concessions by public auction was critical to maintaining the government's

commitment to the reforms (O'Halloran and Ferrer, 1997). The World Bank was therefore concerned in May 1996 when the government granted concessions without auction to two French logging companies. The World Bank sent a letter to the President recommending that the two concessions be revoked. The World Bank never received a reply and the concessions were not canceled. In fact, a third concession was handed out covertly, this time in an area zoned for conservation. When the World Bank protested, the concession was canceled—a decision prompted by an upcoming donor meeting to discuss projects identified in the National Environmental Action Plan (Ekoko, 1997).

In May 1996, 112 *ventes de coupe* were put up for auction for which the applicants presented bids with an annual area tax of 1,000–3,000 CFA/ha. This demonstrated that a concession auction could work in Cameroon and that logging companies were willing to pay an area tax much higher than the 300 CFA in effect at the time of the law. The willingness of companies to bid so much for the *ventes de coupe* was one of the main reasons why the World Bank recommended raising the minimum area tax for the large concessions from 300 to 2,000 CFA/ha. However, the government did not amend the 1996–97 Finance Law and drew up concession application documents using an area tax of 300 CFA/ha. After subsequent negotiations with the World Bank, the government increased the tax to 2,000 CFA/ha through administrative procedures. But the industry argued that such a method was illegal and boycotted the auction, which was held in February 1997. The government received only five bids for the 42 concessions and the auction was aborted.

In August 1997, the government rebid 26 concessions with a minimum area tax of 1,500 CFA/ha, for which 190 companies submitted bids. The results showed that applicants were prepared to pay three or four times more than the minimum area tax. But 16 of the 26 concessions were not awarded to the highest bidder. In most cases, the inter-ministerial committee (made up of representatives of five ministries, the national industry syndicate, and the National Assembly) recommended that concessions be allocated to the company ranked first according to the technical criteria, even if the financial bid was much lower. Then, after the recommendations were submitted to the Prime Minister for approval, six concessions were awarded to individuals who did not even appear on the list reviewed by the commission, but are known to have been key supporters of the regime. Strictly speaking, the law was respected because it reserves for the Prime Minister the right to overrule the committee's recommendations in cases where the national interest is threatened, but the government's decision emphatically broke the spirit of the law.

Illegal Logging

The failure of the August 1997 auction had serious environmental implications. Many individuals awarded concessions did not have the technical or financial means to start logging, let alone prepare management plans. The result was a severe shortage of wood and a boom in illegal logging.

Pressure on the forest had been building since 1993, when the World Bank asked the government to stop any further attribution of licenses until the new law was implemented. According to the French regional policy advi-sor at the time, this was a mistake, given the inevitable delays in implementation, because it penalized companies that needed wood for their sawmills, and encouraged them to engage in "anarchic and illegal logging practices that once in place are difficult to stop."[10]

Working in collusion with provincial governors, companies exploited loopholes that allowed them to circumvent the law. Three permits, *certificat de main levée*, *permis de récupération*, and *permis d'exploitation*, were widely used to this end.[11] A World Bank mission to the East Province in August 1999 concluded that these permits have resulted in the cutting of an almost limitless amount of wood (World Bank, 1999).

Paradoxically, the increase in illegal logging is related to two measures included in the 1994 Forest Law: higher area taxes and the legal recognition of community forests. Higher area taxes have had two effects. First, they have made large concessions more expensive to log than *ventes de coupe*. The minimum area tax payable on *ventes de coupe* is more than on concessions, but the former require no management plans and can be cut in a year, whereas the latter require management plans and the area tax is payable on the whole concession for 30 years. As a result, the area tax burden on wood cut from concessions is three times that on wood cut from *ventes de coupe* on a per volume basis. Not surprisingly, loggers prefer cutting in *ventes de coupe*.

Second, higher area taxes and inadequate government control mean that illegal logging is both easy and profitable.[12] This "push" factor is now matched by a strong "pull" factor. In 1996, MINEF granted villagers the right to receive 1,000 CFA per cubic meter of wood cut. Villagers have often resorted to violence to defend their customary forests against loggers, but now they encourage loggers to cut illegally in exchange for 1,000 CFA per cubic meter. Loggers are happy to pay this tax, because villagers protect them from government interference.[13] According to one observer, for every *vente de coupe* that is logged legally, four are logged illegally.[14]

The 1,000 CFA tax has also aggravated social divisions. Villagers resent the fact that communes often keep the 10 percent of the area tax that villagers are entitled to. This tax should be used to pay for schools, wells, and other public infrastructure requested by the village management committees. Instead, a false invoice is often prepared, no investment is made, and the communes spend the money on beer or political campaigns. The 1,000 CFA tax, on the other hand, goes straight to the villagers, and represents the first direct financial benefit that they have received from logging. This has led to the formation of an alliance between the villagers and loggers against the communes, which threatens to undermine the government's decentralization program.

Community Forests

Some observers believe that MINEF authorized the 1,000 CFA tax to weaken the villagers' interest in acquiring community forests. At the World Bank's insistence, the 1994 Forest Law included provisions granting villages the right to establish community forests. These provisions, unique in Central Africa, represented an important equity objective; but as they appear in the law, they are unclear, contradictory, and open to abuse. Community forests are located in the same zone as the *ventes de coupe*, and some govern-

ment officials have submitted fraudulent requests to secure community forests without the informed consent of the local population. Large sums are at stake. In one case, local MINEF officials working in collaboration with a Lebanese logging company tried to acquire five community forests for a payment of one million CFA and the construction of a community shelter, a total offer of about US$2,500.[15] The timber cut from this area would have been worth over US$10 million.

At the World Bank's insistence, the 1994 Forest Law included provisions granting villages the right to establish community forests. These provisions, unique in Central Africa, represented an important equity objective.

The World Bank has been criticized for not taking into account Cameroon's land reform project in the mid-1970s, which was hijacked by well-positioned government officials who sought title to land over which they had no right.[16] The World Bank's strategy was to delegate responsibility to the British-funded Community Forest Development Project (CFDP), which would establish the legal framework and administrative capacity within MINEF to implement the provisions. The project, which started in 1995, received a hostile reception from some officials because it threatened their ability to subvert the allocation process for personal gain. In November 1998, after a six-month delay, the Minister finally approved a manual outlining the procedures and standards governing the allocation and management of community forests (MINEF, 1998).

While implementation has been problematic, the community forest provisions have made local communities more aware of their rights with respect to the government and logging companies. This has resulted in villagers demarcating their customary forests in order to benefit financially from logging and to protect their land against the claims of adjacent communities. Increased awareness of the law has also led to the almost instantaneous diffusion of information about the tax benefits to which communities are entitled (Karsenty, 1999b).

World Bank Reaction

The World Bank reacted strongly to the outcome of the August 1997 auction, sending a letter to the Prime Minister and following up with a mission in January 1998. However, at an initial meeting, the World Bank told the Minister of Economy and Finance that it understood if, for political reasons, the government was obliged to break the law. This attitude was passed on to the Prime Minister who, when asked at a subsequent meeting by World Bank officials what he planned to do about the auction irregularities, refused to respond, knowing that the issue was not a deal-breaker.

According to the team leader at the time, the World Bank "was at the peak of its power."[17] Although no SAC was in place, even the threat of suspending the SAC III negotiations would have forced the government to review the auction results. The government had its back to the wall because financial assistance was also denied from bilateral donors, including France, whose

support was conditional on Cameroon reaching agreement with the World Bank. A number of options were open to the World Bank, short of implicitly condoning the government's behavior. It could have accepted the results of the auction, but requested that the concessionaires pay an area tax equal to the highest bidder, and then followed up to ensure that the area taxes were paid. Or it could have warned the government that any irregularities in the next auction would lead to canceling the SAC.[18]

Yet, the World Bank chose not to pursue such face-saving options. Some World Bank staff interviewed for this report suggest that the decision not to hold the government accountable was motivated by the World Bank's sensitivity toward France's strategic concerns.[19] According to this argument, forest policy reform was so politically sensitive that if the World Bank forced the government to keep its promises, it would default on its debt, possibly leading to economic collapse and civil unrest. Approval of SAC III would have permitted the conversion of high interest, no-grace-period IBRD loans to low interest, 40-year grace period IDA loans, and helped Cameroon to repay its debt to the World Bank.

World Bank staff closely involved in the SAC negotiations strongly deny this interpretation.[20] In fact, the SAC included strict financial conditionalities, which the government was able to meet because of an unexpected increase in the price of oil. According to these sources, the World Bank's decision not to force the government to back down on forest issues was based on what it believed to be in the best interests of the country. By early 1998, the World Bank had only just established a substantive dialogue with the government over privatization, and restructuring of the banking, energy, and transport sectors. Breaking off relations over the concession auction would have sacrificed this broader policy dialogue, setting back progress in sectors that many staff considered to be critical to Cameroon's development. Given the problems implementing forest policy reform and the delicate nature of its relations with the government, some World Bank staff argued against including any forest conditionalities in SAC III.[21]

Regaining the Initiative

In early 1998, the World Bank official responsible for leading the negotiations since 1993 left the team, and more than six months passed before a new team leader was appointed. The new team leader visited Cameroon in October 1998, two months after SAC III was approved. After lengthy internal discussions, the World Bank decided to include forest conditionalities in the SAC. Thus armed, the mission insisted that the government take two steps: first, clarify the rules governing the bidding process to avoid any possible future misunderstanding, and second, appoint an independent observer who would report publicly on the bidding process. The government agreed to the first, but the Prime Minister, who wanted to preserve his room for maneuver, was opposed to the second.

However, in the face of World Bank threats to cancel the SAC, the Prime Minister issued two decisions (arrêtés) that met these conditionalities. The new auction rules included three changes intended to increase transparency and reduce the scope for fraud. First, bids would be assessed based on a list of yes and no questions. Second, criteria other than

The World Bank's decision not to force the government to back down on forest issues was based on what it believed to be in the best interests of the country.

the actual bid price would represent less than 20 percent of the total score. Finally, bidders were required to deposit a down-payment of two percent of the area tax for the whole concession, which could amount to hundreds of thousands of dollars.

The World Bank continued to maintain pressure on the government. In March 1999, it demanded that many senior MINEF officials be replaced because of poor performance related to the management of the World Bank-supported Campo-Ma'an protected area in southwest Cameroon. This time the World Bank's request was backed up with threats to suspend negotiations over the Chad-Cameroon pipeline, which would terminate at the nearby port of Kribi. With a new management team in place, MINEF published a report showing the extent of illegal logging and providing performance goals against which it could be held accountable (MINEF, 1999). The Ministry also declared that it would cancel the six concessions awarded to supporters of the regime because of their failure to pay the area tax or prepare a forest management plan.

By the end of 1999, the World Bank had regained the initiative that it appeared to have lost after it backed down over the August 1997 auction. Sources outside the World Bank consider the appointment of an independent observer to be an important precedent. The observer's report on the *vente de coupe* auction in September 1999 showed that in many cases the interministerial committee responsible for reviewing the bids ignored the new auction rules (Behle & Associés, 1999), demonstrating once again the government's resilience in the face of externally imposed reforms. Nevertheless, the independent observer was allowed to carry out his functions without interference, and his report was made public, suggesting that there is scope for similar process reforms that increase transparency and accountability in the forest sector.

THE ROLES OF OTHER STAKEHOLDERS

The main protagonists involved in forest policy reform were MINEF, the Presidency, the National Assembly, and the World Bank. The private sector and the French government played secondary roles, and NGOs had minimal input into the discussions.

Private Sector

The logging industry in Cameroon is large and diverse. By 1999, there were over 600 registered logging companies, up from 200 in 1992, of which only 60 had ongoing logging or wood processing operations (Carret, 1998). With the exception of the Lebanese company Hazim, the largest of these are in European hands, with French companies comprising a majority with significant involvement of Italian, Belgian, and Dutch interests (Burnham and Sharpe, 1997). Beneath this first rank of foreign companies, many of which have large sawmills, lies a second rank of companies, which have small sawmills to process a minor portion of their

logs. These two tiers constitute the industry's formal sector. Below them is a third tier of yet smaller companies run by Lebanese, Greek, or Cameroonian nationals. These companies, which constitute the informal sector, typically have very limited capitalization, do not have their own sawmills, and depend on *fermage*.

The largest companies were not active during the drafting stage of the 1994 Forest Law, despite their formidable lobbying power—a position that reflected their ambivalent attitude toward reform. On the one hand, they favored a simpler and more transparent tax system. On the other, reforms implied higher costs and more liabilities. Once the law was passed, however, industry representatives met regularly with World Bank staff.

Companies stood to gain from the new law. First, the World Bank promised that, while the minimum area tax would be increased, it would be largely offset by lower taxes on log exports. Cameroon already had the highest tax rates in Central Africa, and the World Bank did not want to increase the overall tax burden, beyond the additional area tax offered by the companies when the concessions were auctioned (Carret, 1998). Second, the reforms would grant them larger and longer concessions. Third, they supported the World Bank's opposition to a log export ban. Finally, they backed its recommendation that the Office National de Développement des Forêts (ONADEF), which held a de facto monopoly on the provision of forest inventory, mapping, and other technical services, be liquidated.

However, the industry disagreed with the World Bank on two basic points (Carret,

1998). First, the industry was opposed to a significantly higher area tax because, while it represented less than 20 percent of the tax burden, it was a fixed tax and payable up-front and on the whole concession, not just the area logged annually. Second, the World Bank wanted to reduce the protection for domestic sawmills, which it believed encouraged inefficient processing, by raising taxes on processed wood exports, which had previously been untaxed. The industry, on the other hand, argued that inefficient processing was due to the lack of skilled labor and the poor quality of the logs, and called for continued protection for Cameroon's developing industry.

In June 1997, in order to meet the IMF's tax revenue targets, the government introduced two major changes in the Finance Law: export taxes on processed wood were almost doubled, and the reference values used for tax purposes were set at the highest market prices (Carret, 1998). The World Bank opposed these tax increases. In 1995, the Minister for Economy and Finance had reached an informal understanding with the industry that 27-30 billion CFA was a reasonable level of direct taxation. Exports had increased by 20 percent, which would have justified a slightly higher tax burden, but not a doubling. The World Bank was concerned that such increases would reduce the profitability of the logging industry and its international competitiveness. More importantly, it feared that the proposed tax increases would overtax the "good" companies that do pay taxes and reward the "bad" ones, who would find ways not to pay. It argued that more emphasis should be put on improving tax recovery, rather than raising taxes. During the June 1997 mission, the World Bank discovered that the government should

have collected 19 billion CFA in log export taxes between July 1996 and May 1997, compared to the 14 billion CFA that was actually collected. One billion CFA of this shortfall was explained by delays in tax payment, but five billion CFA was never collected (Ferrer, 1997).

As the World Bank predicted, the industry hotly contested the proposed tax changes and went on strike in September 1997. The government quickly backed down and canceled the changes. The World Bank criticized this decision, favoring a compromise solution whereby the export taxes on processed wood would be raised to a more realistic level and the market prices discounted by 15–25 percent. The industry's angry reaction reflected its growing mistrust of MINEF. The Ministry enacted 15 changes in taxation between 1995 and 1998, many of which the industry considered to be arbitrary and unfair.[22] As one industry official put it: "If we obeyed the law, we'd go bankrupt."[23]

The larger companies resented that the formal sector was being asked to shoulder a growing share of the tax burden, since many small companies were able to avoid paying any taxes (Burnham and Sharpe, 1997).In principle, once felled, all logs are individually recorded and taxed at various stages in their movement from the forest to the sawmill or port, but given the lack of control exercised by MINEF staff in the forest, these companies paid little or no tax. When their tax arrears reached major proportions, they should have been legally sanctioned by being stripped of their forest concessions and barred from logging until their back taxes were cleared. However, less scrupulous operators often declared bankruptcy, then reconstituted themselves under a new corporate name, and cleared their tax arrears by paying a small portion of the sum outstanding as a bribe to officials to secure their compliance. The industry was angry at MINEF's apparent complicity in these practices, and its reluctance to enforce any part of the law other than new taxes imposed on the formal sector. Symptomatic of what the industry considered to be the Ministry's lack of seriousness is that it exerted no pressure on companies to prepare forest management plans and failed to respond to those companies that submitted them.

Given the failure of many established companies to win concessions, a shortage of wood to feed the sawmills, constant changes in taxation, the government's reluctance to crack down on tax fraud, and a growing set of costly obligations to local communities, the industry felt under attack from all sides. In response, 15 large European companies operating in Central Africa established the Interafrican Forest Industries Association (IFIA) to give the industry a single voice in forest policy negotiations in Cameroon and elsewhere in Africa.[24]

IFIA was highly critical of the World Bank, which it accused of hiring experts without the necessary experience; constant shifts in policy; presenting *faits accomplis* with no opportunity for discussion; and failing to respond adequately to its written proposals.[25] Contrary to these assertions, the World Bank claims that industry representatives were regularly invited to discuss the content of the new law.[26] Although civil, the discussions apparently went nowhere because of the industry's refusal to agree to concession auctions and higher area taxes—key ingredients of the reform package. Interviews with company officials suggest that they were not

France played an ambivalent role during the reform process—an attitude that reflected its rapprochement with the IMF and its desire to protect its economic interests.

opposed to the reforms proposed by the World Bank per se, but the fact that the reforms failed to take into account the high level of policy instability in Cameroon. This instability substantially increased the cost of doing business and put a premium on security, which translated into a desire on the part of industry for very large concessions, minimal area taxes, and no auctions.[27] The World Bank's reform agenda threatened these objectives. The real target of the industry's anger was not the World Bank, but the Government of Cameroon. For obvious reasons, industry preferred not to blame the government publicly for its problems.

France

France played an ambivalent role during the reform process—an attitude that reflected its rapprochement with the IMF over the need for macroeconomic adjustment in Cameroon, and its desire to protect its economic and geopolitical interests. Cameroon is the second largest economy and France's second largest trading partner in francophone Africa. France had viewed Cameroon as a bulwark against the tide of anglophone influence from Nigeria, its giant neighbor. On several occasions, France had bailed out the Government of Cameroon when confronted with the need to make painful reforms that might have led to political instability. For example, while negotiating with the IMF in 1988, the government convinced France to extend 400 million French francs to rehabilitate several government-owned corporations that had been slated for elimination.

In October 1993, however, the French government pronounced the "Abidjan doctrine," whereby it refused further budgetary support to countries without an IMF agreement in place. This marked a watershed in relations between France and the IMF, and in January 1994 the CFA was devalued by 50 percent against the French franc, an act long advocated by the IMF. France, therefore, did not overtly oppose the World Bank during the forest policy negotiations, since the government's failure to reach agreement on key reforms could have led to canceling of vital macroeconomic support. Neither did it provide the high-level political support that would have strengthened the government's commitment to policy implementation.

France was opposed to specific policy measures, notably a log export ban and concession auctions, which threatened the interests of politically influential French logging companies.[28] The World Bank proposed that the first round of auctions be limited to companies with existing sawmills, which effectively gave large French companies the right of first refusal on concessions located near their sawmills. France was also against higher area taxes, but in this case its opposition was tempered by the fact that French companies were divided on the issue. The second tier of French companies supported the tax reforms, because they could neither negotiate tax breaks nor easily evade taxes. Large companies, on the other hand, had benefited from high levels of government discretion; even after 1994, some were able to negotiate special deals. In 1995, according to well-placed sources, Thanry, the largest French logging company in Cameroon, was exempted from paying export taxes for three years on ayous, one of the most important commercial tree species, in exchange for building a sawmill. Since that species represented half of Thanry's production and the company accounted for one third of Cameroon's wood exports, the financial loss to the government was in the millions of dollars.[29]

France's support to the reform process was confined to providing technical input to drafts of the Forest Law and the Implementation Decree. This included recommendations based on the results of the Aménagement Pilote Intégré (API) project in Dimako in the East Province about minimum concession size, sustainable yield calculations, forest inventory methods, and improved logging practices (CIRAD, 1998). France also offered financing to qualified logging companies (not just French ones) to prepare forest management plans.

French sources suggest that the World Bank tried to go it alone without adequate consultation. World Bank staff deny this accusation and claim that the French government was consulted every step of the way, and that every mission included a briefing for donors, including France. They say that the allegation that France was marginalized misrepresents the World Bank's open approach during the reform process.[30]

NGOs

International conservation NGOs strongly supported the community forest provisions in the 1994 Forest Law, and carried out campaigns to inform local communities of their new rights, much to the annoyance of the logging companies. The World Wide Fund for Nature's office in Cameroon played a key role in raising the profile of forest issues, both domestically and internationally. This heightened sensitivity contributed to President Biya's decision to host a summit meeting in March 1999, which brought together the leaders of Gabon, Central African Republic, Congo-Brazzaville, and Equatorial Guinea, as well as high-level participants from around the world, to jointly announce plans for a new cross-border protected area. According to the World Bank, this summit may represent a watershed in terms of securing high-level political commitment for the reform process.[31]

Domestic NGOs were only legalized in 1990 and were weak at the start of the reform process. But they have since developed rapidly, as shown by their advocacy related to two recent World Bank projects: the 1995 transport sector loan and the proposed Chad-Cameroon pipeline. In both cases, domestic NGOs drew international attention to the potential negative environmental impacts of these projects, and the need to prepare publicly available environmental impact assessment and mitigation plans.

The controversy surrounding the passage and implementation of the 1994 Forest Law raised awareness among domestic NGOs of the inherently political nature of forest policy reform. Some expressed strong support for tying reforms to structural adjustment lending. Others argued that lasting improvements in forest management require that the concession allocation and tax systems be insulated from political pressure, and have called for an overhaul of the legal system to allow private citizens to sue the government and logging companies in the name of public interest. They recognized that tackling forest policy effectively might require linking adjustment lending to institutional reforms outside the forest sector.[32]

THE BOTTOM LINE

The World Bank devoted a huge amount of effort to reforming Cameroon's forest policies, but the results have proved disappointing. Indeed, the flawed first round of concession auctions, the subversion of the community forest allocation process, and pervasive illegal logging, have led some observers to suggest that the situation is worse than before. But others argue that while the reforms have been poorly implemented, they have not been derailed and that the World Bank's intervention has been, on balance, a good thing.

The long and convoluted history of the reform process yields a number of insights. First, forest conditionalities were essential for ensuring the passage of key laws and decrees, but proved ineffective at enforcing the institutional changes needed to implement them. MINEF failed to participate effectively in the reform process because of its internal weaknesses, conflict of interest, and the lack of high-level political support.

Forest conditionalities were essential for ensuring the passage of key laws and decrees, but proved ineffective at enforcing the institutional changes needed to implement them.

During the negotiations, the World Bank put demands on the Ministry for policy papers and studies that it had neither the ability nor authority to carry out. The result was a growing gap between what the World Bank demanded and what the Ministry was able (or willing) to deliver. The World Bank intended to follow up the policy reforms with a forest project to strengthen the Ministry's analytical capacity. It may have been more effective to combine the policy dialogue with targeted World Bank support to increase the staff's sense of ownership of, and commitment to, the reforms.

Second, the World Bank was unable to overcome strong vested interests within the private sector and French government. Many logging companies had benefited from the previous discretionary practices and were opposed to change. Their opposition explains why the views of many industry officials differ markedly from those of the World Bank regarding its willingness to seriously engage them. Although the World Bank often consulted the industry, irrevocable differences of opinion over what constituted sound forest policy may have blocked any meaningful dialogue. While France contributed technical input to the reform process, it withheld political support for fear of destabilizing the regime and upsetting the major French logging companies.

Finally, the World Bank was caught in a dilemma following the failure of the August 1997 auction. On the one hand, the World Bank's credibility required that it hold the government accountable for the auction irregularities; on the other, it did not want to jeopardize its dialogue over key economic reforms. By wavering at a critical point in the negotiations, it avoided provoking a possible political crisis. But, according to World Bank technical staff, it missed a golden opportunity to reinvigorate the forest policy reforms. This decision may have inflicted broader

---

By wavering at a critical point in the negotiations, the World Bank avoided provoking a possible political crisis. But, according to technical staff, it missed a golden opportunity to reinvigorate the forest policy reforms.

---

damage. According to outside observers, there are younger foresters in Cameroon who seem concerned about greater efficiency and transparency, but if they are not supported and encouraged by outside pressure, they could well be subverted by the corrupting influence of their seniors (Burnham and Sharpe, 1997). Every time the government is allowed to get away with breaking the law, the prospects for real change diminish, and the hopes of this group of professionals fall. This example suggests that the long-term commitment by the World Bank that is required to promote accountability and the rule of law in the forest sector is vulnerable to the needs of short-term political expediency.

REFERENCES

Behle & Associés. 1999. Mimeo.

Burnham, Philip and Barrie Sharpe. 1997. *Political, Institutional, Social, and Economic Dimensions of Cameroon's Forestry and Conservation Sectors.* London: University College.

Carret, Jean-Christophe. 1998. *La Reforme de la Fiscalité Forestière au Cameroun: Contexte, Bilan, et Questions Ouvertes.* Paris: CERNA.

CIRAD-Forêt. 1997. "Forest Aid: the Cameroon Rush." Paper presented at the meeting of Funding Organizations on the Forest Sector and Diversity in the Congo Basin, November 20, 1997, Florence.

—1998. "Le Projet d'Aménagement Pilote Intégré de Dimako, Cameroun, 1992-96." Série Forafri, Document 7.

Ekoko, François. 1997. *The Political Economy of the 1994 Cameroon Forest Law.* Working Paper No.3. Yaoundé: CIFOR.

Ferrer, Vicente. 1997. "Cameroon Forest Policy and Taxation: Back to Office Report." June 1997. Washington, D.C.: The World Bank.

Global Forest Watch-Cameroon. 2000. *Situation de L'Exploitation Forestière au Cameroun.* Washington, D.C.: World Resources Institute.

Grut, Mikael, John A. Gray, and Nicolas Egli. 1991. *Forest Pricing and Concession Policies: Managing the High Forests of West and Central Africa.* World Bank Technical Paper 143. Africa Technical Department Series. Washington, D.C.: The World Bank.

Interafrican Forest Industries Association. 1999. "European Foundation for the Preservation of African Forest Resources, Communiqué." October 1999. Paris: IFIA.

Karsenty, Alain. 1999a. "La Fiscalité Forestière et ses Dimensions Environnementales: l'Exemple de l'Afrique Centrale." *Bois et Forêts Tropiques,* 260 (2).

—1999b. "Vers la Fin de l'Etat Forestier: Appropriation des Espaces et Partage de la Rente Forestière au Cameroun." *Politique Africaine,* No. 75, October 1995. Paris: Karthala.

Marchés Tropicaux et Méditerranéens. 1998. "Numéro Hors Série: Cameroun." March 1998.

Ministry of Environment and Forests (MINEF). 1995. "Decree No. 95/531/PM to Determine the Conditions of Implementation of Forest Regulations." Yaoundé, Cameroon: MINEF.

—1998. "Manual of Procedures for the Attribution and Norms for the Management of Community Forests." Yaoundé, Cameroon: MINEF.

—1999. "Planification de l'Attribution des Titres d'Exploitation Forestière." Yaoundé, Cameroon: MINEF.

Ministry of Economy and Finance (MINEFI). 1998. "Contribution du Secteur Forestier à l'Economie Nationale, 1993-98." Yaoundé, Cameroon: MINEFI.

O'Halloran, Eavan and Vicente Ferrer. 1997. *The Evolution of Cameroon's New Forest Legal, Regulatory, and Taxation System.* Washington, D.C.: The World Bank.

Pearce, F. 1994. "France Swaps Debt for Rights to Tropical Timber." *The New Scientist,* January 29, 1994.

Reuters. 1999. "Cameroon in Trouble with the IMF Again." *Reuters*, December 16, 1999.

Transparency International. 1999. Available from http://www.transparency.de/documents/cpi/cpi-bpi_press-release.html

World Bank, The. 1996. "Country Assistance Strategy of the World Bank Group to the Republic of Cameroon." Washington, D.C.: The World Bank.

—1998. "Forests and the World Bank: An OED Review of the 1991 Forest Policy and its Implementation." Washington D.C.: The World Bank.

—1999. "Rapport de la Mission Conjointe MINEF/Banque Mondiale, Province de l'Est." Washington D.C.: The World Bank.

NOTES

1. This chapter draws on "Environmental Adjustment in Cameroon: Challenges and Opportunities for Policy Reform in the Forest Sector" by François Ekoko (1999), which is available at http://www.wri.org/iffeforest.html, as well as interviews conducted by the authors in Cameroon and Washington, D.C. on a not-for-attribution basis. This paper was prepared with financial support from WRI and incorporates material from Ekoko (1997), which was prepared with financial support from the Center for International Forestry Research (CIFOR).

2. The Ministry of Environment and Forests was created in 1992 by separating the forest portfolio from the Ministry of Agriculture.

3. Canada also supported the preparation of a provisional 1:500,000-scale land use map and a reconnaissance-level forest inventory that divided the southern part of Cameroon into permanent forest and non-permanent forest. Future concessions, each consisting of one or more forest management units (*unités forestières d'aménagement*), were to be located in the permanent forest zone, and *ventes de coupe* in the non-permanent forest zone.

4. The previous level, unchanged since independence, was 98 CFA/ha per year.

5. Concessions were to be awarded for a 3-year interim period, during which the company would have to complete an approved forest management plan. During this period, the company could log no more than 2,500 ha per year to help pay for the plan.

6. In addition to MINEF, these included ONADEF, the National Assembly, the Presidency, and the Ministries of Industrial Development and Trade, Tourism, Urbanization, and Housing.

7. Not-for-attribution interview with French Cooperation staff, Yaoundé, October 1998.

8. Not-for-attribution interview with World Bank staff, Washington, D.C., April 1999.

9. Not-for-attribution interview with World Bank staff, Washington, D.C., November 1999.

10. Not-for-attribution interview with regional policy advisor, Yaoundé, September 1999.

11. In the first case, the governor claims that a certain volume of wood has been felled illegally and issues a permit to a company for its removal. In the second case, a company claims that it needs to clear forest to build a road or establish a plantation. In theory, this requires a forest inventory to calculate the stumpage tax. In practice, a false inventory is carried out, a lump sum fee paid to the governor, and the company cuts all the wood it wants. A *permis d'exploitation* entitles cutting up to 500 m^3 in already logged forest, but loggers often cut 50,000 m^3 (World Bank, 1999).

12. In the East Province, source of over half of Cameroon's log production, 109 MINEF staff, equipped with four telephones, two pickups, and two motorbikes were responsible for managing an area the size of Rwanda. By 1992, there was not a single working vehicle. Ministry staff were forced to rely on logging companies

for transport, a situation that did not encourage independent reporting of logging activities.

13. The inability of MINEF staff to sanction illegal practices is reflected by the sharp drop in the number of violations issued against loggers in the Center Province since 1989, and a similar drop in the proportion of violations that were processed. The situation in remoter areas is even worse: between 1989 and 1997, 800 violations were issued in the Center Province, but only 35 in the East Province (Global Forest Watch-Cameroon, 2000).

14. Not-for-attribution interview with social forester, Yaoundé, December 1999.

15. Not-for-attribution interview with SGS staff, Douala, October 1998.

16. Not-for-attribution interview with World Wide Fund for Nature staff, Yaoundé, October 1999.

17. Not-for-attribution interview with World Bank staff, Washington, D.C., November 1999.

18. Not-for-attribution interview with World Bank staff, Washington, D.C., December 1999.

19. Not-for-attribution interview with World Bank staff, Washington, D.C., November 1999.

20. Not-for-attribution interview with World Bank staff, Yaoundé, December 1999.

21. Not-for-attribution interview with World Bank staff, Yaoundé, April 1999.

22. CERNA, a Paris-based industrial research center hired by IFIA, the logging industry association, to carry out a review of forest taxation in Cameroon, argued that the lack of a reliable statistical database on timber production greatly increased the scope for misunderstanding (Carret, 1998).

23. Not-for-attribution interview with logging company staff, Yaounde, November 1997.

24. Since its creation in 1996, IFIA has committed itself to developing guidelines for "practical" forest management plans, drafted a professional code of conduct, and offered technical assistance to a pan-African forest certification system (IFIA, 1999). It has also sought to establish working relationships with a number of conservation NGOs.

25. Written comments from IFIA on draft report, Paris, September 1999.

26. Not-for-attribution interview with World Bank staff, Washington, D.C., November 1999.

27. Not-for-attribution interview with IFIA representative, Washington, D.C., November 1999.

28. Not-for-attribution interview with World Bank staff, Washington, D.C., October 1999.

29. Not-for-attribution interview with SGS staff, Douala, October 1998.

30. Not-for-attribution interview with World Bank staff, Washington, D.C., November 1999.

31. Not-for-attribution interview with World Bank staff, Yaoundé, November 1999.

32. Not-for-attribution interview with domestic NGO staff, Yaoundé, December 1999.

4

INDONESIA

Frances J. Seymour
Hariadi Kartodihardjo

In 1997, two conflagrations swept through Indonesia. Forest fires burned out of control across the archipelago, destroying millions of hectares of forest, causing billions of dollars worth of economic losses, and blanketing the region in a choking haze (Barber and Schweithelm, 2000). Even as the literal fires burned, the Indonesian currency figuratively went up in flames—losing 80 percent of its value over four months in late 1997—consuming the savings, purchasing power, and employment prospects of millions of Indonesians. While each of these crises has been attributed to proximate causes—drought and land clearing in the case of the forest fires, financial contagion in the case of the rupiah's collapse—both had deep and intertwined structural roots in Indonesia's political economy as well. This chapter will examine how the World Bank, in collaboration with the IMF, attempted to address some of the structural

issues in the forest sector through adjustment lending mobilized in the wake of the financial crisis.[1]

BACKGROUND

The World Bank and Indonesian Development

The Government of Indonesia under the Suharto regime enjoyed a special relationship with the World Bank. To address the challenges and opportunities of Indonesian development, in the late 1960s World Bank President Robert McNamara established a resident staff in Indonesia that reported directly to his office. For the next three decades, "World Bank involvement in the country's development efforts was pervasive, and the achievements were many" (World Bank, 1999a, p. ii). These achievements included almost 30 years of uninterrupted growth, which by the early 1990s had vaulted Indonesia into the ranks of the emerging market economies. Thanks in part to World Bank-supported investment in agriculture, infrastructure, health, and education, declining poverty and improving social indicators accompanied the rapid growth. According to a recent history of the World Bank, "Indonesia was the presidentially designated

The Government of Indonesia under the Suharto regime enjoyed a special relationship with the World Bank.

jewel in the Bank's operational crown"
(Kapur, Lewis, and Webb, 1997, p. 493).

A group of U.S.-trained technocrats in government service, the so-called Berkeley Mafia, steered the Indonesian economy through periodic macroeconomic adjustments in the 1970s and 1980s, and managed a gradual liberalization of trade and investment rules in the 1990s. The World Bank supported those adjustments through policy-based lending, but these loans were usually made in return for government actions already taken, rather than conditioned on future actions. Thus, Indonesia was never subjected to a harsh structural adjustment program, such as those imposed by the World Bank in other countries.

However, not everyone shared the World Bank's enthusiasm for the Indonesian development model. Human rights groups condemned Indonesia's brutal invasion of East Timor in 1975, and its repression of civil and political liberties throughout the archipelago. Under the Suharto regime, being labeled an "obstacle to development" (*penghambat pembangunan*) was tantamount to a subversion charge. In the early 1980s, international attention was focused on the destruction visited on tropical forests and indigenous peoples by Indonesia's transmigration program, financed in part by the World Bank, which sponsored migrants from the densely-populated islands of Java and Bali to the outer islands of Sumatra, Kalimantan, and Irian Jaya. A subsequent international advocacy campaign targeted the World Bank-supported Kedung Ombo Dam in Central Java, where the involuntary resettlement of villagers in the inundation area had led to systematic human rights violations. The World Bank's lack of responsiveness to early reports of

Not everyone shared the World Bank's enthusiasm for the Indonesian development model.

abuse uncovered by Indonesian nongovernmental organizations caused many to question World Bank support for the Suharto regime's version of development.[2]

Over time, the World Bank's program in Indonesia increased its attention to environmental and social issues, both in the implementation of so-called safeguard policies—such as those requiring special attention to resettlement—and through greater social and environment sector lending. This increased attention was likely fueled by Indonesia-specific factors, such as a desire not to repeat the Kedung Ombo debacle, as well as broader forces operating in the World Bank overall. In 1993, the World Bank's office in Jakarta established a special unit to address environmental and social issues. It was headed by a senior official with extensive experience in Indonesia, and staffed to provide environmental expertise, social analysis, and outreach to the NGO community.

By the late 1990s, external critics of Indonesia's World Bank-supported development strategy had begun to focus on corruption. Following World Bank President James Wolfensohn's speech at the 1996 Annual Meetings of the World Bank and the IMF, which tied fighting corruption to the World Bank's anti-poverty agenda, the corruption issue could no longer be considered off-limits.[3] In mid-1997, the World Bank denied allegations of large-scale leakage of World Bank project funds in Indonesia, although an internal investigation later confirmed the allegations (Simpson and Phillips, 1998). When the financial crisis hit, many critics pointed to the structural weaknesses in Indonesia's economy, particularly the pervasive corruption and cronyism, to explain the country's initial vulnerability to financial contagion and the depth of the ensuing crisis. In February 1999, the World Bank's internal evaluation department reported that the World Bank's inattention to poor governance and other structural issues had undermined the effectiveness of its assistance to Indonesia over the previous decade, which the report rated as only marginally satisfactory (World Bank, 1999a).

Until the events of mid-1997, the World Bank considered Indonesia to be a model among borrower governments, and Indonesian government officials had a collegial relationship with their World Bank counterparts. Criticism by nongovernmental organizations (NGOs) of the environmental damage and human rights abuses associated with World Bank-supported projects had led to increased attention to these issues, but not to a fundamental change in the relationship. The perception that the World Bank had been complicit in maintaining a regime characterized by pervasive corruption and poor governance compromised the institution's credibility in responding to the 1997 crisis (Simpson and Phillips, 1998; Brauchli, 1998).

The Forest Sector

The forest sector is vital to the political economy of Indonesia.[4] Land designated as state forest covers some 112 million hectares, although the proportion of that area that is actually forested has been declining because of logging, fire, and conversion to other uses. Since the late 1960s, a large proportion of Indonesia's forest land has been managed through logging concessions granted to private and government-owned corporations. Over the last ten years, logging and related industries have contributed an average of 20 percent of Indonesia's total foreign exchange revenues (Kartodihardjo, 1999), and have generated personal and corporate wealth for those involved in forest industries (Schwarz, 1994). In the 1990s, the Ministry of Forestry's Reforestation Fund provided a convenient source of finance for pet projects of Suharto cronies and family members.

By the late 1990s, there was abundant evidence that the rate of forest exploitation was unsustainable. Already, the raw materials needed annually by Indonesia sawmills, plywood factories, and pulp and paper plants exceeded sustainable supply by almost two to one (Kartodihardjo, 1999). This so-called structural timber deficit, the result of a decade of policies to promote domestic processing industries, created incentives for indiscriminate logging, both legal and illegal (Barr, 1999). The historically unprecedented forest fires in 1997, while no doubt exacerbated by El Niño-induced drought, have also been shown to be a direct result of state policies and corporate irresponsibility. Plantation development policies have provided incentives for large-scale land clearing by concessionaires, who found burning to be an inexpensive method of land preparation (Barber and Schweithelm, 2000).

At the local level, the Indonesian timber industry has often been associated with the impoverishment of vulnerable populations, and social conflict. In Java, there is a long history of conflict between forest-edge communities and the paramilitary force guarding state-managed teak plantations (Peluso, 1992). In the outer islands, logging operations have destroyed indigenous peoples' forest gardens, and logging-related pollution and siltation have fouled waterways. Although timber interests tried to blame traditional swidden agriculturalists for the 1997 forest fires, forest-dwelling communities were more victims than perpetrators (Barber and Schweithelm, 2000).[5] Resentment over the inequitable sharing of benefits from forest exploitation—both between central and provincial governments, and between commercial interests, government coffers, and affected communities—was suppressed during the Suharto regime, and now poses a political challenge to his successors.

In 1989, the World Bank initiated lending in the forest sector in Indonesia with a project focused on sector analysis in cooperation with the Ministry of Forestry. Undertaken in collaboration with the U.N. Food and Agriculture Organization (FAO), the project produced 17 volumes of studies. Although some NGOs were invited to a national-level workshop to discuss the results, the affected stakeholders were not truly consulted, nor were the full studies made public.

A second project followed in 1990, with components designed to provide policy advice; improve timber concession management; and develop master plans for research, plantation development, and selected conservation areas. According to the World Bank, the conditions associated with this loan, in conjunction with ongoing policy dialogue, were responsible for almost tripling the fee collected from concessionaires per cubic meter of timber extracted (World Bank, 1996, p. 3). Stakeholder involvement in the

project was again limited. Ironically, the political conditions for the World Bank's success in increasing stumpage fees were enhanced by the extensive media coverage given to an NGO study on the excess profits being enjoyed by timber concessionaires (Ramli and Ahmad, 1993).

In 1994, the Ministry of Forestry signaled to the World Bank that a third forestry project in preparation should not go forward, and the following year the Ministry requested that the second loan be canceled with less than half of the funds disbursed. Implementation of improved concession management systems, including mechanisms for inspection and audit and royalty collection, were among the components canceled, earning the project an "unsatisfactory" rating by the World Bank's final supervision mission (World Bank, 1996, p. 2).

The official reason for terminating World Bank lending to the Ministry of Forestry was that because of the large influx of funds from other donors in the early 1990s following a Tropical Forestry Action Plan roundtable in 1991, loan funds from the World Bank were no longer needed to complete project activities (World Bank, 1996, p. 3). According to numerous individuals interviewed for this study, the real reason was that the World Bank and the Ministry had reached an impasse on policy reforms being promoted by the World Bank, particularly those that would harm the interests of politically powerful concession holders.[6] Canceling the loan gave both parties a face-saving exit. In particular, Mohammed "Bob" Hasan, Indonesia's most prominent timber tycoon and a close associate of President Suharto, is said to have blocked reform of the concession management system.[7] An internal World Bank project evaluation delicately concluded that

> . . . major policy constraints—some of which are beyond the mandate of the Ministry of Forestry—need to be removed, to allow technical improvements currently being generated to bear fruit: incorrect pricing and allocation mechanisms for forest resources; and inappropriate incentive structures for interest groups to pursue sustainability, are two major areas of concern (World Bank, 1996, p. v).

There is other evidence that the World Bank was reluctant to exert its leverage over the government in the context of project lending related to forests. In addition to the two forestry loans mentioned above, in the early 1990s the World Bank also initiated preparation of several biodiversity conservation projects to be cofinanced with funds from the Global Environment Facility (GEF). In the context of an integrated conservation and development project focused on Kerinci Seblat National Park in Sumatra, the World Bank backed down when the government refused to cancel logging concessions in lowland forest areas surrounding the park—even though studies had shown those areas to be the most significant habitat for the wildlife species, such as the Sumatran tiger, that the park was established to protect.

As something of a parting gesture, the World Bank forestry specialist who had been resident in Jakarta from 1992 to 1994 prepared a review of the Indonesian forest sector (World Bank, 1995). The review predicted that a continuation of nonsustainable forest management practices would drive the sector's contributions to output growth and export revenue into decline early in the new millennium. It recommended an extensive program of policy reforms, including a shift from log export taxes to increased royalties, an end to the plywood marketing board monopoly, longer and transferable concessions, concession performance bonds, and a third-party monitoring and enforcement mechanism. The review also recommended policy changes "to facilitate the titling of forest dwelling and adjacent communities in forest land, and also to facilitate the award of concession or stewardship contracts over forest areas, to such groups" (World Bank, 1995, p. 21). Referring to the overall package of recommended reforms, the review noted dryly that "resistance from vested interests can be expected to be strong" (World Bank, 1995, p. 21).

Following the amicable mutual disengagement of the World Bank and the Ministry of Forestry, and the task manager's relocation to World Bank headquarters in Washington, the forest policy reform agenda was allowed to lapse. The World Bank did not invest in a significant consultation process based on the review's findings and recommendations, and most domestic constituencies for reform were probably not even aware of its existence, much less its progressive content related to community forest management.

Thus, at the time of the 1997 crisis, the World Bank had been absent from the Indonesian forest sector for more than three years. The forest management regime was economically, environmentally, and socially unsustainable, with demand for forest products outpacing supply, and a gross imbalance in the distribution of costs and benefits between forest-dwelling peoples and a handful of concessionaires. A five-year experiment in using project lending to leverage needed reforms had ended in 1994 when vested

BOX 4.1

CHRONOLOGY OF ADJUSTMENT AND FOREST POLICY REFORM IN INDONESIA

July 1997	Rupiah begins to depreciate following devaluation of Thai baht. Haze from uncontrolled forest burning reaches Malaysia and Singapore.
October 6	Government of Indonesia seeks aid from the IMF.
October 31	IMF bail-out package announced; no forest policy reform content.
Nov–Jan, 1998	International confidence in the Indonesian economy declines.
January 15	Second IMF package announced. Letter of Intent contains significant forest policy reform content.
January 21	Ministerial decrees abolish forest product monopolies.
February 3–5	World Bank President Wolfensohn visits Jakarta.
March 10	Suharto reelected.
March 15	New cabinet announced; includes timber tycoon Bob Hasan.
April 10	Government announces Supplementary Memorandum of Economic and Financial Policies for World Bank structural adjustment loan (PRSL 1).
April 20–22	Various decrees replace log export taxes with resource rent taxes.
May 4	Announcement of fuel and electricity subsidy removals triggers riots and demonstrations.
May 12–20	Unrest and violence deepen; students occupy parliament building.
May 18	World Bank postpones consideration of structural adjustment loan.
May 21	Suharto resigns; Habibie sworn in as new President.
June 29	Ministerial decree establishes Forestry and Estate Crops Reformation Committee.
July 2	World Bank approves US$1 billion Policy Reform Support Loan. World Bank staff, ministry officials, and bilateral donors discuss forestry SECAL.
August 27	Consultative Group on Indonesian Forestry (CGIF) hosts Forum on Draft Government Regulation on Production Forest Management.
September 16	CGIF hosts meeting on reform process; proposed SECAL floated.
November 2	CGIF hosts forum on draft Basic Forestry Act.

BOX 4.1 | (CONTINUED)

•	December 21	World Bank suspends US$400 million loan tranche because of lack of progress in forest policy reform.
•	January 27, 1999	Government announces Regulation on Production Forest Management.
•	February 9	World Bank approves release of US$400 million.
•	May 20	World Bank approves PRSL II.
•	July 27–28	Consultative Group on Indonesia highlights forest sector reform agenda.
•	September 30	Parliament passes new Basic Forest Law despite World Bank objections.

interests in the status quo had proven more influential than World Bank conditionality.

ADJUSTMENT LENDING AND FOREST POLICY REFORM

The devaluation of the Thai baht in early July 1997, and subsequent events in Indonesia caught the public and private international financial community by surprise. On July 19, 1997, when a new Country Assistance Strategy for Indonesia was being presented to the World Bank's Board of Executive Directors, staff argued that the country was in a strong position to avoid following Thailand into financial crisis (World Bank, 1999b, p. 1). Later that same month, the judgment of World Bank staff and many others was proven wrong as the Indonesian rupiah began to depreciate. Box 4.1 provides a chronology of events.

By early October, Indonesia had been forced to seek aid from the IMF, and on

A five-year experiment in using project lending to leverage needed reforms had ended in 1994 when vested interests in the status quo had proven more influential than World Bank conditionality.

October 31, a first assistance package was agreed upon. The Letter of Intent (LOI) focused on government commitments to banking sector reform, but did not include any reference to environmental objectives or concerns despite having been negotiated literally in the haze of the forest fires, which by then was visible in Jakarta (IMF, 1997). At the request of the IMF, World Bank staff had prepared language on forest policy reform for this LOI, but the forest-related conditions proposed by the World Bank were not included.[8] In a mid-November meeting with

Indonesian and U.S.-based environmental activists, members of the IMF team indicated that while there might have been some policy reform omissions in the agreement, it would have been politically impossible and administratively infeasible to do everything at once.[9]

By early January 1998, the Indonesian government's failure to show evidence of implementing the reforms of the first LOI led domestic and international financiers to vote with their positions, plunging the economy deeper into crisis.[10] On January 15, a second Letter of Intent negotiated with the IMF announced an acceleration and broadening of the earlier commitments to reform. A striking addition to the first package was a series of forest-related and other environmental reform measures. *(See Box 4.2.)* These included commitments to dismantle forest

---

COMMITMENTS IN THE JANUARY 1998 LETTER OF INTENT RELATED TO FORESTRY AND ENVIRONMENT

Commitments Related to the Forest Sector

Point 10   Increase in the taxation of plantations and forestry property.

Point 12   Incorporate the Reforestation Fund into the central government budget, and ensure that funds are used exclusively for financing reforestation.

Point 37   Reduce export taxes on logs, sawn timber, rattan, and minerals, and impose appropriate resource rent taxes.

Point 39   Remove restrictions on foreign investment in palm oil plantations on February 1, 1998 (which could accelerate conversion of natural forests to plantations).

Point 40   Dissolve all existing formal and informal restrictive marketing arrangements, including those for cement, paper, and plywood.

Point 50   Review and raise stumpage fees; auction concessions; lengthen the concession period and allow transferability by June 1998; implement performance bonds; and reduce land conversion targets to environmentally sustainable levels by the end of 1998.

Other Commitments Related to the Environment

Point 9   Gradually eliminate subsidies on fuel and electricity.

Point 13   Cancel 12 major infrastructure projects, including a major power plant (but conspicuously not including a million-hectare project in Kalimantan to convert swamp forest to rice cultivation).

Point 37   Acknowledgment that "export taxes cannot simply be eliminated since they serve as an important means of discouraging overexploitation of Indonesia's natural environment."

Point 50   Draft and establish implementation rules for the new environment law, and accelerate a program for conversion to cleaner fuels, including unleaded gasoline, to improve air quality.

Source: Government of Indonesia, 1998a

---

product marketing monopolies controlled by Bob Hasan and to implement many of the concession management system reforms that had led to the rupture in the World Bank's relationship with the Ministry of Forestry in 1994.

What better way for the Suharto regime to signal seriousness about reform than to sacrifice the economic interests of cronies and family members?

Ownership by the World Bank and the IMF

According to participants interviewed for this study, the IMF team invited World Bank staff to contribute structural reform conditions to the January LOI on extremely short notice, precluding the possibility of conducting any new analysis or consultation with concerned stakeholders. Indeed, when asked why stopping a notorious million-hectare rice project that threatened swamp forests in Kalimantan was not included among the conditions, a World Bank official confessed, "I didn't have a file on it that day."[11] Forest sector elements added to the package were selected from among those already on the shelf from the sector review completed by World Bank staff in 1995.

Why were reforms considered of second-order importance in October suddenly on the IMF's agenda in January? According to participants interviewed for this study, the symbolic significance of the forest sector as an example of poor economic governance and

cronyism was an important motivating factor.[12] What better way for the Suharto regime to signal seriousness about reform than to sacrifice the economic interests of cronies and family members? (Schwarz, 1999) In addition to abolishing Hasan's plywood cartel, the LOI also targeted a clove marketing monopoly and national car manufacturing project, each controlled by one of the President's sons.

In addition to the political symbolism of including forest policy conditions, World Bank and IMF staff saw these conditions as serving economic efficiency objectives as well.[13] Environmental objectives—such as those that would be served by the imposed moratorium on forest conversion—were perhaps tertiary considerations after political and economic concerns.[14] Significantly, the package of forest policy reforms did not include the recommendations from the 1995 sector review related to community rights and roles in forest management.

In April, the World Bank reinforced and refined the forest-related conditionality contained in the IMF package through the first of two structural adjustment or Policy Reform Support Loans, which would be known as PRSL I (US$1 billion) and PRSL II (US$500 million).[15] The government's Statement of Development Policy committed to two sets of structural policy reforms, which gave greater prominence to environmental and social equity objectives than had the January Letter of Intent (Government of Indonesia, 1998b, p. 50–53). Under a section entitled, "Trade and Investment Policy Changes to Increase Productivity," the government reiterated its promise to replace export taxes on forest products with resource royalties ("which would protect the environment"), and stated that the plywood cartel had been dissolved. Under a section entitled, "Policy Changes to Promote the Environmental Sustainability of Development," the government agreed to a June 30, 1998, deadline for changing regulations related to the award of logging concessions. The government further promised a sweeping program of reform of concession system management by the end of the year, including "provisions to encourage participation by local communities, and protection of indigenous forest dwellers." Until this system was implemented, the government agreed to a moratorium on forest land conversion.

By late 1998, many of these conditions remained unfulfilled, including implementation of a concession auctioning system, a performance bond system, and a reduction in the rate of conversion of natural forests (Government of Indonesia, 1998b). The World Bank this cited lack of progress as contributing to its decision to suspend release of the second tranche of PRSL I in December 1998 (Milverton, 1998). A World Bank staffer reported being astonished that senior management was giving such high priority to complying with the forest-related conditions. According to World Bank staff, the government's failure to compliance with key forest-related conditions in PRSL I also proved the final constraint to setting a date for presenting PRSL II to the World Bank's Board in May 1999.[16]

Ownership by the Government of Indonesia

Was the Indonesian government committed to the forest policy conditions contained in

the January Letter of Intent? According to participants in relevant discussions, the technocrats in the government economic ministries who had chafed for years under the economic excesses of the Suharto regime strongly supported the structural reforms mandated by the January LOI—particularly those reforms that targeted politically potent symbols of cronyism such as the clove and plywood monopolies.[17] There was also support within the bureaucracy for environment-related reforms; officials of Bapedal, the Indonesian environmental agency, were said to have been pleased by the inclusion of conditions related to air quality and new environmental legislation.[18]

According to one government official, borrower ownership outside the Ministry of Forestry was captured by the attitude in the Ministry of Development Planning: "(environmental policy reforms) are things we have to do whether or not there is a crisis, so we should take the opportunity."[19] In late March, the Ministry of Development Planning organized an interagency meeting to discuss an environmental agenda in the context of preparation of PRSL I. Lower-level Ministry of Forestry officials and the World Bank staffer covering forestry issues attended the meeting. However, the discussion focused more attention on other environmental issues, such as shifting from leaded to unleaded gas, and coral reef conservation, because the forestry agenda had already been advanced in the January IMF conditions.[20]

Although the specific forest policy reforms contained in the January LOI were discussed in early January with the Ministries of Development Planning, Finance, and

Industry and Trade, Ministry of Forestry officials were not consulted prior to the announcement of the reform package, and were taken completely by surprise. Nevertheless, at least at the beginning, Ministry of Forestry officials reportedly took their responsibility to undertake the reforms quite seriously, feeling that the economy depended on their ability to deliver the reforms that had been agreed to by President Suharto himself.[21] The government's actual compliance with the forestry conditions contained in the January Letter of Intent and PRSL I and II, and shifts occasioned by the 1998 change of national leadership, are described below.

IMPLEMENTATION EXPERIENCE

January to May 1998

A flurry of activity followed the announcement of the forestry conditions contained in the January Letter of Intent. On January 21, 1998, the Ministry of Industry and Trade promulgated nine decrees canceling existing regulations, export quotas, and trading groups related to plywood and rattan. To comply with the tight deadlines included in the IMF conditions, Ministry of Forestry officials began drafting new regulations related to stumpage fees, concession auctions, performance bonds, and use of the Reforestation Fund.

Early on, there were signs that reform would be more apparent than real, as limitations on the government's political will and capacity to meet the IMF conditions emerged.[22] Despite having been formally abolished in January, the plywood cartel continued to operate through February and

Early on, there were signs that reform would be more apparent than real, as limitations on the government's political will and capacity emerged.

March, extracting new fees from plywood exporters (Barr, 1998; Thoenes, 1998). New regulations drafted by the Ministry of Forestry appeared to focus on fulfilling the letter of the IMF agreement rather than the spirit of the objectives they were meant to address. By the end of April, one expatriate observer concluded, "there is still nothing tangible to show in the way of results. The main effect so far has been to force the government to do some serious rethinking and to encourage a much wider debate of the issues and possible solutions"(Fraser, 1998b, p. 5).

By this time, however, the initial high profile of the forest policy reform agenda had been eclipsed by other political and economic developments in early 1998. Similar foot-dragging had taken place in other sectors, as the clove monopoly and the national car project—both linked to the President's children—proved impervious to announced reforms. President Suharto alarmed the international community by naming B. J. Habibie as his choice for Vice President, a Suharto protégé known for his delusions of technological grandeur in the Indonesian aviation and nuclear industries rather than good economic sense. Suharto prompted further consternation, and telephone calls from other world leaders, by announcing that he was considering turning away from IMF advice in favor of a currency board. When he unveiled his new cabinet in March, larded with cronies, economic nationalists, and even his daughter, most observers interpreted this as a signal of defiance of the international community's wishes. In particular, the appointment of Bob Hasan as Minister of Industry and Trade could only be seen as a repudiation of commitments to forest sector reform.

Even to the extent that there was political will for reform scattered among government agencies and officials, reformers faced numerous barriers to implementing the agreed policy changes to meet the IMF deadlines. Many of the fundamental preconditions for the market-based reforms were simply not in place, and could not be established in a matter of months. For example, how could a concession auctioning system be implemented, when there was no baseline data on the condition or value of blocks of forest to be put up for bidding? One Indonesian government official remarked that auctioning concessions without data would be "like selling a cat in a bag."[23] How could a performance bond system be implemented, when the Ministry of Forestry had no outcome-based indicators on which to judge a concessionaire's performance? A summary of criticisms of the reform package is presented in Box 4.3.

Many observers, including reform-oriented ministry staff and expatriate advisors associated with bilateral aid projects, feared that a quick implementation of agreed reforms without those preconditions in place could actually make the forest management situation worse.[24] One of the first areas addressed by the Ministry was timber royalty issues, resulting in a new regulation on resource rent taxes in April. While some observers were distressed by the speed with which the

---

BOX 4.3 | THE RIGHT CONDITIONS?

The conditions included in the January 1998 IMF reform package, and later in the World Bank's follow-on adjustment loans, were consistent with the World Bank's conventional wisdom on forest policy. (*See Box 1.4.*) They focused on promoting efficiency in timber concession allocation and trade in forest products. While many domestic and international constituencies welcomed the package of reforms, they also criticized it for the following reasons:

- **consistency**—Although the IMF conditionality called for a moratorium on forest conversion, it also mandated liberalization in the palm oil sector, which was likely to accelerate pressures on forest conversion.

- **completeness**—The reforms focused on improving efficiency within the existing forest management paradigm, which was based on large-scale corporate concessions, and did not address property rights issues.

- **feasibility**—The reforms did not address the necessary preconditions for many of the efficiency-oriented reforms, such as the need for reliable data on forest quality and monitoring systems (Kartodihardjo, 1999).

- **effectiveness**—Because the reforms did not directly address the demand side of Indonesia's structural timber deficit, as described in this chapter, some argued that efficiency-oriented reforms would only increase incentives for illegal logging (Barr, 1999).

Ministry was promulgating new policy, World Bank staff believed that the symbolic value of making early progress on reform more than compensated for weaknesses in the resulting policy.[25]

In addition, some officials in the Ministry felt that the World Bank and the IMF had erred in defining the conditionality in terms of specific measures to be taken, rather than clarifying the objectives to be reached and leaving the means by which to meet them more flexible.[26] For example, the LOI specified that the Ministry's Reforestation Fund be brought "on budget." While the intent of this condition was to end the misuse of those funds for various pet projects of the Suharto regime unrelated to forestry, integrating the funds into the national budget could also result in a reduction in the amount earmarked for reforestation.[27]

The intricacies of Indonesian government policymaking constrained progress on meeting other conditions; World Bank staff were sometimes confounded by the multiple levels of authority required for each policy change. The fact that World Bank staff, rather than government officials, were shepherding paperwork through the bureaucracy to comply with conditionality indicates the government's limited commitment to the reforms.[28]

As it became clear that many of the agreed reforms could not be effectively implemented in the agreed time frame, or needed to be adjusted to reach intended objectives, World Bank staff encouraged Ministry of Forestry officials to pursue the reforms as an overall package rather than as a checklist.[29] According to one World Bank official, "The [IMF] letter felt very binding [to government officials] in a way I didn't imagine it would," and

> *The fact that World Bank staff, rather than government officials, were shepherding paperwork through the bureaucracy to comply with conditionality indicates the government's limited commitment to the reforms.*

he encouraged them to take the time necessary to develop good policy.[30] However, this flexibility may have inadvertently signaled to the Ministry that conditionality was being relaxed. At minimum, it was difficult for observers to distinguish between the World Bank's encouragement of conscientiousness and its tolerance of footdragging.

A New Regime; New Constituencies

In May 1998, President Suharto resigned following several weeks of increasingly violent demonstrations and rioting. With the smooth transition to an interim Habibie regime and calls for *reformasi total* (total reformation), the political context for forest sector reform appeared to have changed. The Ministry of Forestry was renamed the Ministry of Forestry and Estate Crops (MOFEC), reflecting the addition of a Directorate General previously under the Ministry of Agriculture—and a new Minister, Muslimin Nasution, was appointed. The new Minister had previously served in the Ministry of Cooperatives, and immediately prior to his new post, had served as Vice Chair of the Ministry of Development Planning, where he had helped prepare PRSL I. He quickly signaled that he was a proponent of reform by welcoming an unprecedented student demonstration in the Ministry of Forestry building in Jakarta.

The spirit of total reformation sweeping Indonesia infected forest policy debates as well, generating, in the words of one expatriate advisor, "a hurricane of ideas and demands."[31] While the World Bank-IMF reform agenda had focused almost exclusively on market-oriented reforms designed to improve the efficiency and environmental sustainability of the current, concession-oriented timber production system, the increased political space allowed two additional constituencies to flourish.

The first, led by NGOs and academics, promoted a new paradigm of forest management that recognized the rights and roles of forest communities and the importance of nontimber forest goods and services. The Community Forestry Communication Forum (FKKM), a network convened by Gadjah Mada University and supported by the Ford Foundation, emerged as a focal point of this constituency. By mid-1998, FKKM had published a forest management vision based on principles of social justice, public participation, and accountability, and had articulated a short-term program of proposed reforms (Forum Komunikasi Kehutanan Masyarakat, 1998).

The second forest policy reform constituency that emerged following the fall of Suharto was led by government officials affiliated with Muslim political movements, including Habibie and the new Minister of Forestry and Estate Crops. Similar to FKKM, this constituency expressed concern about social justice; however, this group focused on redistributing forest resource assets through imposition of maximum limits on concession size, and reallocating of concessions to cooperatives. In the Indonesian political context, this position was interpreted as a resurgence

of a perennial effort to redistribute wealth from conglomerates controlled by ethnic Chinese businessmen to cooperatives controlled by the government (Solomon, 1998). This constituency complicated the World Bank reform agenda by driving a parallel series of forest policy changes that were not welcomed by the international donor community, nor by Indonesian researchers, NGO activists, or industry representatives (Sunderlin, 1999).

Interestingly, an additional constituency that did not take a high profile in the forest policy reform debates was the conservation interest group. Despite significant donor support for biodiversity conservation projects and for environmental NGOs throughout the archipelago in the years leading up to the crisis, environmental concerns did not figure prominently in post-crisis debates, much to the consternation of some donor agency staff. According to the Jakarta-based representatives of one international conservation organization, it was seen as unseemly to advocate purely environmental issues, when the social justice aspects of the economic crisis, and the political imperatives of the democratization process needed to be given priority.[32]

Reformation without Any Changes

On June 29, 1998, a ministerial decree established the Forestry and Estate Crops Development Reformation Committee composed of representatives from the Ministry itself, NGOs, universities, and business. Its mandate was to make recommendations to the Minister regarding changes in the Ministry's vision, mission, and organization, as well as with regard to key legislative and regulatory frameworks. The young MOFEC officials who agreed to staff the Committee were seen by more cautious colleagues as risking their careers.[33] The group quickly produced a set of recommendations, but soon ran up against the intransigence of the bureaucracy below the Ministerial level.

In August, the Committee met with senior Ministry officials to discuss a draft revision of the government regulation regarding management of production forests. The Committee recommended that the regulation be recast in terms of integrated forest management rather than narrow timber production objectives, and that it address the issues of community rights to forest resources and participation in forest management, and the decentralization of forest administration. However, the decree promulgated by the Ministry for Presidential approval did not reflect any of these recommendations. World Bank staff pressured the Ministry to undertake further consultations, and to incorporate the results of those consultations into the regulations. Ultimately, World Bank staff intervened and took over the drafting process themselves, in part to remove undesirable text related to the granting of concessions to cooperatives. Later in the year, problems with this regulation delayed release of the second tranche of PRSL I.[34]

Similarly, in October and November 1998, the Committee held consultations on a draft Basic Forestry Law with national and provincial stakeholders, including a national conference in Jakarta (Consultative Group on Indonesian Forestry, 1998). Participants consistently identified key weaknesses in the draft as being the failure to recognize traditional rights over forest land *(hutan adat)*, and an overly centralized approach to forest management. However, the version of the law that emerged from the Ministry of Forestry and Estate Crops for parliamentary consideration did not reflect this stakeholder input. Apparently, bureaucratic resistance to recognition of community rights over forests had again proven successful.[35]

Many observers singled out the lack of transparency in the reform process as a key obstacle to real reform.[36] The recommendations of the Reformation Committee were somehow removed from the regulations and draft legislation that emerged from the Ministry's internal decisionmaking process. Some observers characterized that process as a "black box" that precluded effective participation by interested constituencies (Tjatur, Agus, and Yulia, 1999).

By early 1999, a full year after forest-related conditions were included in the second IMF Letter of Intent, there had been at least some progress in implementing forest sector reforms. The government had abolished Bob Hasan's forest product marketing monopolies. Having held up release of the second tranche of PRSL I, a new concession management regulation was promulgated in January that would increase the government's rent capture by charging higher royalties, remove the required linking of concessions to processing facilities, and establish a performance bonding system with independent inspection teams to monitor compliance (World Bank, 1999c, Annex 1).

By this time, however, proponents of reform had become sufficiently frustrated by lack of progress on more fundamental reforms, and by the characteristics of the reform process itself, that one member of the Reformation Committee had resigned, and several others had lost enthusiasm. One observer characterized the situation as "reformation without any changes" (Tjatur, Agus, and Yulia, 1999).

The implementation stalled over the course of 1999. In September, a policy advisor to a U.K.-supported forestry project prepared a "Report Card on Selected Forest Policy Reforms in Indonesia," awarding mostly grades of "D" and "F" based on the failure of the Ministry of Forestry and Estate Crops to implement commitments made to the World Bank and the IMF (Brown, 1999a). In many instances, compliance with the letter of the commitments was undermined by deviations from the spirit of the commitment. For example, decreases in log and sawn timber export taxes were replaced by nontariff barriers in a form that required exporters to obtain letters of permission. Similarly, while nominal stumpage fees were raised, actual rent capture declined when the Ministry allowed payment in rupiah at highly favorable exchange rates. An advisor to a bilateral forestry project remarked that it was hard for the World Bank not to "check off" the government's compliance with conditions when the World Bank had not specified the objectives to be served.[37]

Evolution of the Reform Agenda

Given the short notice on which World Bank staff were asked to provide forest sector conditions for the January 1998 Letter of Intent, it is not surprising that they were subsequently able to improve both the substance and the process of the World Bank's forest policy reform agenda in Indonesia. As noted above, the April 1998 Statement of Development Policy prepared in conjunction with PRSL I contained more explicit references to

Others in the forest industry were delighted by the prospect of being freed from Hasan's cartels. One World Bank staff member reported being personally thanked for the reforms by an affected Indonesian businessman.

the environmental and equity dimensions of forest policy reform.

More significantly, following the upheavals of May and June 1998, the World Bank initiated a dialogue with a broader group of stakeholders on a more comprehensive reform agenda for the forest sector. In July, a key World Bank forestry specialist met in Europe with government and bilateral agency representatives to discuss the outlines of a supplemental forest policy reform package to be included in a sectoral adjustment loan (SECAL) (Dieterle, 1998). By this time, the World Bank had concluded that a consensus on a forest policy reform agenda among relevant stakeholders, including the government, donor groups, and significant elements of the private sector and civil society, was not only possible, but necessary to reduce the risk that reform achievements would be swept away in subsequent political developments (Douglas, 1998a).

The World Bank circulated an issues paper that was used as the basis for a series of stakeholder consultations on the proposed SECAL (Douglas, 1998b). The paper was remarkable in two respects. First, its priorities were establishing the preconditions ignored by the earlier reform effort, including filling gaps in data and development of performance criteria. Second, it responded to the social justice concerns raised by emergent constituencies in the reformation era, by explicitly calling for community-based conservation and concession management. The paper went so far as to quote extensively from FKKM proposals.

The World Bank's official letter to the Government of Indonesia regarding the proposed SECAL was somewhat more circumspect, referring only to "open[ing] forest areas for use and operation by a wider group of stakeholders" (Fox 1998, p. 8). However, the policy matrix attached to PRSL II in May 1999, specified that draft forest legislation should accommodate "rights and responsibilities for *adat* areas which include forest areas," and required the drafting of a "community forest participation regulation" to ensure community participation in forest management and benefits (World Bank, 1999c, p. 37).

The World Bank was also responsive to stakeholder concerns regarding the lack of transparency and public consultation in the early stages of the reform process. The policy matrix attached to PRSL II included provisions requiring the government to make new maps of forest areas publicly available and initiate "a multi-stakeholder consultative process by which all proposed regulations and legislation will be publicly reviewed and discussed up to the final drafting stage" (World Bank, 1999c, p. 37).

However, the World Bank's success in promoting compliance with these commitments was mixed. After long delays, the Ministry finally posted forest cover maps for Sumatra and Kalimantan on the MOFEC Website in late 1999, but continued to refuse to release the raw data. In June 1999, the World Bank's Jakarta-based country director wrote a letter to the Minister of Forestry and Estate Crops expressing concern about the speed with which the new Basic Forest Law was moving forward, and suggested that further consultation and revisions were necessary before having the relevant parliamentary committee consider the law (Baird, 1999a). However, while providing questionable assurances to the World Bank that the necessary consultations had taken place, the Ministry rushed what many stakeholders considered to be a flawed bill through approval in September 1999.[38]

By the latter half of 1999, the World Bank had begun to characterize its attention to reform in the forest sector explicitly in terms of good governance, and to look outside the MOFEC for leadership of the reform effort. At the July meeting in Paris of the Consultative Group on Indonesia (CGI), the formal donor consortium that coordinates development assistance with the Government of Indonesia, the World Bank secured a commitment from the Ministry of Development Planning to convene a high-level, interagency summit on forest policy reform—a commitment that was honored by the new government that came into power in late 1999.

In sum, the World Bank's approach to the forest policy reform agenda evolved from the initial focus on market-oriented efficiency measures contained in the January 1998 agreement with the IMF to encompass a broader range of issues and constituencies. Conditions attached to PRSL II included strong provisions related to community participation in forest management, as well as provisions related to transparency and participation in the reform process itself. Ultimately, the World Bank acknowledged the connection between forest sector reform and improved governance more generally.

THE ROLES OF OTHER STAKEHOLDERS

Private Sector

Among the key stakeholders said to have been taken by surprise by the January 1998 Letter of Intent was Presidential crony and timber tycoon Bob Hasan. Ironically, at the time the package was being negotiated in Jakarta, Hasan was in Washington, D.C., participating in a meeting of the world's timber industry leaders convened by World Bank President James Wolfensohn.[39] Hasan's continuing ability to influence events thereafter was evidenced by early evasion of the decree abolishing his forest product monopolies, and his appointment to Suharto's cabinet in March 1998, as Minister of Industry and Trade.

Others in the forest industry were delighted by the prospect of being freed from Hasan's cartels. One World Bank staff member in Jakarta reported being personally thanked for the reforms by an affected Indonesian businessman.[40] As long as the reforms focused on increasing efficiency in the business arena, the private sector was supportive. In this way, private sector interests were fully aligned with the reforms being promoted by the World Bank and the IMF. However, businessmen were also concerned about other possible changes that could affect the size and profitability of their operations. In particular, private businessmen (as well as World Bank and IMF officials) were alarmed when populist elements

in the new government began to promote the idea of distributing forest resource assets by limiting concession areas and granting shares to cooperatives (Solomon, 1998)

Ultimately, the World Bank acknowledged the connection between forest sector reform and improved governance more generally.

Bilateral Donors

At the time of the crisis, the bilateral donor community had a large stake in the Indonesian forest sector. By 1995, total donor commitments in the sector had risen to about US$400 million, including large investments in forest management and conservation projects funded by the United States, the European Union, and German and British aid agencies (World Bank, 1996). According to one World Bank official, these agencies had been unwilling to join the World Bank in pressing the Indonesian government for policy reform in the mid-1990s, for fear of jeopardizing smooth relationships with their counterparts.[41]

Expatriate staff of bilateral donor-funded forestry projects were surprised by the inclusion of forest conditions in the January reform package. While initially miffed by the lack of prior consultation, and concerned that the World Bank might displace them by monopolizing policy dialogue with the Ministry, most members of this community were supportive of the proposed reforms.[42] Although they noted the World Bank's four-year absence from the forest sector, they

BOX 4.4

CAMBODIA: LEARNING TO DANCE SMOOTHLY WITH THE WORLD BANK

Background

Exploitation of forest resources has played a significant role in the recent political conflict and economic crisis in Cambodia. Approximately 10.5 million hectares of forest remain in Cambodia, accounting for 58 percent of total land area. Between 1973 and 1993, the rate of deforestation was an estimated 70,000 hectares per year. From 1993 to 1997, the rate of deforestation has accelerated alarmingly to more than 180,000 hectares annually as a result of greater pressure from loggers and local communities. Logging is of enormous commercial importance for Cambodia, and accounted for 43 percent of foreign trade in 1997. Much of this logging is illegal, depriving the central government coffers of as much as US$80 million in foregone tax revenues annually.

Cambodia's military and political structure has been closely involved in much of the illegal logging activity. According to Global Witness, an NGO independently monitoring the Cambodian forest sector, illegal logging revenues fed the election chests of both co-Prime Ministers Rannaridh and Hun Sen. Because high political figures in Cambodia depended on illegal logging profits, reformers in line ministries were limited in the amount of change they could generate in the forest sector.

Cambodia reclaimed membership in the World Bank Group in 1992, after 22 years of domestic conflict. Foreign aid has swelled to 50 percent of the national budget in recent years, a proportion which should provide the aid community considerable leverage for policy reform.

Adjustment Experience

While the World Bank, as the chair of the Consultative Group of donors on Cambodia, has led efforts to assess the forest sector in Cambodia, the IMF has also been key in imposing the World Bank's recommendations through its Enhanced Structural Adjustment Facility (ESAF) loans, initiated in 1994. Bowing to World Bank and IMF conditionality, the Cambodian government instituted a log export ban and created a Forestry Reform Steering Committee within the government. These policy changes were not, however, mirrored in the situation on the ground as illegal logging continued. In late 1996, the IMF acted on its threats to withdraw funding and canceled the fourth tranche of its loan.

With forest issues now firmly on the agenda, the IMF announced in 1997 that any further financial support would be contingent on the government's performance in monitoring log exports and ensuring a transparent flow of forest revenues to the national treasury. Shortly thereafter, however, aid was suspended due to internal political turmoil, as Hun Sen wrested complete power from Rannaridh in a coup d'etat. More recently, as the political situation has stabilized, the donor community put together a US$470 million aid package at the 1999 meeting of the Consultative Group. The aid was explicitly conditioned on forest sector reform. Prime Minister Hun Sen committed to establishing an independent log processing and export monitoring unit, and canceling 12 concessions. Later that year, it was announced that Global Witness had been appointed as the official independent monitor of Cambodia's forest sector.

Results and Analysis

Cambodia represents an extreme case of the deep political entrenchment of logging interests, but also of considerable potential for donor leverage. This leverage, however, has cut both ways. With Cambodia so heavily dependent on aid, donors have hesitated to withdraw funds because of

BOX 4.4 | (CONTINUED)

humanitarian concerns, which has undermined the credibility of conditionality. Until recently, the Cambodian government has managed to keep the aid stream flowing without conceding much reform in the forest sector.

Yet, appointing an independent agency to monitor Cambodia's forests suggests that coordinated donor pressure for reform can yield important results, even in a situation of limited government ownership of the reform agenda. The pace of reform may be slow in Cambodia, because forest issues are bound up with the broader problems of post-conflict reconstruction in the country. In the mid-1990s, concerned Cambodian officials were fearful that there was no future for the forest sector in their country. But by mid-1999, international pressure for reform had encouraged and empowered many reform-minded individuals within the government. By raising the profile of forest issues, the international community had succeeded in getting forest sector reform on the agenda of the government, and had helped to free pro-reform individuals and agencies from their political handcuffs.

In 1999, government officials claimed to be moving forward on implementing the reform agenda, while at the same time expressing some frustration with the overly rigid timing and inappropriate sequencing of World Bank-mandated reforms. Said one, "We need to learn to dance smoothly with the World Bank."

Sources: Global Witness. 1996. "RGC Forest Policy & Practice & the Case for Positive Conditionality: A Briefing Document for the 1996 Meeting of the Consultative Group." London: Global Witness. www.oneworld.org/globalwitness.

—1997. "Consultative Group Meeting on Cambodia, Paris, 1-2 July 1997: Analysis of the Forestry Issue, Compilation of Attendee Statements and Recommended Next Steps." London: Global Witness. www.oneworld.org/globalwitness.

—1997. "Just Deserts for Cambodia?" London: Global Witness. www.oneworld.org/globalwitness.

—1999. "RGC Puts Reputation on the Line on Forestry Reform." London: Global Witness. www.oneworld.org/globalwitness.

—1999. "Global Witness Appointed Independent Monitor of Forestry Sector." London: Global Witness. http://carryon.oneworld.org/globalwitness/press/pr_991 202b.html

Hun Sen, Samdech. 1999. "Opening Speech of Samdech Hun Sen, Prime Minister of the Royal Government of Cambodia to 1999 CG Meeting." www.worldbank.org/extdr/offrep/eap/khcg99/opspeech-pm.htm.

Okonjo-Iweala, Ngozi. 1999. "Consultative Group for Cambodia: Chairman's Opening Remarks." Washington D.C.: The World Bank. www.worldbank.org/html/extdr/offrep/eap/khcg99/opre-marks.htm

—1999. "Cambodia's Reconstruction Depends on Sustained Commitment of Coalition Government and International Donors." Washington D.C.: The World Bank.www.worldbank.org/html/extdr/offrep/eap/khcg99/oped.htm.

Royal Government of Cambodia. 1998. "Cambodia National Environmental Action Plan 1998–2002." Kingdom of Cambodia: Royal Government of Cambodia.

The Economist. "The Fight Against Illegal Loggers," April 3, 1999, p. 34.

World Bank, The. 1999. "Cambodia: A Vision for Forestry Sector Development." Washington D.C.: The World Bank.

—1999. "Cambodia Wins Solid Support from Donors." News Release 99/2107/EAP, February 26, 1999, www.worldbank.org/html/extdr/extme/2107.htm.

—"The World Bank and Cambodia: Country Brief." Washington D.C.: The World Bank. http://wbln0018.worldbank.org/eap/eap.nsf

World Bank, The, UNDP, and FAO. 1996. "Sector Report for Cambodia-Forest Policy Assessment." Washington D.C.: The World Bank.

rallied to assist World Bank colleagues and Ministry of Forestry officials to move forward with the reform agenda.

At the request of the World Bank, the Consultative Group on Indonesian Forestry (CGIF)—which was supported by a German-funded project—stepped forward to play a coordinating role in convening donors, government officials, and eventually NGOs to discuss how to implement the reforms. Others, including the staff of projects funded by the United States, the European Union, and the United Kingdom, provided experts and analysis to guide design of new policies. While conceding the validity of some criticisms leveled at the substance and process of reforms promoted by the World Bank and the IMF, a report generated by one bilateral project concluded that "the reforms themselves are *exactly* what the Indonesian forest industry needs" (1999b).[43]

In July 1999, the new World Bank country director mentioned forestry issues in his opening remarks to the Paris meeting of the CGI (Baird, 1999b). Representatives of other donor agencies reportedly spoke forcefully of the need to address forest policy reform, elevating forestry issues to the top tier of the CGI agenda, along with the situation in East Timor, and attracting attention from government agencies other than the Ministry of Forestry and Estate Crops.[44] Box 4.4 describes recent experience in Cambodia, where the World Bank, the IMF, and the broader donor community collaborated to leverage forest policy reform in the context of adjustment lending.

Domestic and International NGOs

The World Bank entered the Indonesian crisis with many domestic and international NGOs questioning the World Bank's credibility. Participants in a civil society forum in Jakarta with World Bank President James Wolfensohn in February 1998, said they had "warned the World Bank years ago that economic growth hinged on an overhaul of Indonesia's rigid political system" (Torchia, 1998, p. 1).[45] Evidencing some ambivalence about international intervention early in the crisis, an international NGO network called on the World Bank, the IMF, and the Asian Development Bank to ensure that their actions would not result in worsening social or environmental conditions, but also urged them to "use their leverage not only to see that the Indonesian government implements economic reforms, but also impress upon the Government of Indonesia that economic reform without political reform will be insufficient to stem the loss of international confidence in Indonesia" (INFID, 1998a). Just prior to Suharto's fall from power, the same network called on the World Bank and the IMF "to condition further economic assistance to Indonesia on fundamental political reform" and "to improve their own transparency and accountability in order to increase the legitimacy of their exercise of this conditionality" (INFID, 1998b).

With a few exceptions, the community of NGOs within Indonesia concerned about forest issues was not well-informed about the workings of the international financial institutions, and was not sure how to react to the January 1998 reform package. On the one hand, like their international counterparts, they were pleased to see the IMF challenging such potent symbols of the excesses of the Suharto regime as Bob Hasan's plywood monopoly. On the other hand, they were also skeptical about the motives of the World Bank and the IMF, particularly with respect to the institutions' support of economic liberalization and privatization, which were seen as serving the interests of international investors.[46]

In addition, the opinions of many domestic NGOs were influenced by those of international research and funding organizations active in the Indonesian forest sector, such as the International Council for Research on Agroforestry (ICRAF) and the Ford Foundation, whose staff privately criticized various aspects of the reforms.[47] In particular, these groups were critical of the failure of the reforms to promote a more fundamental reorientation of forest management policy from a social justice perspective. During the flourishing of the spirit of *reformasi* in mid-1998, international organizations and domestic groups coordinated through the FKKM played an active role in promoting community participation and recognition of indigenous peoples' resource rights in discussions of new forestry legislation and regulations.

NGO distrust of the World Bank's motives and lack of understanding of the mechanics of adjustment lending constrained the World Bank's ability to develop a constituency for reform within the Indonesian NGO community. In September 1998, at a meeting convened by the Ford Foundation at the request of the World Bank, NGO activists refused to discuss the specifics of a proposed sectoral adjustment operation focused on the forest sector, because of their misperception that World Bank funds would be channeled to the Ministry of Forestry.[48] Similarly, the World

Bank's interest in collaborating with NGOs to monitor implementation of reform in the field was compromised by the latter's unwillingness to accept funds from the World Bank. One group placed the World Bank and the IMF on a blacklist of funding sources along with transnational timber corporations (Plume, 1999).

International advocacy groups were ambivalent about the forestry-related conditions contained in the January reform package. On the one hand, they could not help but celebrate the setbacks dealt to vested interests in unsustainable logging practices, and called on the World Bank and the IMF to use disbanding of the plywood and other cartels as a litmus test for further support to the government (Fried and Rich, 1998). On the other hand, they wondered why equally egregious threats to forests, such as the ill-conceived million-hectare rice production scheme in the swamps of Kalimantan, were not targeted by the World Bank and the IMF. A "Joint-NGO Request to the IMF for Immediate Intervention" to halt the project was forwarded to IMF Managing Director Michel Camdessus, implicitly acknowledging the legitimacy of such intervention (Barclay et al., 1998). In 1999, in a report exposing the flourishing of illegal logging, domestic and international NGOs recommended that the World Bank, the IMF, and other donors "be held responsible for upholding actions to stop illegal logging and reform forestry law" (Environmental Investigation Agency and Telapak, 1999, p. 40).

International NGOs also criticized the specific forest policy reform content. They noted remarkable inconsistencies in the package, including a call for a moratorium on forest conversion while at the same time liberalizing investment in the oil palm plantation sector, a major driver of such conversion (Fried and Rich, 1998). They observed that the reforms seemed to be oriented toward increasing the efficiency of the existing, corporate-oriented concession system, and did not deal with more fundamental issues of property rights and community roles in forest management.

THE BOTTOM LINE

Are the prospects for improved forest management in Indonesia better or worse off as a result of the World Bank and the IMF including forest policy reforms in adjustment lending? And to what extent can the actions of the Bank and the IMF be separated from the effects of the larger historic events in May of 1998? Although Indonesia's transition to a post-Suharto era is still underway, it is possible to draw some preliminary conclusions.

Experience in Indonesia shows that the World Bank's attention to governance issues in the reform process itself, particularly transparency and stakeholder consultation, is essential to empower domestic constituencies for reform.

Some progress in reform of the forest sector has been achieved. The breakup of the forest product marketing monopolies, while delayed, was important as a political symbol and in terms of economic efficiency. In addition, the existence of a reform process has served to open up the dialogue on forest policy reform, and has created a forum for NGOs, bilateral donors, and other constituencies to debate and advance their views. To the extent that this process can maintain momentum with the new government that assumed power in late 1999, the significance of the World Bank and the IMF's "getting the Ministry of Forestry's attention for the first time in centuries"—in the words of one World Bank staffer—should not be underestimated.[49]

However, the slow and uneven pace of reform can be traced to many factors, some of which were under the control of the World Bank and the IMF. First, the initial package of reforms was inconsistent and incomplete. While these weaknesses are easily attributable to the unreasonable deadline given by the IMF to the World Bank for coming up with structural conditions in the second LOI, it is also true that the World Bank had not been substantively engaged in the forest sector for the four years prior to the crisis. As a result, World Bank staff did not have the benefit of updated analysis or stakeholder consultation to support the design of those conditions. More consistent engagement in the sector following terminations of existing and planned loans to the Ministry of Forestry in 1995 might also have tempered the mixed reception afforded the World Bank's abrupt re-entry onto the forest policy stage.

Second, the original forest policy conditions contained in the January LOI were articulated in terms of specific measures rather than desired outcomes, were associated with unrealistic deadlines, and in some cases reflected a lack of understanding of the Indonesian policymaking process. The subsequent need for the World Bank to adjust the conditions and the deadlines sent mixed signals to the government, and made it difficult for outsiders to know whether noncompliance was the result of lack of political will or lack of feasibility. In addition, the articulation of conditions in terms of specific measures allowed the Ministry of Forestry to comply with the letter of the conditions while undermining their spirit.

Third, the initial focus of the World Bank and the IMF on efficiency-oriented reform, without explicit attention to the social justice aspects of alternative forestry management regimes, compromised the initial ownership of the reform program among key constituencies, including domestic and international NGOs. While World Bank staff may have judged correctly that a structural adjustment loan was not the right vehicle for promoting such institutional change, they could have done a better job of signaling the broader scope of the long-term reform agenda.

Fourth, experience in Indonesia shows that the World Bank's attention to governance issues in the reform process itself, particularly transparency and stakeholder consultation, is essential to empower domestic constituencies for reform. Over time, the World Bank has shown itself to be increasingly willing to exert pressure on the government to disclose information about the reform process and to engage stakeholders in more meaningful participation.

Finally, the Indonesia case demonstrates the limitations of the adjustment instrument to promote change in the forest sector. In 1995, the World Bank's own assessment of its experience with project lending in the forest sector in Indonesia concluded that "the need to deal comprehensively with institutional constraints is a major lesson which arises from experience with this project" (World Bank, 1996, p. iv). Four years later, it is clear that institutional constraints continue to be the major obstacle to reform, despite the significant political and economic changes that have occurred in the interim.

REFERENCES

Agence France Presse. 1997. "Indonesian Timber Baron Denies Big Companies Are to Blame for Fires." *Agence France Presse.*

Baird, Mark. 1999a. "Letter No. M-051/ENV/VI/99 to Dr. Ir. Mulimin Nasution, Minister for Forestry and Plantation." The World Bank. June 18, 1999. http://www.worldbank.org/html/extdr/offrep/eap/cgi99/bairdstatement.htm

—1999b. "Indonesia: From Crisis to Opportunity." Presentation at Consultative Group for Indonesia, Paris, July 27, 1999.

Barber, Charles Victor. 1998. "Forest Resource Scarcity & Social Conflict in Indonesia." *Environment* Vol. 40, No. 4 (May 1998).

Barber, Charles Victor, and James Schweithelm. 2000. *Trial by Fire: Forest Fires and Forestry Policy in Indonesia's Era of Crisis and Reform.* Washington D.C.: World Resources Institute.

Barclay et al. 1998. "Joint-NGO Request to the IMF for Immediate Intervention." Jakarta, February 26, 1998.

Barr, Christopher M. 1998. "Bob Hasan, the Rise of Apkindo, and the Shifting Dynamics of Control in Indonesia's Timber Sector." *Indonesia* No.65 (April 1998). Cornell University Southeast Asia Program.

—1999. "Banking on Sustainability: A Critical Assessment of the World Bank's Structural Adjustment Reforms in Indonesia's Timber Sector." Draft manuscript prepared for World Wildlife Fund and CIFOR, September 1999.

Brauchli, Marcus W. 1998. "World Bank Is Hurt by its Failure to Anticipate the Indonesia Crisis." *Wall Street Journal,* July 14, 1998.

Bresnan, John. 1999. "The United States and the Indonesian Financial Crisis." Edited by A. Schwartz and J. Paris, *The Politics of Post-Suharto Indonesia.* New York: Council of Foreign Relations.

Brown, David W. 1999a. "Report Card on Selected Policy Reforms in Indonesia." Jakarta: Indonesia-UK Tropical Forestry Management Programme. Unpublished.

—1999b. *Addicted to Rent: Corporate and Spatial Distribution of Forest Resources in Indonesia, Implications for Policy in the Reformasi Era.* Jakarta: Indonesia-UK Tropical Forest Management Programme.

Consultative Group on Indonesian Forestry, and Ministry of Forestry and Estate Crops. 1998. *Report of CGIF Meeting 15th Round: Draft Basic Forestry Law.* Jakarta: Consultative Group on Indonesian Forestry and Ministry of Forestry and Estate Crops.

Dieterle, Gerhard. 1998. "Summary Report on an Informal Meeting on Structural Reform in Indonesian Forestry." Jakarta: Consultative Group on Indonesian Forestry.

Douglas, Jim. 1998a. "Sector Adjustment for Forests in Indonesia: Issues." Paper read at Consultative Group on Indonesian Forestry/Forum Konsultasi Kehutanan, October 30, 1998, at Indonesia.

—1998b. "World Bank Involvement in Sector Adjustment for Forests in Indonesia: The Issues: World Bank." Paper distributed at Pertemuan Informal Grup Knoservasi, October 30, 1998.

Environmental Investigation Agency and Telapak Indonesia. 1999. *The Final Cut: Illegal Logging in Indonesia's Orangutan Parks*. Washington, D.C.: EIA US.

Forum Komunikasi Kehutanan Masyarakat. 1998. *Zaman Baru Kehutanan Indonesia*. Yogyarkarta: Forum Komunikasi Kehutanan Masyarakat.

Fox, Geoffrey. 1998. "Attachment 2 of Letter to Indonesian Minister of Public Works and Minister of Forestry & Plantation on Water Resources and Forestry Sector Policy Reform: World Bank." Washington D.C: The World Bank. September 8, 1998.

Fraser, Alastair I. 1998a. "Indonesia Forestry Sector: Impact of the Economic Crisis and IMF Proposed Measures." Status Report: 16th March, Jakarta: Department for International Development.

—1998b. "Indonesia Forestry Sector: Impact of the Economic Crisis and IMF Proposed Measures." Status Report: 30th April, Jakarta: Department for International Development.

—1998c. "Indonesia Forestry Sector: Impact of the Economic Crisis and IMF Proposed Measures." Status Report: 31st May, Jakarta: Department for International Development.

Fried, Stephanie, and Bruce Rich. 1998. "Letter from 55 NGOs from 19 Countries to IMF Managing Director and World Bank President." April 16, 1998.

Government of Indonesia. 1998a. "Indonesia – Memorandum of Economic and Financial Policies." In *Second Letter of Intent*. Jakarta: Government of Indonesia.

—1998b. "Statement of Development Policy." Jakarta: Government of Indonesia.

International Campaign for Ecological Justice in Indonesia. 1998. "Debt, Poverty and the IMF." *Down to Earth* No.38 (August 1998): 5.

International Monetary Fund. 1997. *IMF Approves Stand-By Credit for Indonesia* (Press Release No. 97/50, November 11, 1997, http://www.imf.org/external/np\sec\pr\1997\PR9750.HTM.

International NGO Forum on Indonesian Development (INFID). 1998a. "INFID Statement on the Economic and Political Crisis in Indonesia." Jakarta and The Hague: INFID.

—1998b. "11th INFID Conference Statement on Economic Reform and Corruption." Bonn: INFID.

Kapur, Devesh, John P. Lewis, and Richard Webb. 1997. *The World Bank: Its First Half Century*. 2 vols. Vol. I. Washington D.C.: Brookings Institution Press.

Kartodihardjo, Hariadi. 1999. *Belenggu IMF & World Bank: Hambatan Struktural Pembarharuan Kebijakan Pembangunan Kenhutanan di Indonesia*. Jakarta: Lembaga Alam Tropika Indonesia (LATIN).

Milverton, Damian. 1998. "World Bank Suspends Two Loans to Indonesia." *Dow Jones News*, December 21, 1998.

Peluso, Nancy Lee. 1992. *Rich Forests, Poor People: Resource Control and Resistance in Java*. Berkeley: University of California Press.

Plume, Catherine. 1999. "Trip Report to Forest Watch Indonesia." Washington D.C.: World Resources Institute. Mimeo.

Ramli, Rizal, and Mubariq Ahmad. 1993. *Rente Ekonomi Pengusahan Hutan Indonesia*. Jakarta, Indonesia: Wahana Lingkungan Hidup Indonesia (WALHI).

Schwartz, Adam. 1994. *A Nation in Waiting: Indonesia in the 1990s*. St. Leonards: Allen & Unwin Pty Ltd.

Schwartz, A. and Paris, J., eds. 1999. *The Politics of Post-Suharto Indonesia*. New York: Council of Foreign Relations.

Simpson, Glenn R., and Michael M. Phillips. 1998. "World Bank Sounds Alarm on Corruption in Indonesia." *Wall Street Journal*.

Solomon, Jay. 1998. "Habibie's Plan for Asset Sales Worries IMF." *Asian Wall Street Journal*, October 27, 1998, 1 and 14.

Sunderlin, William D. 1999. "The Effects of Economic Crisis and Political Change on Indonesia's Forest Sector, 1997–99." Bogor: Center for International Forestry Research (CIFOR).

Thoenes, Sander. 1998. "Indonesian Wood Cartel Resists IMF Reforms." *Financial Times*, February 13, 1998.

Tjatur, Agus, and Yulia. 1999. "Reformasi Setengah Hati." *Indikator*, No. 12. Tahun 1, January 28 – February 3, 1999.

Torchia, Christopher. 1998. "World Bank President Draws Criticism at Forum of Community Leaders." *Associated Press*. February 4, 1998.

Wolfensohn, James D. 1998. "Letter to Zoemrotin K. Soesilo and Asmara Nababan of the International NGO Forum on Indonesian Development." Washington D.C.: The World Bank. February 24, 1998.

World Bank, The. 1995. "Draft Forestry Report: The Economics of Long Term Management of Indonesia's Natural Forests." Washington D.C.: The World Bank.

—1996. "Implementation Completion Report: Indonesia - Second Forestry Institutions and Conservation Project." Report No. 15294, Washington D.C.: The World Bank.

—1999a. "Indonesia: Country Assistance Note." Washington D.C.: The World Bank.

—1999b. "Indonesia: Country Assistance Strategy - Progress Report." Report No. 18963, Washington D.C.: The World Bank.

—1999c. "Draft Report and Recommendation of the President of the International Bank for Reconstruction and Development to the Executive Directors on a Proposed Policy Reform Support Loan II in the Amount of US$500 Million to the Republic of Indonesia." Washington D.C.: The World Bank.

NOTES

1. This chapter draws on "Toward an Environmental Adjustment: Structural Barriers to Forestry Development in Indonesia" by Hariadi Kartodihardjo, which is available at http://www.wri.org/wri/governance/iffeforest.html or published in Indonesia as *Belenggu IMF & World Bank: Hambatan Struktural Pembaharauan Kebijakan Pembangunan Kehutanan di Indonesia* (Kartodihardjo 1999), as well as interviews conducted by the authors in Jakarta and Washington, D.C., on a not-for-attribution basis.

   Both authors were participants in some of the events described in this chapter. Frances Seymour serves on the Non-Indonesian Steering Committee of the International NGO Forum on Indonesian Development, and helped facilitate meetings in Washington between Indonesian activists and officials of the World Bank and the IMF. Hariadi Kartodihardjo was appointed to the Forestry and Estate Crops Development Reformation Committee in June 1998 and served until mid-1999.

2. In 1986, advocacy groups from Indonesia and donor countries formed a network parallel to the official donor consortium to promote an alternative vision for Indonesian development. The organization is now known as the International NGO Forum on Indonesian Development (INFID).

3. While senior Bank officials had periodically raised the corruption issue with President Suharto (Kapur, Lewis, and Webb, 1997), public acknowledgment of the issue had remained taboo.

4. For a good summary of the political economy of forests in Indonesia, see Barber (1998).

5. In September 1997, timber magnate Mohammad "Bob" Hasan was quoted as saying not only that the fires were caused by small farmers, but that activists who said otherwise were associated with Communists (*Agence France Presse*, 1997).

6. Personal communication with World Bank official, April 1999.

7. For an excellent summary of Bob Hasan's background, political ties, and commercial empire, see Barr (1998).

8. According to participants, an initial solicitation of two pages of text on environmental issues was followed by requests for condensation to a page, a paragraph, and finally a single point. (Not-for-attribution interviews with World Bank officials, November 1998.)

9. Personal communication, November 1999.

10. For an excellent, play-by-play analysis of the events in Indonesia from October 1997 to March 1998, and the response of the international community, see Bresnan (1999).

11. Not-for-attribution interview with World Bank official, November 1998.

12. Not-for-attribution interview with World Bank official, November 1998. This judgment was later captured in a footnote to the Bank's presentation to the board regarding a second

adjustment loan to Indonesia: "Forestry is not only strategically important to the economy due to the enormous value of natural resources involved, but forest management has been characterized by nepotism and private appropriation of resource rents. Hence, reforming forest policy not only improves efficiency but demonstrates a commitment to improved governance" (The World Bank, 1999c).

13. Not-for-attribution interview with World Bank official, November 1998.

14. Nevertheless, the inclusion of other, nonforest conditions in the reform package—related to implementation of a new environmental law and attention to air quality issues—is evidence that staff worked to include environmental elements on their own terms.

15. The PRSL II was also supplemented by a parallel Social Safety Net Adjustment Loan in mid-1999.

16. Not-for-attribution interview with World Bank official, June 1999.

17. Not-for-attribution interview with bilateral project advisor, November 1998.

18. Various not-for-attribution interviews with World Bank officials and Indonesian government officials, November 1998.

19. Not-for-attribution interview with Indonesian government official, October 1998.

20. Not-for-attribution interview with Indonesian government official, October 1998.

21. Not-for-attribution interviews with Indonesian government officials and bilateral project advisors, November 1998.

22. A series of status reports on "Indonesia Forestry Sector: Impact of the Economic Crisis and IMF Proposed Measures" produced by the leader of a U.K.-funded project provides a useful chronology and analysis (Fraser, 1998a,b,c).

23. Not-for-attribution interview with Indonesian government official, October 1998.

24. The DFID status report dated May 31 states, "A major cause of concern over these matters is that decisions will be rushed, without proper thought and analysis, which may result in a less than optimal outcome" (Fraser 1998c).

25. Not-for-attribution interviews with World Bank official and Indonesian government officials, October 1998.

26. Not-for-attribution interview with Indonesian government official, November 1998.

27. Legislation on decentralization passed in September 1999, stipulates that 40 percent of Reforestation Fund proceeds will be returned to the regions as a special budget allocation not specifically tied to reforestation (Mubariq Ahmad, personal communication).

28. Not-for-attribution interview with World Bank official, June 1999.

29. Not-for-attribution interviews with bilateral project advisor, November 1998.

30. Not-for-attribution interview with World Bank official, June 1999.

31. Not-for-attribution interview with bilateral project advisor November 1999.

32. Not-for-attribution interview with NGO staff, November 1998.

33. Not-for-attribution interview with Indonesian government officials, October 1998.

34. Not-for-attribution interview with World Bank official, June 1999.

35. By June 1999, the inadequacy of the draft law had become the target of protests by students, NGOs, professional associations, and the former ministers of environment and forestry.

36. Not-for-attribution interview with bilateral project advisor, November 1998.

37. Not-for-attribution interview with bilateral project advisor, November 1998.

38. Not-for-attribution interview with World Bank official, September 1999.

39. In addition to other timber industry leaders, participants in the meeting included senior officials from World Resources Institute, World Wide Fund for Nature, Conservation International, and International Union for Conservation of Nature and Natural Resources.

40. Not-for-attribution interview with World Bank official, June 1999.

41. Not-for-attribution interview with World Bank official, January 1999.

42. Not-for-attribution interview with bilateral project advisors, November 1999.

43. The report goes on to caution that "[o]bservers should think twice before throwing stones at the Bank, at least where its forestry agenda in Indonesia is concerned" (Brown, 1999b, p. 74).

44. Not-for-attribution interview with World Bank official, September 1999.

45. In subsequent correspondence, Wolfensohn stated that "the *political* reforms of the Indonesian system that your letter mentions *must* be the responsibility of the Indonesian people. International agencies such as the World Bank cannot do that" (Wolfensohn, 1998).

46. For example, a newsletter reported that, "There has been mounting criticism too of the economic conditions set by the IMF because they serve the interests of the international financial community rather than the needs of Indonesia itself." And, "The current IMF programme is paving the way for greatly expanded foreign domination of Indonesia's economies" (International Campaign for Ecological Justice in Indonesia, 1998).

47. Not-for-attribution interview with staff of Indonesian NGOs and international organizations, October-November 1998.

48. Not-for-attribution interview with staff of Indonesian NGOs and international organizations, October-November 1998.

49. Not-for-attribution interview with World Bank official, June 1998.

5

KENYA

Frances J. Seymour
John Mugabe

B y the mid-1990s, the World Bank had been providing assistance to Kenya for improved natural resources management for more than two decades. Despite an impressive array of political pronouncements, environmental policies, and government agencies charged with environmental stewardship, the Government of Kenya had

---

In recent years, Kenya has experienced irreversible environmental degradation that undermines prospects for long-term economic growth and socio-political stability.

---

an equally impressive record of failing to implement policies necessary to reverse environmental degradation. In early 1996, a handful of World Bank officials began floating the idea of a structural adjustment operation focused exclusively on environmental policy reform. This chapter will examine the World Bank's experience in promoting the idea of "environmental adjustment," and will attempt to identify the reasons that an environmental adjustment operation never materialized.[1] The Kenya case illustrates how gov-

ernance issues arise in the context of environmental policy reform. It also provides an interesting example of how adjustment lending is related to project lending in the forest sector, and to another key World Bank instrument, the Country Assistance Strategy.

BACKGROUND

Environmental Policy and Implementation in Kenya

In recent years, Kenya has experienced irreversible environmental degradation that undermines prospects for long-term economic growth and socio-political stability. Soil and water degradation threatens the sustainability of Kenya's agriculture sector, which in the late 1990s has generated about a third of the country's Gross Domestic Product (GDP), and employed more than 70 percent of the population. Wildlife tourism provides an important source of foreign exchange. While savannas are home to the more familiar wildlife species that attract tourists, forest ecosystems provide habitat for a large proportion of the country's biological diversity. Forests also furnish essential watershed functions for the entire nation, as well as providing timber and fuelwood. Although constituting only a small percentage of Kenya's land area, forests have been depleted or lost at a rate of thousands of hectares per year (Mugabe and Krhoda, 1999).

While Kenya's rapid rate of population growth has contributed to environmental degradation, economic policies and political factors have also played a significant part (Kahl, 1998). Government policies have often failed to reflect the full economic value of natural resource exploitation. *For example,* World Bank staff estimate that Kenya has captured less than 10 percent of the value of roundwood on-the-stump and collected less than 35 percent of the royalties due from logging of plantation-grown pine and cypress.[2] Property rights regimes have also presented perverse incentives. *For example,* by taking ownership and user rights over wildlife away from private landowners, the Wildlife Conservation and Management Act removed incentives to conserve wildlife outside of protected areas (Marekia, 1991).

For several decades, the Government of Kenya has recognized the need to institute measures to arrest environmental degradation. For example, a policy paper published in 1965 made clear statements on natural resources management and noted the importance of integrating environmental concerns into development planning (Republic of Kenya, 1965). The 1974–1978 Development Plan articulated the need to manage the environment for ecological, sociocultural and economic benefits, and recognized that the lack of appropriate institutional arrangements and policies was limiting environmental management. The 1994–96 Development Plan stressed that "success in achieving social sustainability will largely depend on conserving and protecting the natural resource base on which future development depends" and explicitly called for integrating environmental considerations into the policy-making process (quoted in Mugabe and Krhoda, 1999, p. 5).

Kenya has numerous policies, laws, and agencies to address environmental problems. More than 70 different laws either directly or indirectly apply to natural resources management, and Kenya has signed and ratified most of the major international environmental agreements. The country has more than 20 institutions and departments dealing with environmental matters: the Ministry of Environmental Conservation, the Ministry of Natural Resources, the National Environment Secretariat, the Forest Department, the Kenya Wildlife Service, the Kenya Forest Research Institute, and the National Museums of Kenya, among others. In addition, Kenya is notable in the region for the numerous NGOs engaged in environmental activities.

Despite this institutional infrastructure, Kenya has continued to experience natural resource degradation and increasing environmental destruction. Generally, the Government of Kenya has not shown deliberate efforts to institute and implement new and adequate policies and legislation, partly because of the absence of a strong and consistent civil service constituency to push for reforms (Juma, Torori, and Mwangi, 1995). The inadequacy of government efforts has also stemmed from the lack of institutional capacity to implement and monitor environmental policies, laws and programs. Implementing agencies have lacked institutional linkages, adequate infrastructure, human capital, and sufficient legal authority and political autonomy. The political will necessary to overcome short-term vested interests, which favor natural resource exploitation, in order to promote long-term sustainable development has not been realized.

A particularly salient manifestation of the political factors underlying natural resource management problems in Kenya has been the increasingly common phenomenon of land grabbing, defined as "the irregular allocation of public lands to well-connected individuals and companies" (Klopp, 1998). Much recent forest loss has resulted from government-approved, politically motivated, and dubiously legal excisions of forest land from protected areas and reserves and plantations. According to one analysis, land grabbing is the result of an increased use of land for political patronage in a context of increased electoral competition (Klopp, 1998). A Kenyan government official remarked, "If an election were held every year, there would be no forest left."[3]

The World Bank and Adjustment Lending

Since independence, the World Bank has played a significant role in Kenya's development, through project lending, and more recently, through structural adjustment. Kenya was the first country in Sub-Saharan Africa to receive a structural adjustment loan from the World Bank in 1980 (O'Brien and Ryan, 1999). The government adopted stabilization and structural adjustment programs financed by the World Bank and the IMF largely to enable the country to respond to economic instability resulting from such factors as the oil shock of 1973–74 (which generated trade imbalances) and the government's fiscal indiscipline. The structural reforms focused on reducing deficit spending,

limiting public borrowing from the banking sector, rationalizing public expenditure, removing price controls, and improving the performance of state corporations. Since 1986, Kenya has received additional structural and sectoral adjustment loans that have targeted the agriculture sector (liberalization of marketing systems and removal of import barriers), civil service reform or restructuring (with emphasis on rationalizing the operations of several ministries), privatization of selected public enterprises, and reform of the education and health sectors (with emphasis on the creation of cost-sharing arrangements).

Recent forest loss has resulted from government-approved, politically motivated, and dubiously legal excisions of forest land from protected areas and reserves and plantations.

The success of structural adjustment lending to Kenya has been mixed. In a number of sectors (e.g., privatization of public enterprises) some achievements have been made while in most areas reforms have not been fully instituted. A study by Gurushri Swamy (1994) assessing the success of the first adjustment program concludes that it was characterized by "a total lack of compliance, partly because of design and timing problems, but also because the commitment to the stated policy changes was limited to a small coterie of top civil servants. Trade reforms were not carried out, and grain marketing was not liberalized." Stabilization programs negotiated with the IMF were successful in removing exchange rate restrictions, and instituting tight fiscal policies in the mid-1980s (O'Brien and Ryan, 1999). However, fiscal indiscipline continued, resulting in high domestic borrowing, high interest rates, and inflation.

As described in a recent World Bank research report, Kenya's 18-year engagement with the international financial institutions through adjustment lending has been characterized by a "stop-go pattern" that repeats every few years (O'Brien and Ryan, 1999). During a "go" phase, the donor community provides support for government commitments to reform. After a few years, when donors have become dissatisfied with the government's failure to meet agreed conditions, a "stop" phase begins, resulting in delays in disbursements and a decline in new commitments. A particularly notable "stop" phase occurred in 1991, when at a meeting of Kenya's Consultative Group, the donors decided to suspend all adjustment lending pending progress on corruption and governance issues (O'Brien and Ryan, 1999).

The World Bank, Forestry, and Environment

While environment-specific considerations were not part of the World Bank's adjustment operations, attempts were made to address forestry and wildlife concerns in the agricultural sector reforms. However, lending to such environmental domains as wildlife and forestry has largely been on a project basis, some of which have been designed to stimulate certain policy reforms and strengthen natural resources management institutions. For example, World Bank intervention resulted in the transformation of the former Wildlife Conservation and Management Department, a public body, into the Kenya Wildlife Service, a government-owned corporation.

The World Bank has been involved in the Kenyan forest sector through almost 30 years of project lending. The forest policy reforms emphasized by the World Bank have largely focused on promoting efficiency in industrial forestry, for example, through enlarging industrial plantations and strengthening the capacity of forestry institutions. The World Bank has tended to promote institutional reforms that would relocate the management of industrial plantations from the Forest Department to the private domain. Its concern has been that the Forest Department lacks the ability to ensure efficient operational and financial management of the plantations (World Bank, 1990). According to Forest Department officials, the World Bank's approach to the forest sector was influenced by the structural adjustment programs underway at the time, and thus focused on privatization of public enterprises and reduced government expenditure (Mugabe and Krhoda, 1999). An additional objective of reform was to review and upgrade forest policies and legislation.

These concerns were integrated into the fourth Forestry Development Project, which the World Bank approved in 1991. Although the original project documentation and negotiations included a variety of conditions related to institutional and policy reforms, the failure of other donors to come through with promised cofinancing for other project components led to a more narrow focus on plantation development and maintenance. According to World Bank assessments, project objectives were compromised by the need for institutional and regulatory reforms for plantation management (in particular to allow the private sector and community groups a larger role), the need for enforcement of a clear policy on excisions of plantation lands, and the persistence of extremely low royalty rates charged for plantation timber (World Bank, 1998; Ganguly, 1998).

In addition to project-specific lending, the World Bank had also provided support for developing a broader environmental policy framework for Kenya. In 1994, the Government of Kenya formally adopted the National Environmental Action Plan (NEAP), which had been prepared with World Bank support (Republic of Kenya, 1993). The NEAP proposed a number of recommendations to integrate environmental concerns into overall

economic development planning, including a new institutional structure and the formulation of national environmental legislation. It also stressed the importance of improving forest protection and management—objectives which the Forest Department further elaborated in a Forestry Master Plan in 1994.

By late 1995, frustrated by the Government of Kenya's failure to follow through on environmental policy commitments, the World Bank decided to elevate the environmental policy dialogue above the sectoral level.[4] In February 1996, the Government of Kenya produced a Policy Framework Paper (PFP)—the result of negotiations with the World Bank and the IMF—which described a program of agreed economic reforms for 1996–1998 (Government of Kenya, 1996). At the suggestion of the World Bank, the Government of Kenya published and made public the PFP, which until then was a confidential document. The PFP asserted the government's concern for the state of indigenous forests and their biodiversity, and stated a commitment to implement the NEAP through a series of policy, institutional, and legislative reforms. According to participants in the negotiations, World Bank staff were responsible for the environmental content of the PFP, which was incorporated on a "no objection" basis by IMF officials.[5] Box 5.1 provides a summary of the PFP's environment-related content.

THE PROPOSED "ENVIRONMENTAL ADJUSTMENT" LOAN

At the same time that the 1996–1998 PFP was being formulated, the then Regional Director for East Africa and other Washington-based World Bank staff began

---

BOX 5.1 | **ENVIRONMENT-RELATED COMMITMENTS CONTAINED IN THE 1996–1998 POLICY FRAMEWORK PAPER**

- Present to parliament an environmental bill for enactment into law by September 1996;
- Present to parliament a Forestry Policy Paper by March 1996;
- Enact new forestry legislation by September 1996;
- Begin implementation of the recommendations of a Kenya Wildlife Service study on land use policy by June 1996;
- Establish a national Land Use Commission by December 1997; and
- Present to parliament a revised wildlife bill for enactment into legislation by December 1996.

floating the idea of an environmental adjustment loan within the World Bank, with Kenyan government officials, and with selected members of the international and Kenyan NGO communities. The World Bank presented the adjustment loan, the first and so far only one of its kind, as an instrument to leverage implementation of the environmental policy reform commitments articulated in the NEAP and the PFP. The adjustment operation would target reforms in such key sectors as forestry, wildlife, and land management, and would address various fiscal and economic policies that generate incentives for environmental destruction.

In early 1996, coincident with the publication of the PFP, World Bank officials met with Kenya's Ministry of Finance officials to discuss the environmental adjustment idea. In that discussion, World Bank staff emphasized the economic costs that Kenya was incurring by not instituting reforms in the forest sector specifically and the environmental area more generally.[6] It was anticipated that the credit would generate proceeds to reduce fiscal constraints, reduce reliance on domestic borrowing, and enable low-cost, long-term financing of identified government projects. An estimated US$90 million would be made available through this operation and would contribute to the government's efforts to address a budget deficit.

While the World Bank and the Ministry of Finance did not identify specific reforms to be targeted in the proposed operation in their initial discussions, they agreed upon a process to explore the feasibility and focus of an environmental adjustment program. Box 5.2 provides a chronology of related events and stakeholder involvement.

The Taskforce

In November 1996, following several months of negotiations with the World Bank, the Government of Kenya established an environmental adjustment taskforce under the leadership of the Ministry of Environment and Natural Resources (MENR) that included representatives of various ministries, NGOs, and the private sector. In light of the government's usual reluctance to involve stakeholders in the development of policy options (O'Brien and Ryan, 1999, p.32), the World Bank's success in encouraging broader membership on the taskforce is significant. The taskforce was mandated to accomplish the following: (a) review the extent to which various policies, laws, and institutional reforms recommended by the NEAP and the PFP had been or were being implemented; (b) identify and discuss specific environmental reforms that would be included in PFP 1999–2001; and (c) identify, discuss, and develop specific environmental reforms that could be addressed in the context of an environmental adjustment credit.

The taskforce held six meetings and organized one national workshop. World Bank staff members attended taskforce meetings as resource persons, while IMF staff did not participate in any of the deliberations of the taskforce. A large part of these meetings was spent on discussing general environmental issues and identifying gaps in the implementation of environmental reforms contained in the PFP rather than on the specific reform opportunities presented by inclusion of environment-related conditionalities in a structural adjustment operation. According to participating government officials, the work of the taskforce suffered from a lack of intellectual leadership from the MENR, as well as a

BOX 5.2

CHRONOLOGY OF EVENTS RELATED TO ENVIRONMENTAL ADJUSTMENT AND STAKEHOLDER INVOLVEMENT IN KENYA

	EVENTS AND STAKEHOLDER INVOLVEMENT
1993–1994	Preparation and adoption of NEAP, consultative process involving NGOs and the private sector. First funding from World Bank for a comprehensive environmental process/program in Kenya.
1994–1995	Preparation of draft environmental policy and legislation, initiation of policy and legal reform in wildlife and forest sectors. World Bank, Government of Kenya, and wide NGO consultations on the reforms.
1995	Preparation of PFP by the Government of Kenya, World Bank, and IMF with no NGO or private sector involvement, but in early 1996 PFP became a public document.
Feb 1996	World Bank officials meet with Ministry of Finance to discuss an environmental adjustment (EA) operation.
	Ministry officials receptive and agree on the need for a national task force on EA within the Ministry of Environment and Natural Resources (MENR).
May–Dec 1996	World Bank and MENR in discussions on EA taskforce modalities.
Nov 1996	ACTS and WWF host workshop on EA emphasizing the role of the NGO community in the EA development and implementation.
Dec 1996	EA Taskforce established and first meeting held.
Feb 1997	EA workshop for Government of Kenya, World Bank, NGOs, and the private sector.
April–July 97	Two meetings of EA taskforce held; draft Terms of Reference for EA Credit Identification. Mission planned for August-September 1997 discussed.
July 1997	Government of Kenya - IMF negotiations collapse.
August 1997	EA Identification Mission cancelled; consultations on Country Assistance Strategy (CAS) underway.
January 1998	World Bank terminates Fourth Forestry Development Project.
September 1998	CAS focused on governance presented to World Bank's board.

The proposed environmental adjustment package was envisioned to encompass a significant institutional reform component, as well as engagement of the land issue, one of the most politically sensitive in Kenyan politics.

lack of clear and consistent guidance from the World Bank (Mugabe and Krhoda, 1999).

However, the Washington-based World Bank task manager did prepare a draft concept paper on environmental adjustment that was discussed by the taskforce at its June 1997 meeting. According to the document, an adjustment credit would support the efforts of the government to stabilize Kenya's long-term growth prospects by implementing fiscal, institutional, policy, and legal reforms which would ensure the sustainable use of its natural resources and to put in place regulatory mechanisms which would limit future environmental costs"(World Bank, n.d.). Specific reforms to be targeted by the adjustment operation, which would be measurable or easily identifiable, had been discussed by some members of the taskforce and World Bank officials. These included the following:

- Institutional and legal reforms—particularly those aimed at strengthening national institutions to enforce environmental standards, carry out environmental impact assessment, and enforce environmental legislation. In addition, the adjustment operation would provide leverage for restructuring of the MENR, rationalize the operations of the Forest Department, and establish a more

effective institutional structure to manage Kenya's indigenous forests.

- Land reforms—particularly the establishment of an independent Land Commission to formulate new policy and prepare a national lands bill. Several World Bank officials were keen to use EA to leverage land reforms through the commission process. The beginning point would have been PFP 1996–98 in which the Government of Kenya committed itself to establishing the commission.

- Economic and fiscal reforms to increase incentives for environmentally sound land use practices, and to increase the use of clean technologies by industry.

Thus, in addition to more traditional efficiency-oriented reforms typical of adjustment programs, the proposed environmental adjustment package was envisioned to encompass a significant institutional reform component, as well as engagement of the land issue, one of the most politically sensitive in Kenyan politics.[7] Proponents of the reform agenda inside and outside the World Bank were concerned about how the adjustment instrument could be adapted to leverage meaningful progress toward such long-term, institutionally complex goals. At the time of the June taskforce meeting, it was expected that a World Bank Identification Mission scheduled for August 25 to September 12, 1997, would explore those issues in more detail.

Government Ownership

World Bank staff report that Ministry of Finance officials were quite receptive to the idea of an environmental adjustment operation when it was first mooted in early 1996.[8] Indeed, Ministry of Finance officials reportedly themselves suggested to World Bank staff that such a vehicle could be used to address the difficult issues of land and water rights. Despite this well-placed constituency for environmental reforms in the ministry usually responsible for dealing with the World Bank on adjustment issues, government officials decided that an environment-oriented initiative must be led by the responsible line agency, and assigned leadership of the EA task force to the Ministry of Environment and Natural Resources.

At first, World Bank staff thought that MENR leadership could be workable, believing that there was a sufficiently broad-based government commitment to implementing the PFP reforms.[9] However, having a taskforce charged with designing an adjustment operation chaired by a line agency proved confusing and contentious. Although the MENR would have the responsibility for defining environmental adjustment, budget control and funds would remain in the hands of the Ministry of Finance. Some line agency officials suspected that the Ministry of Finance was using the MENR to mobilize non-environmental funds. This became a particularly sensitive point as it became clear over the course of 1997 that the World Bank was not willing to move forward with additional phases of project lending to support the forest sector and NEAP activities in the absence of significant institutional reforms. From interviews conducted for this study, it is clear that government officials did not understand the linkage between the World Bank's dissatisfaction with the pace of reform in the forest sector and its promotion of an environmental adjustment loan.[10]

The uncertainty of the MENR with respect to its EA mandate was evidenced at the first taskforce meeting, at which the Permanent Secretary had difficulty in interpreting the taskforce Terms of Reference. The Ministry was also resistant to efforts at assessing the extent to which the Government of Kenya was implementing environmental reforms in the PFP.[11] The taskforce prepared an assessment, which demonstrated that most of the reforms in PFP had not been implemented, meaning that the Government of Kenya had defaulted on many of the commitments it had made to the World Bank, the IMF, and the Kenyan people.

In addition to the MENR, several other government departments and ministries were involved in the taskforce discussions: the Ministry of Lands and Settlement, the Office of the President, the Ministry of Planning and National Development, the Forest Department, the Kenya Wildlife Service (KWS), the National Museums of Kenya, the Ministry of Water Resources, the National Environment Secretariat (NES), and the Secretariat of the NEAP, among others. Many of these agencies were largely interested in environmental adjustment as a vehicle for financing environment-related projects, and did not understand the distinction between project-specific and structural adjustment loans.[12] Many representatives of the ministries and departments did not fully understand that the purpose of an environmental adjustment operation was to leverage structural reforms. As a result, progressive elements within the bureaucracy that might have supported the proposed reforms were not mobilized as a constituency. Some Forest Department officials, who wanted to prevent forest excisions approved by other government agencies, did not understand that the proposed reforms would have strengthened the department's legal autonomy and authority, and their ability to block such forest conversions.

To the extent that they did understand the adjustment operation's potential to leverage policy reform, it was evident that most line ministries did not want the adjustment to cover those reforms that would undermine their own influence and tenure. Within the Forest Department, a significant constituency was opposed to reform, because it would have removed rent-seeking opportunities. Similarly, officials from the Ministry of Lands and Settlement were opposed to preparing and adopting a new land policy and legislation, which would likely relocate certain authorities and responsibilities away from the Ministry and its Commissioner of Lands.

Internal bureaucratic battles among environmental agencies also undermined government leadership of the environmental adjustment process. Some MENR officials wanted EA activities to be administered by NES, which served as the policy department of the MENR. Higher level officials, including the Permanent Secretary and his Deputy, were assigning administrative functions associated with the EA taskforce to the NEAP Secretariat, which had better infrastructure and political connections. At one taskforce meeting, the Deputy Permanent Secretary stated that the MENR saw Environmental Adjustment (EA) as a process that would enable the government to provide funds for the NEAP's implementation. Though the NEAP process was quickly losing credibility within the World Bank's circles, it still enjoyed the government's trust.

World Bank Ownership

Within the World Bank, the initial proponent of an environmental adjustment loan for Kenya was the Washington-based Regional Director. Several members of the Kenya country team, including environment specialists based in Washington and Nairobi, as well as several officials in the World Bank's central Environment Department, were also supportive of the idea. Soon after discussions had been initiated with the Government of Kenya, however, an internal reorganization at the World Bank resulted in a country director being assigned to Kenya (replacing the role of the previous regional director), and the country director position was moved to Nairobi. Other staffing changes included the relocation of one of the environment specialists from Nairobi to Washington, turnover in the Country Economist position, and the appointment of a new NGO liaison in the Nairobi office.[13]

In February 1997, several Kenyan NGO representatives met with the new World Bank country director in Nairobi in an attempt to gain his support for the environmental adjustment process. According to participants in the meeting, the new director expressed skepticism about the proposed environmental adjustment operation. He indicated that he did not believe that there was adequate data and analysis to demonstrate to politicians the economic costs of environmental degradation and the benefits of reform, and challenged the NGOs to provide such analysis. He did not see environmental issues as a priority for the Government of Kenya; the World Bank's priority agenda with the government was economic governance issues, especially corruption (Mugabe and Krhoda, 1999).

Other World Bank staff members based in Nairobi were similarly disinclined to invest in supporting the environmental adjustment process. Many were new and not in a position to effectively sell the idea. By mid-1997, Nairobi-based World Bank staff, in particular the new NGO liaison, were investing heavily in a participatory process to develop a new Country Assistance Strategy, which was not integrated with the ongoing environmental adjustment discussions.[14] Thus, only when the Washington-based task manager was in Nairobi did the World Bank take a high profile in environmental adjustment-related discussions.

THE PROCESS STALLS

In July 1997, negotiations between the Government of Kenya and the IMF collapsed, resulting in the suspension of the Enhanced Structural Adjustment Facility (ESAF), which had provided the framework for the World Bank's environmental adjustment discussions. Without such a framework in place, there was no scope for World Bank adjustment lending of any kind. As a consequence, the environmental adjustment Identification Mission scheduled to begin in late August was canceled, never to be rescheduled.

The suspension of ESAF ended the environmental adjustment discussions, although the process might not have moved forward even without such a disruption. By mid-1997, the taskforce had failed to generate a critical mass of support for the idea. At the same time, the prospects for government leadership emerging had diminished with the approach of an election later that year. Taskforce participants remarked that senior civil servants at MENR were not prepared to make any long-term commitments mainly

because of the uncertainty associated with their own positions in government. Moreover, they faced difficulties in getting cabinet approval for many policy matters as the ministers were retreating to their political constituencies and focusing little attention on their ministerial responsibilities.

The question thus arises as to the wisdom of the World Bank's initiating a dialogue on environmental adjustment in the first place, and subsequently disengaging after the ESAF collapse in mid-1997. In interviews conducted for this case study, various perspectives emerged. In one view, given the government's manifest lack of commitment to address issues of natural resource ownership and access—as evidenced by its failure to implement related reforms contained in the PFP—it was a mistake to pilot the environmental adjustment idea in Kenya.[15] In another view, it was appropriate for the World Bank to give the government an opportunity to demonstrate its credibility—and use its leverage to invite other stakeholders into the dialogue—and equally appropriate for the World Bank to walk away from the process when no such credibility emerged.[16] A third view is that the ESAF collapse precipitously ended the environmental adjustment discussions prior to an Identification Mission—too early in the process to judge where those discussions might have led.[17]

There is evidence to support each of these perspectives, although the initial support for the concept of environmental adjustment from the Ministry of Finance and enthusiasm from elements of the NGO community imply that the World Bank's initiation of these discussions was worth a try. However, events later in 1997 and early 1998 further called into question the government's and the World Bank's ownership of the environmental policy reform agenda.

In the run-up to the elections, land grabbing intensified, leading to the loss of some 26,000 hectares of plantation forest.[18] In early 1998, the World Bank finally closed its Fourth (and final) Forestry Development Project with an unexpended balance, after it had become clear that the Forest Department had no intention of implementing the institutional reforms that had been agreed to in the context of that project. Forest Department officials were surprised by the World Bank's willingness to disengage from the forest sector.

Yet there is no evidence that the World Bank's senior managers took the opportunity—at the close of almost three decades of project lending—to communicate to high-level Kenyan officials why the institution was terminating lending in the sector. A year later, the World Bank's voice was conspicuously absent when leaders of other international institutions spoke out against a blatant appropriation of public forest land in the Karura Forest in Nairobi and a related attack on peaceful demonstrators. Observers inside and outside the World Bank concluded that World Bank senior managers were unwilling to risk the institution's relationship with the Government of Kenya over forest and land issues.

Given the collapse of ESAF, another interesting question is how the World Bank pursued its environmental policy reform agenda in Kenya in the absence of an adjustment instrument. As mentioned above, at the same time the environmental adjustment discussions were terminated in mid-1997, the World Bank was embarking on an unusually participatory process to develop a new

There is no evidence that the World Bank's senior managers took the opportunity—at the close of almost three decades of project lending—to communicate to high-level Kenyan officials why the institution was terminating lending in the sector.

Country Assistance Strategy (CAS). In July-August 1997, and again in December, the World Bank held consultations with a range of stakeholder groups (World Bank, 1998). Several NGO representatives who participated in the CAS process tried to introduce specific environmental issues, especially de-gazettement of forests and associated land grabbing, in the context of broader governance concerns, around which CAS discussions centered.

The resulting CAS, which was presented to the World Bank's board in September 1998, focused almost exclusively on poor governance as "the central development challenge in Kenya," and did not elaborate strategies in any specific sectors (World Bank, 1998). In particular, the CAS does not mention environmental or natural resources issues, other than to rank environment as a low priority for the country and the World Bank, even though the World Bank's curtailment of lending in the forest sector earlier in the year could be seen as the leading edge of its new intolerance for corruption and lack of progress on reform (World Bank, 1998).

While EA discussions between the World Bank and government officials made explicit the link between environmental problems and poor governance—and indeed, accounted for the EA's proposed focus on institutional and legal reforms related to the allocation of land and other resources—the CAS did not make the reciprocal linkage.[19] In addition, the environment sector's low priority in the CAS, especially in the context of an overall reduction in lending, translated into a lack of support and incentives for World Bank staff to continue analysis and consultation related to environmental policy reform.

THE ROLES OF OTHER STAKEHOLDERS

Nongovernmental Organizations

Domestic and international NGOs both played roles in defining and promoting the concept of environmental adjustment in Kenya. According to World Bank officials, one of the reasons Kenya was chosen as the country in which to initiate environmental adjustment discussions was that a relatively large and mature NGO community could be expected to serve as a constituency for environmental policy reform. Indeed, a World Bank official reported that he would not have pursued the environmental adjustment idea if several Kenyan NGO leaders had not given their explicit encouragement.[20]

Early on, World Bank proponents of environmental adjustment floated the concept to NGOs, including the African Centre for Technology Studies (ACTS) in Nairobi and the World Wildlife Fund (WWF) in Washington. In 1996, these two organizations facilitated an NGO dialogue among organizations in Nairobi and Washington parallel to the World Bank's discussions with the Government of Kenya, and monitored

World Bank-Government of Kenya discussions. The two organizations hosted a workshop in Nairobi in November 1996, that was attended by representatives of domestic and international NGOs.[21] Following these discussions, ACTS published a paper that assessed the potential of environmental adjustment from an NGO perspective (Mugabe et al., 1997).

The following month, the government invited several NGOs to participate in the EA taskforce. The inclusion of NGO representatives on the taskforce was at the recommendation and insistence of the World Bank. In their negotiations with the government, World Bank officials had called for an open and transparent process that would draw from civil society, consistent with the World Bank's new emphasis on working with NGOs and creating opportunities for their participation in World Bank-supported policy processes.

Several factors constrained the effective participation of NGOs in the EA process. First, for many NGOs, the World Bank lacked credibility as an agent of environmental policy reform. Kenyan NGOs observed that the World Bank had been engaged in a long series of environmental policy processes, in particular the NEAP, without ensuring follow through on implementation. One NGO representative maintained that the World Bank was not the best agency to promote environmental adjustment in Kenya because of its contribution to environmental degradation in many parts of the world, in addition to its poor record in promoting environmental reforms in Kenya. The adjustment label was also problematic, because in Kenya, as elsewhere, NGOs associate the World Bank's structural adjustment programs with social hardship, erosion of institutional capacity, and infringement on national sovereignty. Thus, while many NGOs agreed with the stated objectives of the proposed environmental adjustment program, they were hesitant to openly support the World Bank. In the words of one NGO participant, the EA process and the associated taskforce were "perceived as too much of a 'bank thing' to really get involved in."[22]

Second, few of the NGOs were sufficiently fluent in economic analysis, engaged with relevant policy arenas, including the World Bank, or broad-gauged enough to play strategic roles in shaping the proposed environmental adjustment operation. Similar to their counterparts in government, many NGOs assumed that the adjustment operation would finance government line agencies to undertake environmental projects. Few were familiar with the PFP, even after it became a public document. Although the World Bank informally circulated a study on the economics of environmental degradation to a few NGOs on the taskforce, the study was not available early enough in the process to empower their participation in taskforce discussions with rigorous analysis. One NGO leader observed that partly because of fatigue at government inaction on environmental policy, the NGO community did not adequately invest in exploring the potential ramifications of EA.[23]

The NGO community was also insufficiently organized to exercise influence. For those NGOs who did see the potential for adjustment to address their policy reform interests, they tended to focus on only one subsector. The Kenya Forest Working Group (KFWG) mainly concentrated on how EA could be used to get the government to stop illegal degazettement of forests. Similarly, the Kenya Pastoralists' Forum focused on land reforms and the reallocation of wildlife user rights to pastoralists. As a result, despite the World Bank's efforts to include NGOs in environmental adjustment-related discussions, NGO participation did not translate into a constituency sufficiently strong to overcome the lack of government ownership of the reform agenda.[24]

The Private Sector and Other Donors

The private sector's involvement in discussions on environmental adjustment in Kenya was limited. While the taskforce had a representative of the Kenya Association of Manufacturers (KAM), the representative's participation was minimal. He saw EA as a tool to help restructure the industrial forest management regime, particularly by enlarging the role of the private sector. The sector's main interest was to ensure the privatization of commercial plantations in order to reduce costs associated with government licensing, and to destroy the monopolies of a few politically connected firms. However, these considerations were rarely debated in the taskforce. Many MENR officials, particularly the then Permanent Secretary and Deputy Permanent Secretary, considered such issues to be outside the taskforce's mandate, and argued that the issues were being handled within the context of World Bank forest sector project lending by a study on forest institutions.

Discussions of environmental adjustment were largely confined to the World Bank and the Kenyan government, and the many bilateral and multilateral donors operating in the country were not brought into the process. One official from a bilateral donor agency remarked: "We had heard about the World Bank discussing with Kenya some form of structural adjustment for the environment at our donors' meeting briefly attended by one staff from Washington and the Permanent Secretary of Environment. It was World Bank and Government of Kenya business. Our input was not sought."[25] According to World Bank officials, it would have been premature to start involving other donors prior to the World Bank and the government more fully defining the proposed program.[26] However, the effectiveness of a coordinated effort among donors to suspend adjustment lending pending governance reforms in 1991 suggests that having donor involvement in the environmental adjustment agenda might have been important if EA discussions with the government had moved forward.

THE BOTTOM LINE

The failure of the World Bank and proponents of environmental policy reform in Kenya to realize an environmental adjustment program stems from many factors. First and foremost was the lack of a critical mass of support or a strong champion within the Kenyan government. While agreeing that in retrospect, borrower ownership was clearly lacking, a World Bank staffer remarked that when the process was initiated in 1996, "we were all fooled" by the government's stated commitments to reform.[27]

It proved a strategic mistake to accept the government's decision to select line ministry officials—who were used to relating to the World Bank in the context of project lending—as leaders of the environmental adjustment taskforce, rather than cultivating leadership from Ministry of Finance officials who understood the potential benefits of

reform to the Kenyan economy. Many government officials who participated in taskforce discussions did not understand the concept of environmental adjustment. Moreover, there was insufficient capacity within the government to undertake its own analysis to guide discussions with the World Bank. Some line agency officials felt betrayed by the World Bank's unwillingness to continue supporting the forest sector and the NEAP secretariat, and therefore did not support environmental adjustment. In an internal memo in 1996, a World Bank forestry specialist cited the proposed environmental adjustment loan as "an ideal vehicle to re-start the dialogue on forest sector policy and institutional reform, in a context where the Office of the President and other lead political agencies in Kenya can be directly engaged in the process" (Douglas, 1996). Because such lead political agencies were not sufficiently involved in the process that took place, the potential of environmental adjustment to leverage forest policy reform in Kenya was not adequately tested.

To a degree unusual in the context of designing a structural adjustment operation, the World Bank did attempt to open up the process to NGOs and other nongovernment stakeholders, by encouraging the government to publish the PFP and include NGOs on the environmental adjustment taskforce. However, the low credibility of the World Bank and the adjustment instrument in the eyes of NGOs, as well as the NGO community's lack of sophistication and coordination, meant that NGO participation did not translate into a significant constituency for environmental adjustment.

The lack of ownership by the World Bank, particularly in the Nairobi office, precluded the possibility of increased World Bank engagement leveraging more intense and higher-level in-country support. It is difficult-to assess whether more active World Bank engagement of government officials, NGOs, the private sector, or other donors early on might have made a difference in constituency-building leading to more borrower ownership. More widely-available analytical work making a compelling case for environmental policy reform through structural adjustment lending—including its efficiency, equity, and governance dimensions—would certainly have been helpful.

Another factor influencing World Bank and borrower ownership was unfortunate timing. Within the World Bank, a reorganization moved supporters of environmental adjustment out of key positions, while the election cycle distracted senior Kenyan civil servants. Although initiated during one of the periodic "go" phases of the World Bank's relationship to the Kenyan government, the onset of a "stop" phase began before the World Bank could undertake an Identification Mission. In any event, the unexpected collapse of ESAF in mid-1997 precluded the possibility of an adjustment operation of any kind.

Following the ESAF collapse, it would appear that the World Bank missed an opportunity to continue to focus attention on needed environmental policy reforms in the context of the participatory Country Assistance Strategy (CAS) process. In particular, the World Bank could have used the CAS process to highlight the relationships between poor governance, land grabbing, and social and environmental impoverishment. The CAS's ultimate focus on governance issues was as, or more, appropriate for the forest sector as for other sectors, especially in light of the World Bank's decision to terminate lending to the sector. Some observers interpreted the World Bank's failure to raise forest and broader land issues with government officials at the highest levels as a lack of seriousness about both forestry and governance issues.

Finally, with the end of project lending in the forest sector and a CAS conditioning further lending on governance reforms, World Bank staff were not able to continue work on environmental governance issues in the absence of sectoral projects or a prospective adjustment operation. This illuminates the institution's difficulty in unbundling lending from policy analysis and stakeholder engagement.

In sum, the World Bank's attempt to initiate the first environmental adjustment loan failed to result in a policy reform program in Kenya because of a lack of World Bank and borrower ownership, unfortunate timing, and insufficient linkage of forestry and governance issues. However, the idea of utilizing adjustment lending to promote environmental policy reform remains intriguing as a vehicle for mainstreaming environmental issues into what is currently the World Bank's most significant lending instrument. The Kenya experience, while not a success, has not discredited the concept of environmental adjustment, and the World Bank may promote the idea elsewhere in East Africa.

REFERENCES

Bragdon, S. 1990. *Kenya's Legal and Institutional Structure for Environmental Protection and Natural Resources Management: An Analysis and Agenda for the Future.* Washington D.C.: Economic Development Institute, The World Bank.

Douglas, Jim. 1996. "Kenya: Forestry Development Project." Washington D.C.: The World Bank. Internal World Bank Memo.

Ganguly, Sushma. 1996. "Letter to Permanent Secretary Ambuka Regarding Kenya Forestry Development Project (CR.2198-KE), Mid-Term Review Mission." Washington D.C.: The World Bank.

Government of Kenya. 1996. "Economic Reforms for 1996–1998: The Policy Framework Paper." Nairobi: Government Printer.

Juma, C., Torori, C. and Mwangi, A. 1995. "Institutional Capacity for Natural Resources Management in Kenya." Report Submitted to the United States Agency for International Development (USAID). Washington D.C.: USAID.

Juma, C. and Ojwang, J.B. eds. 1996. *In Land We Trust: Environment, Private Property and Constitutional Change.* Nairobi: African Centre for Technology Studies Press.

Kahl, Colin H. 1998. "Population Growth, Environmental Degradation, and State-Sponsored Violence: The Case of Kenya, 1991–93." *International Security* Vol. 23, No. 2 (Fall 1998): pp.80–119.

Klopp, Jacqueline M. 1998. "The Politics of Land Grabbing in Kenya." Paper prepared for delivery at the 1998 Annual Meeting of the American Political Science Association, in Boston, MA.

Marekia, N. 1991. "Managing Wildlife in Kenya." In *Gaining Ground*, edited by A. Kiriro and C. Juma. Nairobi: African Centre for Technology Studies Press.

Mugabe, J., Seymour, F. and Clark, N. 1997. *Environmental Adjustment in Kenya: Emerging Opportunities and Challenges.* Nairobi: African Centre for Technology Studies Press.

Mugabe, John and George Krhoda. "The Politics of Public Policy Reform in Kenya: The Case of Environmental Adjustment." Nairobi, Kenya. Mimeo.

O'Brien, F.S. and T.C.I. Ryan. 1999. *Aid and Reform in Africa: Kenya Case Study.* Washington, D.C.: The World Bank. Available at: www.worldbank.org /research/aid/africa/papers.html

Republic of Kenya. 1965. "African Socialism and its Application to Planning in Kenya." Sessional Paper No. 10 of 1965. Nairobi: Government Printer.

—1971. "National Report on the Human Environment." Nairobi: Government Printer.

—1993. "National Environment Action Plan (NEAP)." Report E0092. Nairobi: Government Printer.

Swamy, G. 1994. "Kenya: parchy, intermittent commitment." In *Adjustment in Africa: Lessons from Country Case Studies*, edited by Husain, I. et al. Washington D.C.: The World Bank.

World Bank, The. 1990. *Kenya: Forestry Development Project*. Staff Appraisal Report No. 9005-KE. Washington, D.C.: The World Bank.

—1998. "Project Completion Report: Fourth Forestry Development Project." Washington, D.C.: The World Bank.

—(no date.) "Draft Concept Paper on Kenya Environmental Adjustment Credit." Paper prepared by the World Bank and discussed by the EA Taskforce at its meeting June 18, 1998.

—1998. "Kenya: Country Assistance Strategy: Improving Economic Governance for Sustainable Development." Washington, D.C.: The World Bank.

NOTES

1. This chapter draws on "The Politics of Public Policy Reform in Kenya: The Case of Environmental Adjustment," by John Mugabe and George Krhoda, which is available at http://www.wri.org/wri/governance/iffeforest.html as well as interviews conducted by the authors in Nairobi and Washington, D.C. on a not-for-attribution basis. This chapter also draws on "Case Study #3: Environmental Adjustment in Kenya" by Frances J. Seymour and Karyn Fox, draft paper circulated at WWF workshop on Mainstreaming Biodiversity into Country and Sector Development Strategies, September 1996.

   Both authors were participants in some of the events described in this chapter. John Mugabe serves as Director of ACTS and was a member of the Inter-ministerial Taskforce on Environmental Reforms. As Director of Development Assistance Policy at World Wildlife Fund, Frances J. Seymour participated in meetings with World Bank officials and representatives of U.S. and Kenyan NGOs to discuss the proposed environmental adjustment operation during 1996.

2. Personal communication with World Bank official, September 1999; and Ganguly (1998).

3. Not-for-attribution interview with Kenyan government official, December 1998.

4. Not-for-attribution interview with World Bank officials, March 1999.

5. Not-for-attribution interview with World Bank officials, March 1999.

6. Not-for-attribution interview with World Bank officials, March 1999.

7. One Kenyan government official in Nairobi remarked that the proposed Land Commission "impinges on every big boy in this town." (Not-for-attribution interview with Kenyan government official, December 1998.)

8. Not-for-attribution interview with World Bank officials, March 1999.

9. Not-for-attribution interview with World Bank officials, March 1999.

10. Not-for-attribution interview with Government of Kenya officials, December 1999.

11. Some MENR officials claimed that it was too early to review the 1996–98 PFP and that the Presidential Economic Commission, which was responsible for overseeing implementation of the PFP, should provide consent to any process to review the PFP. However, after several informal meetings between some NGO representatives and the then Permanent Secretary of the MENR, he became convinced of the potential usefulness of the 1996–98 PFP review in the context of the environmental adjustment process.

12. Not-for-attribution interviews with Government of Kenya officials, December 1998.

13. Not-for-attribution interviews with World Bank officials, March 1999.

14. Not-for-attribution interviews with World Bank official, December 1999.

15. Personal communication with Peter Veit, November 1999.

16. Not-for-attribution interview with World Bank official, November 1999.

17. Personal communication with World Bank official, September 1999.

18. Personal communication with World Bank official, September 1999.

19. Jacqueline Klopp stresses the need for the donor community "to censure all forms of corruption, including those that most immediately affect the majority of Kenyans." (Klopp, 1998)

20. Personal communication with World Bank official, September 1999.

21. Participants included representatives from such agencies as World Neighbors, East African Wildlife Society, Kenya Forest Working Group, the Kenya Energy and Environment Organizations (KENGO), the African Wildlife Foundation, Greenbelt Movement, Earth Council, Kenya Pastoralists' Forum, the World Resources Institute, World Conservation Union (IUCN), and Action-Aid Kenya.

22. Personal communication with NGO activist, January 2000.

23. Personal communication with NGO activist, January 2000.

24. Personal communication with NGO activist, January 2000.

25. Not-for-attribution interview with bilateral donor official, February 1999.

26. Not-for-attribution interview with World Bank officials, March 1999.

27. Personal communication with World Bank official, September 1999.

6

CONCLUSION

The cases in this report demonstrate that under the right conditions, the World Bank has been able to effect key forest policy changes in the context of adjustment lending, tipping the scales in favor of reformist elements and against vested interests. Under the wrong conditions, the World Bank's efforts have been met with frustration for both the World Bank and the borrower, and a stalemate in the reform agenda.

In Papua New Guinea, progressive forces in the government bureaucracy and their allies in the World Bank were successful in using adjustment lending to consolidate policies that reined in rampant logging, and for several years prevented attempts by vested interests to roll back those reforms. Experience in the Philippines provides another example of the use of adjustment lending by reformist elements to shift domestic politics toward forest policy reform. *(See Box 1.3)*. In Indonesia, the World Bank and the IMF took advantage of the 1997 financial crisis to shine a spotlight on governance issues in the forest sector and to force the dismantling of forest product monopolies.

Those examples of limited success are also counterbalanced by significant failures and omissions. In Indonesia and Cameroon, the World Bank has so far been unable to transform government commitments into meaningful change in concession allocation and management systems. None of the cases provide evidence of the effective promotion of reforms focused primarily on equity or environmental objectives. In Kenya, an

Under the right conditions, the World Bank has been able to effect key forest policy changes in the context of adjustment lending, tipping the scales in favor of reformist elements and against vested interests.

attempt to promote a more broadly conceived environmental adjustment program never even reached the point of an identification mission, much less a lending operation. Experience in the Solomon Islands in the early 1990s provides further evidence of the limits of the World Bank's leverage over forest policy in the context of structural adjustment. *(See Box 2.1.)*

The case studies thus raise a number of questions regarding where, when, and how the World Bank should attempt to promote forest policy reform through adjustment lending. Under what conditions is conditionality effective? How important is ownership by the borrower and the World Bank? What can the World Bank do to build and sustain coalitions for change? The remainder of this chapter will summarize the insights on these under-what-conditions questions provided by the case studies, and their implications for the World Bank.

TWISTING ARMS AND TIPPING SCALES

The recent literature on adjustment lending stresses the dominance of domestic political factors in determining policy outcomes in borrower countries. Quantitative studies of factors influencing the success or failure of adjustment programs have concluded that variables under the control of external actors, including the level of effort expended by the World Bank, are not significant (World Bank, 1998). Similarly, a previous study of World Bank conditionality and forest policy reform concluded that as long as the balance of domestic political forces favored logging interests, there was nothing the World Bank could do to stimulate reform (Ross, 1996).

Indeed, the poor record of the World Bank's "arm twisting" style of attempting to leverage policy reform through conditionality is leading to a new conventional wisdom based on the principle of selectivity. According to this school of thought, captured in the World Bank's *Assessing Aid*, since donors cannot "buy" commitment to reform through policy-based lending, such lending should be targeted only at those governments already

demonstrably committed to the "right" policy frameworks (World Bank, 1998). This prescription rests on five conclusions: that there is one readily discernible right policy framework and that the World Bank knows what it is; that conditionality cannot be effective without borrower ownership; that it is straightforward to distinguish between clients that do and do not have the necessary commitment; that the World Bank's own ownership of the reform agenda is not a significant variable; and that the World Bank cannot generate borrower ownership where it is lacking.

The case study experience described in this report challenges each of these conclusions. The remainder of this section summarizes the nuances added by the case studies to current thinking about conditionality, World Bank ownership, and borrower ownership. The following section will also discuss the process of determining the right policy framework and building coalitions for change.

Conditionality and Policy Change

In Papua New Guinea, the World Bank's willingness to hold the line on the concession allocation system forced a new government backed by logging interests to reluctantly back down from letting those interests reassert control over the forest sector. In this case, World Bank staff worked closely with reformist elements inside the government to design appropriate conditionality. Even though the policy regime proved fragile over the long term, the World Bank's exercise of conditionality bought time against what would have been the irreversible impacts of a major unleashing of uncontrolled logging activity. The Suriname case, described in Box

1.2, also highlights the importance of sustained international intervention to buy time for domestic reform.

Can forest policy conditionality be effective without such borrower ownership? In Indonesia, the World Bank in cooperation with the IMF employed conditionality at a strategic moment to stimulate key changes in forest policy, even when the borrower's commitment to those reforms was far from certain. The inclusion of forestry issues in Indonesia's January 1998, bail-out package rocketed those issues to the first tier of good governance challenges on the national agenda, something that previous World Bank projects and a year of unprecedented forest fires had failed to do. After some foot-dragging, agreed reforms resulted in non-trivial power shifts within and among the timber industry and related government agencies.

Why might conditionality be more effective in the context of adjustment lending, when conditions attached to forest projects have consistently proven ineffective? The case studies suggest two reasons. First, the mere inclusion of forest-related conditions in an adjustment loan raises the conditions' profile from dialogue with sectoral agencies to a national priority on the agenda of more powerful ministries of finance and planning. In Indonesia, increases in stumpage fees pro-

moted under forest sector projects were only achieved after being included in the World Bank's policy dialogue with the Ministries of Finance and Planning. In the Philippines, the SECAL had the effect of raising forestry issues above the level of the Department of Environment and Natural Resources. *(See Box 1.3.)*

Second, at the sectoral level, World Bank project loans face competition from bilateral projects funded by grants. In Indonesia, the explicit reason for discontinuing cooperation with the World Bank in the forest sector in 1995 was the availability of less costly finance for project activities. In adjustment lending, however, the World Bank has no competitors,[1] so the price paid by borrower governments for rejecting conditions is higher.[2] It is significant that the governments of Papua New Guinea, Cameroon, and Indonesia were all experiencing economic crises at the time that they agreed to the World Bank's forest-related conditions for new lending.

Conditionality and Implementation

In Kenya, the World Bank was driven to propose an environmental adjustment operation precisely because the government had consistently failed to follow environmental policy reform commitments with implementation. However, the case study experience demonstrates that adjustment conditionality is not an effective instrument for leveraging policy changes that depend on reform of the institutions responsible for implementing those changes. While the World Bank's principal interlocutors in structural adjustment lending—ministries of finance and planning—are often able and willing to implement policy changes in tax rates and other reforms

---

The mere inclusion of forest-related conditions in an adjustment loan raises the conditions' profile from dialogue with sectoral agencies to a national priority.

---

amenable to the stroke of a pen, ministries of forestry are much less amenable to reforming themselves.

In every case study country, the World Bank singled out the lack of institutional capacity as the principal impediment to long-term, sustainable forest management.

This finding is quite significant, since in every case study country, the World Bank singled out the lack of institutional capacity as the principal impediment to long-term, sustainable forest management. In Indonesia, *follow-through* on commitments to implement auctions and performance bonds was undermined by the lack of a system to measure and monitor performance, as well as by the lack of political will within the relevant ministry. In Cameroon, World Bank staff intentionally designed new regulatory and fiscal regimes for the forest sector so as to require the least capacity on the part of the government, in particular, removing opportunities to exercise discretion and, therefore, corruption.

Adjustment lending is poorly suited to supporting implementation and institutional reform because of its short timeframe, limited to the disbursement period of one to two years. In Indonesia, Papua New Guinea, and Cameroon, the World Bank envisioned following up on policy changes leveraged through adjustment lending with sectoral loans (Indonesia) or specific projects (Papua New Guinea and Cameroon) designed in part

to address institutional capacity issues. Experience in those countries demonstrated that project lending to improve forest management undertaken prior to the kinds of reforms promoted through adjustment lending was ineffective. There is not yet a record of experience to judge whether or not a reversal of the sequence will enjoy greater success.

Design of Conditionality

The case study experience illuminates a lively debate about the kinds of conditions that are most effective in promoting reform. In both Cameroon and Indonesia, the government was able to evade the spirit of the World Bank's conditionality while complying with its letter. According to some officials in borrower governments, forest policy conditions should focus more on desired outcomes than on specific measures. Even reformist officials sometimes resent the World Bank's micromanagement, and several interviewed for this study expressed a preference for being empowered to achieve an objective without having their hands tied to specific means. At the same time, World Bank officials with significant experience in adjustment lending expressed strong skepticism that such an approach would be effective.[3]

In Indonesia, academics and activists interested in forest policy reform felt that an important function of World Bank-imposed conditionality would be to require transparency and public participation in the reform process itself, to open up forest policymaking. By insisting on publication of draft regulations and legislation and consultation with domestic stakeholders, the World Bank was able to increase its perceived legitimacy and credibility in the eyes of key constituencies for change outside of government. Similarly, observers of recent developments in Cameroon and Cambodia stress the significance of independent forest monitors required by World Bank conditionality.

The proper sequencing of reforms is also a critical challenge in the design of conditionality. The 1998 Indonesia reform package was criticized for mandating reform of the concession management system without due attention to the necessary preconditions that would have to be in place for such reform to be effective. First among these was the need for baseline information on the extent and quality of forest resources, criteria and indicators for improved forest management, and an effective system for evaluating concession performance. Similarly, some observers claim that World Bank-supported community forest provisions in the Cameroon reform process have actually made things worse by failing to anticipate the ability of unaccountable local elites to capture the benefits, which should have been predictable based on experience with land reform efforts in the 1970s. In such cases, the credibility of World Bank reform efforts may be jeopardized if imposed conditions are *prima facie* infeasible to implement.

World Bank Ownership

With all the attention given to the necessity of borrower ownership of reform in adjustment lending, there is a danger of slighting the importance of World Bank ownership of the reform agenda. The case studies suggest a strong relationship between the strength of the World Bank's commitment to forest policy reform and the likelihood of success in the context of adjustment lending. The link between forest policy reform and the broader adjustment agenda can cut either way: the

full weight of the World Bank's leverage can be brought to bear on forest-related issues, or the forest agenda can be sacrificed to preserve the World Bank's relationship with the borrower.

In the Papua New Guinea case, a persistent World Bank country team outraged by the government's bad faith was backed up by an unusually strong country director able to mediate between forestry specialists and macroeconomists within the World Bank. This group overrode World Bank culture and

---

The case studies suggest a strong relationship between the strength of the World Bank's commitment to forest policy reform and the likelihood of success in the context of adjustment lending.

---

contradictory signals from the vice presidential level to hold the line on forest conditionality by suspending disbursement of the adjustment loan. In Indonesia, the World Bank's commitment to forest policy reform was apparently supported all the way up the chain of command, such that the government's failure to comply with forest-related conditions was the last sticking point in a tranche release delay in late 1998.

By contrast, the Cameroon and Kenya stories illustrate the costs of inconsistent support and commitment within the World Bank. In the Cameroon case, the technical staff responsible for forest policy felt betrayed when more senior managers, who were not willing to disrupt the broader relationship with the borrower, ignored the government's allocation of concession to low bidders in 1997 in contravention of World Bank-sponsored reforms. In Kenya, a Washington-based task manager's efforts proved insufficient to focus the government's attention on the opportunity for environmental adjustment without stronger support from the country director, other staff at the resident mission in Nairobi, or more senior management.

Attention to environmental and natural resources management issues is rare in the context of adjustment lending. According to interviews conducted for this study, constellations of World Bank staff sufficiently committed to that portion of the reform agenda to buck existing incentive systems are rarer still. Thus, attaining a sufficient degree of World Bank ownership of forest policy reform may be among the more difficult conditions to get right.

Borrower Ownership

The adjustment literature's treatment of borrower ownership suffers from the assumption that the borrower is a unitary actor. The case studies expose the oversimplification that results from just dividing borrowers into two groups, those with or without ownership. Even where there are strong individual champions for reform, such as the head of the DENR in the Philippines *(see Box 1.3)*, or reformist elements in government, as was the case in Papua New Guinea, they must wage a political struggle against those with vested interests in maintaining the status quo. In Indonesia, the Ministry of Forestry was deliberately excluded from early discussions of the reform agenda, under the correct assumption

that these bureaucrats would be among those most resistant to reform. In these cases, reformers enjoyed at least partial success in leveraging World Bank conditionality to promote policy change.

In other cases, borrower ownership proved insufficient. In Cameroon, the parliament's unwillingness to go along with commitments made by the President frustrated attempts to establish a rational forest policy framework. The President's tepid efforts to seek parliamentary approval raised questions about how committed to change the highest levels of government were, despite reformist elements within the bureaucracy. In Kenya, government commitment to reform was similarly called into question by weak leadership of the environmental adjustment planning process. While some government officials expressed genuine support for the reform program, no single well-placed individual sufficiently understood or cared about the opportunity enough to exercise leadership or rally support inside or outside of government. Even though World Bank officials had targeted Kenya as a test case for environmental adjustment precisely because of Kenya's strong NGO community and the high profile of natural resource management issues in the political economy, these elements proved insufficient for generating a sustained reform process.

Considering the complexity of domestic politics in each of the four case study countries, it is not clear that it would have been possible to discern in advance which cases had enough borrower ownership, inside and outside government, to merit the World Bank pursuing a reform agenda. The Papua New Guinea case best illustrates this complexity, in which many reformers inside the government bureaucracy were themselves expatriates, and where policy stances were later reversed upon the advice of a former official of the World Bank. Experiences in the Solomon Islands *(see Box 2.1)*, and in Cambodia *(see Box 4.4)*, provide further evidence of the difficulty of discerning the political prospects of reform proponents compared with those favoring logging forces.

The dichotomous approach to borrower ownership begs an interesting question: what is the appropriate World Bank response to cases that lie somewhere between complete ownership of the reform agenda and a total lack of commitment to change? Only in rare cases are there no latent constituencies for reform in either the government or civil society. In cases where some parts of a borrower government—or the private sector or the NGO community—are in favor of reform, yet are faced by staunch opposition from entrenched vested interests, can the World Bank utilize the adjustment process to "tip the scales" from insufficient to sufficient ownership? The following section suggests some insights from the case studies.

BUILDING COALITIONS FOR CHANGE

The case studies hint that engaging broad stakeholder groups before and during the adjustment process is an effective way for the World Bank and reformist elements in the client country to cultivate a critical mass of domestic political support for forest policy reform. The Philippines case presents a good example of the borrower leading the constituency-building process. *(See Box 1.3)* However, only in Papua New Guinea did the World Bank undertake a significant and comprehensive outreach effort, therefore much of the evidence regarding the potential of stake-

holder engagement is about opportunities lost rather than captured. At minimum, the cases demonstrate that a failure to engage key stakeholder groups can leave a reform program vulnerable to attack, and illustrate the difficulties encountered by the World Bank in attempting to reach out to a large group of actors and to incorporate a range of issues in the adjustment process.

Broadening the Agenda

The content of the forest policy reform agenda is a key driver of domestic political support or opposition. Policy changes restricted to the World Bank's efficiency-oriented conventional wisdom *(see Box 1.4)* are likely to provoke strong opposition from those with vested interests in maintaining the rent-seeking opportunities in existing forest policies. At the same time, the indirect benefits of such policy changes, through allocation of increased government revenue to poverty alleviation or reduced forest degradation, are likely to be contested or poorly understood by constituencies for forest policy reform. Further, depending on the institutional context, efficiency-oriented reforms may even lead to perverse social or environmental consequences.

The case studies indicate that opportunities for coalition-building increase as the adjustment reform agenda is expanded and constituencies are engaged. In Cameroon, Indonesia, and Papua New Guinea, potential constituencies for reform were either left dormant, or actively alienated, by their perceptions that the World Bank was insufficiently open to incorporating forest policy objectives related to social equity and environmental protection into the adjustment process.

Consistent with the traditional focus of adjustment lending on macroeconomic policy reform, forest-related conditionality in the adjustment operations analyzed tended to focus on efficiency objectives. In the words of one World Bank task manager, "I still consider getting anything of significance on forests onto the adjustment agenda, especially that of the IMF, to be a victory."[4] To the extent that there were other objectives, such as signaling a break with cronyism in Indonesia, reforms were chosen based on their consistency with efficiency justifications. As a result, the reform agenda was denied the support of, and sometimes even was faced with opposition by, natural constituencies for change in the forest sector.

The Indonesia case provides the clearest example of the above-mentioned situation. Even though the World Bank's own 1995 sector review had recommended recognizing the rights and roles of forest-dwelling communities in forest management, these recommendations were not in the January 1998 bail-out package. As a result, many NGOs, academics, and donors active in Indonesian community forestry or environmental movements perceived the World Bank-IMF reform agenda as being limited to improving the efficiency of a fundamentally flawed forest management paradigm, and did not see an opportunity to pursue their objectives—including a rethinking of how property rights for forest resources are allocated—in the context of adjustment. Only when discussions of a possible forest sector SECAL were initiated later in the year was this wider set of issues put on the table.

Expanding the adjustment umbrella to encompass broader objectives also has implications for forest policy reforms designed to

The World Bank's attempts to include NGOs in policy formulation and implementation were constrained by the World Bank's limited legitimacy and credibility in the eyes of those stakeholders, and by the efficiency-orientation of its reform agenda.

meet efficiency objectives. In Papua New Guinea, a significant segment of the NGO community was alienated by the World Bank's refusal at the time of the adjustment loan to consider imposing a log export ban, despite NGO concerns about the grand-scale corruption associated with log exports and the desire to nurture small-scale processing activities at the community level. According to the World Bank, the log export ban would lead to inefficient domestic industry. NGOs saw the World Bank's rejection of their concerns as being based on an ideological commitment to economic liberalization that overrode domestic considerations.

Domestic Constituencies

The case studies illustrate how the World Bank's attempts to include NGOs in policy formulation and implementation were constrained by the World Bank's limited legitimacy and credibility in the eyes of those stakeholders, and by the efficiency-orientation of its reform agenda. In both Indonesia and Kenya, domestic NGOs were suspicious of the World Bank's motives, even in situations where World Bank staff were trying to promote progressive forest policy reform and engage in a genuine consultative process. In

Indonesia and Papua New Guinea, NGOs reacted to the World Bank's initial focus on reforming industrial forestry and the lack of emphasis on social equity and environmental protection by keeping the World Bank at arm's length.

At the same time, where the World Bank did engage in consultation, meaningful NGO engagement was constrained by the lack of sophistication and coordination of domestic NGO communities in borrower countries. In Kenya, where the World Bank chose to pilot the concept of environmental adjustment with the encouragement of some NGO leaders, the NGO community failed to exploit the opportunity that was offered. In Indonesia, the NGO community's lack of understanding about the mechanics of adjustment lending led to a misperception about how funds from a sectoral adjustment loan would be allocated and used. In Papua New Guinea, the legitimacy of those NGOs who most vocally supported the forest conditions was undermined by questions about whose interests those groups represented.

In Papua New Guinea, the World Bank was taken by surprise early in the preparation of an Economic Recovery Program when controversy swirled around a proposed provision concerning land registration, which was later dropped. World Bank staff had failed to highlight publicly the pro-rural and pro-landowner components of the so-called sustainable development reforms that were a significant part of the reform package, so other interest groups less favorably affected were able to dominate public debate. As a response, the World Bank launched a concerted outreach effort to gain support for the reform program from NGOs. The results of this effort, especially public statements supporting the World

Bank made by a particular individual from the NGO community, at least headed off international NGO opposition. However, because of limited staff on the ground and savvy about domestic politics, the outreach effort was vulnerable to manipulation by domestic political interests not necessarily consistent with the forest policy reform agenda.

In Cameroon, the World Bank-supported reform program was similarly vulnerable to populist attacks, which were voiced in the parliamentary debate on new forest legislation. However, the relative dearth of organized civil society groups, downwardly accountable local government officials, or other representatives of the rural population that stood to gain from the reform program would have posed a challenge to any World Bank effort to include those constituencies in the reform dialogue.

In Indonesia, the World Bank's approach was characterized by a gradual evolution from the almost unilateral imposition of conditions through the IMF bail-out package in January 1998, to its mid-1999 posture of strongly encouraging the government to consult relevant stakeholders on draft forestry legislation. While the former approach resulted in limited success of some efficiency-oriented reforms, constituencies for more complex policy changes, such as reform of the concession allocation and management system, were unwilling to settle for a closed decisionmaking process.

International Constituencies

The evidence from the case studies regarding the benefits of engaging the broader international community of public and private sector

stakeholders is ambiguous. In Papua New Guinea and Cameroon, moving forward on a reform program required at least the tacit support of former colonial governments, respectively Australia and France. The extent to which frictions related to forest sector projects and policies between these governments and the World Bank undermined what might have been more active support for the World Bank's reform agenda is not clear. In Indonesia, although the bilateral donors active in the forest sector were surprised by the reform package in January 1998, they quickly rallied to play supportive analytical and convening roles. In Kenya, despite the large bilateral donor agency presence in the forest and other environment-related sectors, the World Bank did not attempt to marshal their support for the proposed environmental adjustment program. The Cambodia case provides a good example of donor coordination in forest-related conditionality.
(See Box 4.4)

The cases suggest that the World Bank's engagement with international NGOs can help to shape the agenda and hold the World Bank and borrower governments accountable for their commitments. In Indonesia, international NGOs drew attention to inconsistencies in the World Bank reform package. Australian NGOs provoked a commitment from the World Bank President to engage NGOs in Papua New Guinea, and international environmental activists later tacitly endorsed the reforms related to forests in the adjustment loan. International conservation groups with programs in Cameroon supported reforms related to community forestry, and—to the dismay of the government and the logging industry—publicized their existence to rural villagers. In Cambodia, an international human rights organization

raised the profile of government complicity in illegal logging, and was later appointed by the government as the official monitor of the forest sector in compliance with World Bank conditions. In Kenya and other cases, international and domestic groups linked through NGO networks influenced each others' thinking about structural adjustment and forest policy reform.

Cameroon was the only case in which the World Bank is known to have had significant direct engagement with international private sector actors in the forest sector. In that case, World Bank staff consulted regularly with the European timber companies with interests at stake in the reform program. Nevertheless, the industry engaged in periodic denunciations of the World Bank's program, boycotted a concession auction in 1997, and went on strike to protest a new tax on wood entering domestic sawmills, causing the government to back down.

To summarize, the effectiveness of World Bank-led reform programs, as well as their perceived credibility and legitimacy in the eyes of nongovernment stakeholders, can in some cases be enhanced by World Bank efforts to reach out to greater constituencies, and to include broader reform objectives. The appearance (or reality) that World Bank-supported reform agendas are limited to achieving economic efficiency objectives in the context of inequitable and environmentally unsustainable forest management regimes denies proponents of reform the support of key domestic constituencies. While such efforts are no guarantee of success, failure to take these steps can certainly limit its prospects.

IMPLICATIONS FOR THE WORLD BANK

The case study experience summarized in this report has implications for the World Bank at two levels. At the operational level, the foregoing analysis suggests several changes in the World Bank's procedures, staffing, and incentives that would increase the potential for using adjustment lending as an effective instrument for forest policy reform. At the strategic level, the analysis illuminates the opportunities and challenges presented by the recent shift in the World Bank's portfolio toward increased adjustment lending, as well as the institution's new emphasis on promoting good governance.

OPERATIONAL IMPLICATIONS

Safeguard Policies

To support the development of domestic political coalitions for reform in borrower countries, the World Bank needs to enhance its credibility with key stakeholder groups as a proponent of environmentally friendly policy change through adjustment lending. The World Bank's credibility problems are clearly highlighted when internal contradictions in a reform package undermine environmental objectives.

One way to prevent the unintended negative environmental impacts of adjustment lending that currently damage the World Bank's credibility is to apply environmental assessment procedures to adjustment loans. For example, such an assessment of the 1998 Indonesian reform package—even a quick desk review—would have flagged the potential for the liberalization of investment in the palm oil sector to increase deforestation.

Sustained Sectoral Engagement

The World Bank can be more effective in promoting forest sector reform through policy-based lending if the necessary analysis and contacts are in place prior to the adjustment operation. In Papua New Guinea, the World Bank was well-positioned to influence the complex and contentious arena of forest policy reform in 1995 when economic distress presented both a crisis and an opportunity. Since their initial engagement in the sector through the TFAP process in 1989, World Bank staff had developed significant expertise and contacts through sector analysis, project lending, and sustained policy dialogue. As a result, the World Bank was armed with the technical and political knowledge necessary to design conditions that would be effective in staving off an attempt by logging interests to reassert control over the sector.

In contrast, the World Bank's resident staff in Indonesia had allowed forest policy analysis and engagement to lie fallow after the rupture in the relationship with the Ministry of Forestry in 1995. Faced with the opportunity of including forest sector reforms in the 1998 bail-out package in a matter of hours, World Bank staff had no choice but to draw from recommendations contained in a sector review almost four years out of date. In

The World Bank can be more effective in promoting forest sector reform through policy-based lending if the necessary analysis and contacts are in place prior to the adjustment operation.

initiating the subsequent dialogue, the Jakarta-based task manager had to rely on the staff of other donor agencies to introduce him to key Ministry officials, as he had no contacts of his own. The World Bank's credibility as a leader of the reform effort was, thus, initially hampered by its lack of recent engagement in the sector.

The effectiveness and legitimacy of World Bank intervention in the forest sector through adjustment lending could also be improved by investing in up-to-date analysis that addresses the social equity and environmental implications of proposed changes in the forest management regime.[5] Such analysis could serve as an important basis for a broader agenda of reform than the currently narrow focus on efficiency objectives, as well as a platform for intellectual commitment to reform on the part of domestic constituencies inside and outside of government. In both Cameroon and Papua New Guinea, the legitimacy of the adjustment conditions could have been increased if their benefits to rural communities had been better understood and communicated.

However, according to interviews with World Bank staff, current policy and practice in budget allocation tie funds for sectoral engagement to lending volumes. This means that investment of staff time and analysis must be commensurate with anticipated lending. However, the case studies in this analysis indicate that in some cases there may be a reverse correlation between the need for investment in sectoral engagement and lending volume. The World Bank therefore needs to reform its budgeting process to provide resources for sustained engagement in key countries and sectors even in the absence of a projected lending program.

Stakeholder Engagement

The World Bank needs to invest more resources in communicating with key stakeholder groups about the nature and purpose of adjustment lending and listening to their priorities and concerns. The case studies reveal that when adjustment lending is applied to an unconventional sector, such as forestry, or environmental policy reform more generally, government and nongovernment actors alike are confused about how adjustment actually works. The perceived legitimacy of proposed adjustment loans was undermined by the belief of Kenyan government officials and NGO activists in Indonesia that the loans would channel funds directly to line ministries charged with forest management, although in neither case was it true. In addition, increased communication can strengthen the World Bank's commitment to stay the course: in Papua New Guinea, the World Bank's resolve on withholding the second tranche release may have in part been driven by the need to live up to its prior public pronouncements.

Of equal importance for both effectiveness and legitimacy is the need to move beyond an outreach mode to establishing a dialogue with key stakeholders and incorporating their insights into the design and implementation of the proposed reform program. While the knowledge of institutional and political constraints will always be asymmetrical, increased communication between World Bank staff and domestic reform constituencies can help to narrow the gap.

Thus, had World Bank staff been in contact with the informal community of forest policy reformers in Indonesia (including Ministry of Forestry officials, donors, academics, and NGOs) in the months prior to the 1998 reform package, the conditionalities could have been more carefully tailored to prevailing challenges and opportunities. The Indonesia experience highlights the importance of maintaining an engagement with relevant stakeholders even in the absence of an active lending program. While resource constraints preclude the World Bank's involvement in all sectors in all countries at all times, the political, economic, social, and ecological significance of the forest sector in Indonesia would arguably merit the World Bank's attention.

Conditionality Engineering

The number and nature of forest-related conditions should reflect emerging lessons about their effectiveness.[6] As described above, the World Bank has tended to have more success using adjustment conditionality to leverage a small number of high-profile policy changes, rather than to effect a large number of incremental steps necessary for their implementation. The timing and sequencing of forest-related conditions present a particular challenge, given the limited disbursement period of adjustment loans. The rush to meet unrealistic deadlines for developing and implementing reforms can lead to bad process and bad policy. As illustrated by the Indonesia case, implementing reforms designed to improve the efficiency of forest management prior to dealing with property rights issues can cause internal contradictions within the reform program.

One option for the World Bank to explore is to supplement conditions designed to stimulate policy decisions with process-oriented conditions that specify characteris-

tics of the decisionmaking process for implementing those decisions, as well as outcome-oriented conditions that specify the objective to be met. For example, a condition requiring formulation of a new system for collecting rent would be accompanied by conditions regarding transparency and consultation in the formulation process. In Indonesia, reform constituencies outside the Ministry of Forestry have convinced the World Bank that one of the most important roles it can play is to open up forest policy-making to public scrutiny and participation, although to date its success has been mixed.

Staffing and Incentives

Many of the prescriptions outlined above run counter to the World Bank's current staffing, budgeting, and incentive systems. Broadening the adjustment agenda to include nontraditional issues and constituencies requires a different set of skills and attitudes on the part of World Bank staff: to conduct stakeholder analyses, the World Bank will need more social scientists; to move beyond efficiency objectives, macroeconomists will need to share responsibility for the reform agenda with others; and to avoid alienating potential members of coalitions for change, arrogance will need to be replaced by collegiality.

Appropriate staff skills and attitudes must also be supported by institutional incentives. As noted by Robert Wade in the recent history of the World Bank, "[A]nything that requires 'environment' to be handled other than as a subnational sector is difficult to organize and sustain, for it runs against established budgetary and reward systems" (Wade, 1997, p. 732). The case studies indicate that the World Bank's ownership of the reform agenda and effectiveness in promoting it are often dependent upon the personal commitment and style of individual task managers and country directors.

However, extensive staff investment in analysis (in the World Bank's terminology, "Economic and Sector Work") and stakeholder engagement in the forest sector over the long term, especially when decoupled from an active lending program, are neither supported by current budget allocation mechanisms nor encouraged as a path to career advancement. Indeed, one World Bank staff member interviewed for this study suspected that efforts to mainstream environmental considerations into adjustment lending may have damaged the careers of the staff involved. Clearly, finding ways to create "incentives for sustainable interest within the Bank" (Wade, 1997, p. 723) in tackling such difficult issues as forest policy reform is, thus, one of the major challenges for the World Bank to address.

STRATEGIC IMPLICATIONS

Selectivity

An influential World Bank research report, *Assessing Aid*, asserts that "[t]he role of agencies such as the World Bank is not to arm-twist governments to do what they are reluctant to do" (World Bank, 1998, p. 59), arguing that donors should focus their resources on countries with governments that have already demonstrated their commitment to reform. And yet, at least with respect to the forest sector in Papua New Guinea and Indonesia, such arm twisting was welcomed by domestic constituencies for reform, and at minimum resulted in setbacks to those with

The case studies indicate that the World Bank's ownership of the reform agenda and effectiveness in promoting it are often dependent upon the personal commitment and style of individual task managers and country directors.

vested interests in unsustainable logging. Similarly, it would be difficult to argue that the World Bank and the IMF should not have pressed the Cambodian government to clamp down on illegal logging, even though the government was clearly reluctant to do so (*see Box 4.4*).

A strict application of selectivity based on strong borrower ownership of the reform agenda would have ruled out the World Bank's interventions in these cases. The proposition that conditioned assistance should be limited to those countries already committed to reform ignores the possibility that World Bank conditionality can itself empower domestic constituencies for reform. Conditionality can alter the political dynamics of forest issues, if only by raising the profile of these issues on the national agenda.

The same World Bank report concludes that for assistance to be effective in countries with weak institutions and policies, there is a need to identify "champions of reform," and for aid to support innovations that "involve engaging civil society" (World Bank, 1998, p. 116). Experience from the case studies related to the forest sector is fully consistent with these conclusions, but as indicated above, suggests that the World Bank's internal incentive systems do not yet reward staff for "supporting reformers rather than disbursing money" (World Bank, 1998, p. 116). When the World Bank terminated project lending to the forest sector in Indonesia in 1995, there was no mechanism available to maintain engagement in the sector. While it can be argued that the World Bank exercised appropriate selectivity in the Kenya case by not moving forward with the proposed environmental adjustment loan, it is also true that the efforts of World Bank staff to cultivate support for reform were not adequately supported.

The Governance Agenda

In recent years, leadership of the World Bank has increasingly emphasized governance concerns. In his 1999 address to the Board of Governors, President Wolfensohn asserted that if countries "do not have good governance . . . their development is fundamentally flawed and will not last and proposed an ambitious agenda for the World Bank to promote good governance" (Wolfensohn, 1999).

The case studies show that for the World Bank to be effective in promoting reform in the forest sector, governance issues must be addressed centrally. In Papua New Guinea and Indonesia, the World Bank was able to catalyze forest policy reforms when the adjustment instrument was used to challenge "the rules of the game" in the forest sector, elevating forestry-related governance concerns to the top of the policy agenda. In Cameroon, by contrast, World Bank management was unwilling to give priority to similar concerns when the government backtracked on commitments, sending a signal to corrupt elements in the government—as well as to a younger generation of aspiring reformers— that some corruption will be tolerated. The increased use of adjustment conditions to promote transparency and consultation in forest policy decisionmaking is a specific mechanism for linking forestry and governance concerns.

Conversely, the case studies also indicate that in some countries, for the World Bank to be effective in promoting good governance, forest issues must be addressed. In Papua New Guinea, Indonesia, and Cameroon, forest issues are important enough in real and symbolic terms to the national political economy that to talk about good governance without reference to the forest sector would be incomplete at best. In Kenya, many observers inside and outside the World Bank interpreted the World Bank's failure to speak out on the Karura forest episode as evidence that the World Bank lacked seriousness about its governance agenda with the Moi regime. Even though a participatory process to develop a new Country Assistance Strategy resulted in a focus on governance concerns, the World Bank missed an opportunity to frame the environmental adjustment agenda in broader governance terms. These findings support the suggestion that the environment and natural resources arena is "a particularly suitable place" to pursue a governance agenda (Hyden, 1999).

THE BOTTOM LINE

Can the World Bank be an effective proponent of forest policy reform through adjustment lending? The case studies suggest that the answer is a qualified "yes"—under the right conditions. On the part of the borrower, those conditions include constituencies for reform within the borrower government or civil society, and opportunities for meaningful policy changes that do not require extensive institutional reform to implement. On the part of the World Bank, those conditions include strong and consistent commitment to the reform agenda and engagement with key stakeholders in defining and communicating the objectives and strategy for reform.

While sustained policy reform and implementation ultimately depend on the interplay of domestic political forces, forest-related conditions imposed by the World Bank have been effective in raising the profile of forest issues on the national agenda, prodding governments to commit themselves to new policies, and providing support to the efforts of domestic constituencies for reform. Experience in the case study countries indicates that variables within the control of the World Bank can sometimes influence the domestic politics of the forest-related issues, and, hence, borrower ownership, broadly defined. However, the World Bank has been much less effective in using adjustment lending to leverage the long-term institutional changes that are often necessary to implement significant reforms.

The World Bank's effectiveness is ultimately influenced by both its legitimacy and credibility, as support, or lack of opposition, from key constituencies is critical for success. The case studies confirm that key stakeholders often do not believe that the World Bank is a credible champion of forest policy reform in the context of structural adjustment lending. The World Bank's credibility can be enhanced by long-term in-country involvement in the sector, good analysis and outreach emphasizing the benefits of reform, and an expansion of the reform agenda to include equity and environmental objectives. Conversely, the World Bank's credibility can be undermined by imposing forest-related conditions out of sequence, including non-

forest related conditions that negatively affect forests, and backing down when borrowers flout agreed conditions. Overcoming the World Bank's credibility deficit will require significant changes in the current staffing and incentive patterns.

Finally, the case studies indicate that the World Bank's use of adjustment-related conditionality to leverage forest policy reform can be seen as legitimate even by World Bank critics when: government policy is manifestly against the public interest (for example, when irreversible damage to forests is threatened in the near term); there are some domestic constituencies for reform in the borrower country; the World Bank can make a compelling case that alternative policies would better serve sustainable development objectives; and the World Bank's intervention is sufficiently grounded in local realities to provide a reasonable chance of success without significant unintended negative consequences. The World Bank's legitimacy can be further enhanced by working to make the forest policy reform process more transparent, accountable, and participatory, both in its own activities and through its leverage over borrower governments.

Under the right conditions, in the borrower country and on the part of the World Bank, the World Bank can be an effective proponent of forest policy reform through adjustment lending. These findings suggest that adjustment lending, the World Bank's most significant instrument, presents an important opportunity for mainstreaming social, environmental, and governance objectives into the World Bank's work. The findings also offer a sobering challenge to the institution to get the conditions right.

REFERENCES

Catán, Thomas, and Gwen Robinson. 1999. "Papua New Guinea's Fraught Bond Debut." *Financial Times*, June 30, 1999.

Hyden, Goran. 1999. "Environment and Natural Resource Management: The New Frontier of Democracy & Governance Work?" Gainesville, FL: University of Florida. Mimeo.

Nelson, Joan. 1999. *Reforming Health and Education: The World Bank, The IDB, and Complex Institutional Change.* Washington D.C.: Overseas Development Council.

Ross, Michael. 1996. Conditionality and Logging Reform in the Tropics. In *Institutions for Environmental Aid*, edited by R. O. Keohane and M. A. Levy. Cambridge, MA: MIT Press.

Wade, Robert. 1997. "Greening the Bank: The Struggle over the Environment, 1970–1995." In *The World Bank: Its First Half Century*, edited by D. Kapur, J. P. Lewis and R. Webb. Washington D.C.: Brookings Institution Press.

Wolfensohn, James D. 1999. "Coalitions for Change: Address to the Board of Governors." Address to the Board of Governors at the World Bank Annual Meetings, September 28, 1999. Washington D.C.: The World Bank. Available at: http://www.worldbank.org/html/extdr/am99/jdw-sp/index.htm

World Bank, The. 1998. *Assessing Aid: What Works, What Doesn't, and Why.* Washington, D.C.: The World Bank.

NOTES

1. An important exception is highlighted by the Cameroon case: from 1989–1993, significant financial support from the France enabled the government to avoid adjustment.

2. Just how much higher is demonstrated by recent experience in Papua New Guinea. To avoid World Bank conditionality, in mid-1999 the government unsuccessfully attempted to attract bond finance through private capital markets at interest rates up to three times that offered by the World Bank (Thomas and Robinson, 1999).

3. This opinion was expressed by several World Bank participants in the April 1999, workshop at WRI.

4. Personal communication, September 1999.

5. Practitioners from the World Bank and NGO representatives who attended the April 1999, workshop at WRI felt strongly about this point. The recommendation that the World Bank invest in better sector analysis is also consistent with Joan Nelson's prescription to multilateral development banks to "make haste slowly" in social sectors and focus on establishing the preconditions and constituencies for change (Nelson, 1999, p. 93).

6. This was a point of least consensus among persons interviewed for this study and participants in the April 1999, workshop at WRI.

APPENDIX: RESEARCH DESIGN

The central analytic question of this study is: to what extent, and under what conditions, can the World Bank be an effective proponent of forest policy reform through structural adjustment lending?

APPROACH

Our approach was to examine a limited set of cases where the Bank intentionally attempted to incorporate environmental goals into adjustment lending. Our primary interest was in the *process* by which adjustment lending was initiated, formulated, negotiated, and implemented.

By contrast, other reviews of adjustment lending have utilized cross-country regression analysis (Killick, 1997; Mosley, Harrigan, and Toye, 1995; World Bank, 1998), with a view to isolating factors associated with the success or failure of adjustment loans. This approach was not suitable for our purpose for three reasons. First, many of the factors we believed to be important—degree of borrower ownership, extent of civil society engagement by the Bank—were not amenable to quantification. Second, the number of cases where the World Bank used adjustment lending for forest policy reform was too limited to provide robust regression results. Third, a binary measure of success was too crude to capture the range of outcomes we wished to assess.

By emphasizing process, we faced two methodological issues. First, how were we to evaluate the effectiveness of the World Bank in promoting policy reform? A clear answer was hampered by the lack of a counter-factual—what would have happened in the absence of adjustment lending—against which to measure success. Keeping this problem in mind, our approach sought to identify the elements of success and failure in the policy reform processes considered here—"the right conditions." Moreover, while the ultimate test of effectiveness is improved environmental and social outcomes, in this study we restricted ourselves to the formulation of policy conditions in adjustment loans and, where information was available, the translation of those conditions into national policy. Hence, we assumed that policy reform is a necessary if not sufficient condition to achieving sound outcomes in the forest sector.

Second, given our emphasis on process, what was our assessment of the scope and content of reforms? On the scope, we acknowledged that the state of the forests is not influenced exclusively by forest policy, but as much, or more, by decisions taken outside the forest sector. These include projects in other sectors that affect land-use and, hence, forest patterns (Kaimowitz and Angelsen, n.d.) and macroeconomic policies that shift incentives in favor of forest exports (Cruz and Repetto, 1992). Yet, forest policy remains an important part of the puzzle and is the piece we chose to focus on in this study.

On the content of forest policies, we acknowledged that there are ongoing debates over the various elements of forest policy reform introduced through adjustment lending. For example, the linkage between improved efficiency in industrial logging and improved environmental outcomes is controversial. In this study, we did not attempt to enter these debates, but rather explored, through each case study, the links between the process of formulating reforms and the ultimate content of those reforms, as well as the connection between process and the likelihood of eventually implementing reforms.

RESEARCH QUESTIONS

The research questions were grouped around three categories:

Stakeholders and context. Who are the stakeholders in forest policy reform in the country and in the World Bank, what was at stake for each of these actors, and what is the political and economic context within which the adjustment operation was formulated and implemented?

Content. What was the environmental content of the adjustment loan, how was it articulated, how was it understood and contested by different stakeholders, and how was it implemented in the loan?

Borrower ownership and donor strategy. How accurately did World Bank staff assess borrower ownership, how effectively did they identify and engage with key state and nonstate actors, what was the nature of this engagement, and, in light of this engagement, to what extent and how was conditionality applied and enforced?

METHODOLOGY

We used these questions to guide our research in four case study countries—Papua New Guinea, Cameroon, Indonesia, and Kenya—working in collaboration with a research partner in each country. The principal methods were semi-structured interviews with key informants from government agencies, civil society, and the private sector in each country, as well as with World Bank and IMF officials, all on a not-for-attribution basis. This information was supplemented by official government and donor agency reports, secondary analysis of adjustment programs, and press coverage.

In addition, in April 1999, we held a roundtable discussion on the preliminary results from the cases. Participants in the discussion included the principal case study authors, World Bank and IMF staff with expertise in the case study countries, and resource-persons with independent expertise in one or more of the case study countries.

CASE STUDY SELECTION

The set of possible cases was defined by the countries in which the World Bank has intentionally incorporated forest policy reform objectives into its adjustment lending. This was a relatively limited set. In selecting among these, we sought a geographic spread across the cases. We were unable to identify appropriate cases in Latin America or Central and Eastern Europe and the Newly Independent States. We sought to avoid a clustering of cases in East Asia, the region where adjustment lending for forest policy reform has been most intensively applied. Thus, Philippines, Indonesia, Papua New Guinea, and Cambodia were all candidate cases, but only two of these were selected for full case studies. In addition, there was an inevitable dimension of pragmatism involved in the selection process. Specifically, we drew on cases where the primary authors could build on existing knowledge and contacts, and we decided not to pursue further cases that had been comprehensively studied by other scholars, notably the Philippines case, discussed in Box 1.3 (Ross, 1996). This led us to select three primary case studies: Papua New Guinea, Cameroon, and Indonesia. In all these cases, the Bank had intentionally included forest policy reform objectives into a broader adjustment loan.

In addition, we opted to add a fourth case, Kenya, which stands apart from the other three. In Kenya, an environmental adjustment loan designed entirely to address environmental objectives was proposed, but not agreed to or implemented.

Finally, we conducted a series of shorter and less comprehensive analyses based largely on secondary sources to complement these primary cases. These shorter studies, on Cambodia, Philippines, Solomon Islands, and Suriname, are peppered throughout the report in text boxes.

Our approach sought to discover and outline causal mechanisms inductively through the careful analysis of cases. Hence, the case studies were chosen on the basis of the phenomenon we wished to study (here, the intentional application of adjustment lending for environmental objectives), rather than on the basis of a set of independent variables. We favored the former approach for two reasons. First, from a theoretical viewpoint, we believed the intensive approach to be the best way to identify causal factors and processes. By contrast, selection based on independent variables required that we have confidence that those independent variables capture most, if not all, the variation in outcomes across cases. Second, from a pragmatic point of view, selection across likely independent variables would have been unlikely to give us a sufficient spread in outcomes, since the number where the World Bank applied adjustment to environmental objectives is small.

It is instructive to note some patterns across the cases, including the text box level cases. First, in all the case study countries, forestry is either of considerable economic or symbolic importance. Second, many of the cases, with the notable exception of Indonesia, tend to be small countries of little geopolitical significance and, hence, countries where donor intervention fails to be heavily scrutinized in the international arena. Third, many of the countries have a reputation for poor governance as indicated, for example, by a low ranking on the Corruption Perceptions Index compiled by Transparency International.[1] Fourth, the cases represent a range of adjustment instruments, from structural adjustment loans in most cases to a sectoral adjustment loan in Philippines, to an adjustment loan exclusively for environmental reform in Kenya.

REFERENCES

Cruz, Wilfrido, and Robert Repetto. 1992. *The Environmental Effects of Stabilization and Structural Adjustment Programs: The Philippines Case.* Washington D.C.: World Resources Institute.

Kaimowitz, David, and Arild Angelsen. no date. "The World Bank and Non-Forest Sector Policies that Affect Forests." Bogor, Indonesia: CIFOR. Mimeo.

Killick, Tony. 1997. "Failings of Conditionality." *Journal of International Development* 9 (4): 483–495.

Mosley, Paul, Jane Harrigan, and John Toye. 1995. *Aid and Power: The World Bank and Policy-Based Lending.* New York: Routledge.

Ross, Michael. 1996. "Conditionality and Logging Reform in the Tropics." In *Institutions for Environmental Aid*, edited by R. O. Keohane and M. A. Levy. Cambridge, MA: MIT Press.

World Bank. 1998. *Assessing Aid: What Works, What Doesn't, and Why.* Washington, D.C.: World Bank.

NOTES

1. Indonesia, Kenya, and Cameroon all ranked between 70 and the lowest ranking of 80 in the index. Papua New Guinea was not included. The index is available at: http://www.transparency.de/documents/cpi/index.html

ABOUT THE AUTHORS

Frances J. Seymour is the Director of the World Resources Institute's Institutions and Governance Program. Her work focuses on international financial flows and institutions, and sustainable development challenges in Southeast Asia. Prior to joining WRI, she served as Director of Development Assistance Policy at World Wildlife Fund, and spent five years in Indonesia with the Ford Foundation.

Navroz K. Dubash is a Senior Associate in the Institutions and Governance Program at WRI. His work explores the impact of financial globalization on problems of environment and development. Before joining WRI, he served with the Environmental Defense Fund as coordinator of the international Climate Action Network, and has also worked in India on local institutions for the management of groundwater resources.

Jake Brunner is a Senior Associate in WRI's Information Program and coordinates WRI's policy research in Central Africa. He also advises USAID's Africa Bureau and its missions on the use of remote sensing and GIS for the agency's natural resource management projects. Prior to this, Mr. Brunner taught remote sensing and GIS at London University and Oxford University.

François Ekoko is a Forest Programme Specialist at the United Nations Development Programme in New York. He currently works on institutions and governance issues, and forest policy. Previously with the Center for International Forestry Research in Cameroon, his publications have focused on forest policy, poverty and deforestation, and governance.

Colin Filer heads the Social and Environmental Studies Division of the National Research Institute in Papua New Guinea, and is currently on secondment to the Australian National University, where he is working on the Resource Management in Asia Pacific Project in the Research School of Pacific and Asian Studies. He has published widely on matters of forest policy, biodiversity conservation, and the social impact of mining and petroleum projects in Papua New Guinea.

Hariadi Kartodihardjo is a Professor at the Faculty of Forestry, in Bogor Agricultural University, Indonesia. Dr. Kartodihardjo is in active collaboration with several local NGOs and is one of the founders of the Indonesian Ecolabeling Institute. He also served as an advisor to the Ministry of Forestry as a member of The Forestry and Estate Crops Development Reformation Committee.

John Mugabe is Executive Director of the Nairobi-based African Centre for Technology Studies (ACTS). He is the author of several publications on technology and environmental policy. His recent research has focused on international politics and policy on biotechnology and its impacts on global economic change.

World Resources Institute

The World Resources Institute (WRI) is an independent center for policy research and technical assistance on global environmental and development issues. WRI's mission is to move human society to live in ways that protect Earth's environment and its capacity to provide for the needs and aspirations of current and future generations.

Because people are inspired by ideas, empowered by knowledge, and moved to change by greater understanding, the Institute provides—and helps other institutions provide—objective information and practical proposals for policy and institutional change that will foster environmentally sound, socially equitable development. WRI's particular concerns are with globally significant environmental problems and their interaction with conomic development and social equity at all levels.

The Institute's current areas of work include economics, forests, biodiversity, climate change, energy, sustainable agriculture, resource and environmental information, trade, technology, national strategies for environmental and resource management, and business liaison.

In all of its policy research and work with institutions, WRI tries to build bridges between ideas and action, meshing the insights of scientific research, economic and institutional analyses, and practical experience with the need for open and participatory decision-making.

WORLD RESOURCES INSTITUTE
10 G Street, N.E.
Washington, D.C. 20002, USA
http://www.wri.org/wri